Biology
for the IB Diploma

Workbook

Matthew Broderick

CAMBRIDGE
UNIVERSITY PRESS

CAMBRIDGE
UNIVERSITY PRESS

University Printing House, Cambridge CB2 8BS, United Kingdom

One Liberty Plaza, 20th Floor, New York, NY 10006, USA

477 Williamstown Road, Port Melbourne, VIC 3207, Australia

4843/24, 2nd Floor, Ansari Road, Daryaganj, Delhi – 110002, India

79 Anson Road, #06 –04/06, Singapore 079906

Cambridge University Press is part of the University of Cambridge.

It furthers the University's mission by disseminating knowledge in the pursuit of education, learning and research at the highest international levels of excellence.

www.cambridge.org
Information on this title: www.cambridge.org/9781316646090 (Paperback)

First published 2017

20 19 18 17 16 15 14 13 12 11 10 9 8 7 6 5 4 3 2 1

Printed in Spain by GraphyCems

A catalogue record for this publication is available from the British Library

ISBN 978-1-316-64609-0 Paperback

Contents

How to use this book

Chapter outline

Each chapter begins with a chapter outline to briefly set out the learning aims and help with navigation through the topic.

> ### Chapter outline
>
> In this chapter you will:
> - describe how the evolution of multicellular organisms allowed cell specialisation and cell replacement
> - compare the complex cell structure of eukaryotes to that of prokaryotes
> - outline how the structure of biological membranes makes them fluid and dynamic
> - outline how membranes control the composition of cells by active and passive transport
> - outline the unbroken chain of life from the first cells on Earth to all cells in organisms alive today
> - describe how cell division is essential and controlled.

Key terms

A list of Key terms at the start of each chapter provide clear, straightforward definitions for the Key vocabulary.

> ### KEY TERMS AND DEFINITIONS
>
> **Cell cycle** – the sequence of events that takes place from one cell division until the next; made up of interphase, mitosis and cytokinesis.
>
> **Endosymbiosis** – theory that proposes that mitochondria and chloroplasts evolved from bacteria.
>
> **Eukaryotic** – organism whose cell contains a membrane-bound nucleus.
>
> **Fluid mosaic model** – the accepted model of the structure of a membrane that includes a phospholipid bilayer in which proteins are embedded or attached to the surface.
>
> **Prokaryotic** – organism whose genetic material is not contained in a nucleus.

Exercises

Each chapter contains a number of Exercises that relate to each chapter topic. Exercises can help to practice and consolidate learning.

Exercise 4.1 – Species, communities and ecosystems

1 A lion and a panther are two different species, although they may have some similarities and may even live in the same area at the same time.
   a Define *species*.
   b Sometimes, it is possible for closely related species to interbreed. Suggest what the offspring might **not** be able to do.
   c Figure 4.1 shows a photograph of a *zonkey*. Using the name, *zonkey*, deduce the two species that have been interbred to produce this genetic hybrid.

Exam-style questions

Each chapter concludes with a list of Exam-style questions. These Exam-style questions provide an opportunity to practise what has been covered in each topic and prepare for the types of question that will appear in the IB Biology Diploma exams.

? Exam-style questions

1 **The movement of molecules across a partially permeable membrane is not affected by which factor? [1]**
   A Concentration gradient of the particles diffusing
   B Surface area of the membrane
   C A selective membrane
   D Temperature

2 **The correct movement of water molecules in osmosis is: [1]**
   A From high solute concentration to low solute concentration
   B From low water concentration to high water concentration
   C From low solute concentration to high solute concentration
   D Between solutes of equal concentration

3 **Observe the following statements about cell theory.**
   I   Living organisms are composed of cells.
   II   Cells are the smallest units of life.
   III Cells come from pre-existing cells.

   Which combination of statements about cell theory is true from the statements above? [1]
   A I and III only
   B I and II only
   C I, II and III
   D None of the above

Introduction

This workbook has been written to support students studying the IB Diploma Biology syllabus at both Standard Level (SL) and Higher Level (HL). The book aims to support understanding of the content; it also offers structured support to guide students towards examination success and an appreciation of the importance of biology in our world today.

The content follows the chapters of the biology syllabus and can be covered in any order that the student chooses. However, it is recommended that you align this with in-class instruction as the questions are designed to support this. Each chapter begins with the main learning objectives and lists the key terms that best outline the chapter ahead.

Each chapter aims to develop the fundamental building blocks of knowledge through the simpler Assessment Objective (AO1) command terms. As each chapter develops, more of the AO2 and AO3 command terms are used, usually with some real-life, contextualised applications. The articles and background information for the questions are all based on recent biological affairs and are designed to get students thinking about the nature of science that naturally embeds itself throughout the book.

Answers have been provided at the back of this book and contain as many alternatives as possible. As the student develops into an independent, critical-thinking biologist, it may be that they can expand on the mark schemes offered. Answers to the exam-style questions are structured to prepare the student for the examinations. The exam-style-questions cover papers 1, 2, and 3. The mark schemes are comprehensive to guide students towards the *best* answer, as opposed to simply a *good* answer.

Skills grid

AO	Command term	1. Cell biology	2. Molecular biology	3. Genetics	4. Ecology	5. Evolution and biodiversity	6. Human physiology	7. Nucleic acids	8. Metabolism, cell respiration and photosynthesis
1	Define	1.1.4 1.3.4	2.2.3 2.3.1 2.4.5 2.5.1 2.5.7 ESQ 9	3.3.1 3.5.3	4.1.1 4.1.2 4.2.3 4.2.4 4.3.2	5.1.1 5.1.3 5.1.4 5.2.1 5.2.2 5.4.1 5.4.3 ESQ 9	6.1.3 6.3.2 6.4.1 6.5.1 6.6.1	7.1.1 7.2.1 7.3.3 7.3.4 ESQ 15	8.1.2 8.2.1 8.3.1 ESQ 14
1	Draw	1.2.1 1.3.5 ESQ 4	2.1.2 2.3.1 ESQ 8		4.2.2 ESQ 10		6.1.1 6.1.3 ESQ 12	7.1.1 ESQ 14	
1	Label	1.2.1 ESQ 4	2.3.1 ESQ 8		4.2.2 ESQ 10	5.1.3	6.1.1 6.2.4 ESQ 12	7.1.1 ESQ 14	8.3.4
1	List		2.2.4	3.5.3	4.1.2 4.3.2	5.2.2 5.3.1	6.2.2 6.2.5 6.2.7 6.3.2 6.3.3 6.3.5 6.4.1 6.6.2	7.2.1 7.3.3	8.2.1
1	Measure	1.2.2							
1	State	1.1.1 1.1.4 1.2.1 1.2.2 1.3.5 1.4.1 1.5.1 1.5.4 1.6.1	2.1.1 2.1.3 2.1.4 2.1.5 2.1.6 2.2.1 2.2.2 2.2.4 2.3.2 2.3.3 2.4.3 2.4.5 2.4.6 2.5.1 2.5.3 2.5.4 2.5.6 ESQ 7 ESQ 10	3.2.1 3.3.1 3.3.2 3.3.3 3.4.1 3.4.2	4.1.2 4.1.4 4.1.5 4.1.6 4.2.1 4.2.3 4.2.4 4.3.1 ESQ 9 ESQ 10	5.1.1 5.1.3 5.1.4 5.1.5 5.3.1 5.3.2 5.3.3 5.3.4 5.4.2	6.1.1 6.1.2 6.2.4 6.2.5 6.2.6 6.3.5 6.4.1 6.5.1 ESQ 9 ESQ 10	7.1.1 7.1.2 7.1.3 7.2.1 7.3.1 7.3.3 7.3.4	8.1.2 8.1.3 8.2.1 8.2.2 8.3.1 8.3.3 ESQ 9
2	Annotate	1.2.1	2.3.1		4.1.4 4.2.1		6.2.4	ESQ 14 ESQ 15	8.1.2 8.1.3 8.2.2 ESQ 13
2	Calculate	1.1.1 1.2.2 1.5.4	2.2.6 2.4.6	3.3.3 3.4.1 3.4.2 ESQ 11	4.1.2 4.2.3 4.3.3 4.4.1 ESQ 9	5.4.3	6.2.3 6.2.6		8.1.1 8.2.3

AO	Command term	1. Cell biology	2. Molecular biology	3. Genetics	4. Ecology	5. Evolution and biodiversity	6. Human physiology	7. Nucleic acids	8. Metabolism, cell respiration and photosynthesis
2	Describe	1.2.2 1.3.1 1.5.2	2.1.5 2.2.5 2.3.3 2.5.7 ESQ 7 ESQ 9	3.1.1 3.2.1 ESQ 14	4.1.5 4.3.1	5.1.5 5.2.1 ESQ 11	6.1.1 6.3.1 6.4.1 6.6.1 6.6.2 ESQ 9 ESQ 11	7.1.1 7.3.2 7.3.3 ESQ 16	8.1.2 8.2.2 8.2.3 8.2.4 8.3.2 8.3.4
2	Distinguish		2.2.4 2.4.1		4.1.3 4.1.6 4.4.1	5.1.3 5.4.1 ESQ 9 ESQ 12	6.1.3 6.2.2 6.2.4 6.4.1 6.6.1 ESQ 11	ESQ 16	8.2.1 8.3.2 ESQ 13 ESQ 14
2	Estimate	1.3.5			4.2.3 4.3.2	5.4.2	6.1.1 6.3.5	7.1.3 ESQ 6	
2	Identify	1.1.4 1.2.1	2.1.3 2.3.1 2.3.3	3.1.1 3.1.2 3.2.1 3.3.1 3.4.1 ESQ 4 ESQ 6 ESQ 7 ESQ 8 ESQ 12 ESQ 13	4.1.3 4.1.4 4.2.1 4.2.3 4.3.1 ESQ 7	5.1.1 5.1.2 5.1.3 5.3.2 5.3.4	6.1.1 6.1.3 6.2.5 6.6.2 ESQ 2 ESQ 3 ESQ 4 ESQ 5 ESQ 8	7.1.1 7.1.2 7.2.1 7.3.3 ESQ 4 ESQ 5 ESQ 8 ESQ 9 ESQ 12 ESQ 13	8.1.3 8.2.1 8.3.1 8.3.2 8.3.5 8.3.6 ESQ 4 ESQ 12
2	Outline	1.1.1 1.4.1 1.6.1 ESQ 3	2.1.4 2.1.5 2.2.4 2.3.3 2.4.1 2.4.5 2.5.2 2.5.4 2.5.5 2.5.6 ESQ 9	3.1.1 3.3.1 3.4.1 3.4.2 ESQ 13 ESQ 14	4.1.4 4.2.3 4.3.1 4.3.3 4.4.1 4.4.2	5.1.1 5.1.2 5.1.5 5.2.1 5.2.2 5.3.1 5.3.2 5.4.1 5.4.2 ESQ 9 ESQ 11	6.1.1 6.1.2 6.2.3 6.2.7 6.3.1 6.3.3 6.3.4 6.3.5 6.4.1 6.5.1 ESQ 9	7.1.1 7.1.2 7.1.3 7.3.2 7.3.4 ESQ 14 ESQ 15	8.1.2 8.2.1 8.2.2 8.2.3 8.2.4 8.3.1 8.3.2 ESQ 13
3	Analyse		2.5.5	3.2.1 3.3.1	4.2.3 4.3.3	5.3.2 5.4.1 ESQ 10	6.1.1 6.3.1 ESQ 11	7.2.1	8.2.2
3	Comment		2.1.3 2.1.6 2.4.1	3.2.1 3.2.2 3.5.1 3.5.3	4.1.6 4.2.3	5.1.1 5.2.2	6.2.1 6.3.2 ESQ 11	7.1.1 7.3.3 7.3.4	8.1.1 8.2.4 8.3.1
3	Compare	1.1.2 1.4.1	2.5.4 ESQ 10	3.2.2		5.1.3 ESQ 9	6.2.1		8.3.2
3	Compare and contrast		2.1.4 2.4.1 2.5.6		4.2.3	5.1.3 5.3.3	6.2.2 6.6.1		8.1.3 8.3.2 ESQ 14
3	Construct	1.1.3	2.4.2	3.4.1 3.4.2	4.1.5 4.2.1	5.3.4 ESQ 13	6.2.3		

AO	Command term	1. Cell biology	2. Molecular biology	3. Genetics	4. Ecology	5. Evolution and biodiversity	6. Human physiology	7. Nucleic acids	8. Metabolism, cell respiration and photosynthesis
3	Deduce		2.4.4		4.3.1	5.1.1 5.2.3 5.3.3	6.1.3 6.2.5 6.3.1 6.5.1 6.6.1	7.1.2 7.2.1 7.3.2 7.3.3 ESQ 14	8.2.2 8.3.2 8.3.4 ESQ 8
3	Design	ESQ 5	2.1.5 2.3.2		4.3.3 4.4.2		6.1.3		8.1.3 8.2.1
3	Determine		2.4.3	3.1.2 3.2.2 3.4.1 3.4.2 ESQ 13	4.3.1 ESQ 9	5.1.5 5.4.1	6.2.3		8.2.1 8.2.2 8.2.3
3	Discuss	1.1.4	2.3.3 2.5.5 ESQ 11	3.1.2 3.3.2 3.5.2 3.5.3	4.2.3 4.3.2	5.2.2 5.4.1	6.2.1	7.1.1 7.2.1	8.1.1 8.3.5
3	Evaluate	1.1.5	2.1.6 2.2.7		4.3.1 4.3.3 4.4.2	5.4.3	6.1.3 6.3.2 6.6.2	7.1.3	8.3.1
3	Explain	1.1.2 1.3.5 1.4.1	2.1.5 2.2.5 2.3.2 2.3.3 2.5.3 2.5.5 2.5.7 ESQ 10	3.1.1 3.2.1 3.3.1 3.5.1 3.5.2 ESQ 13	4.1.3 4.2.2 4.2.4 4.3.1 4.3.3 4.4.2 ESQ 10	5.1.4 5.1.5 5.2.1 5.2.3 5.3.1 5.4.1 5.4.2 5.4.3 ESQ 11	6.1.1 6.1.2 6.2.3 6.3.1 6.3.3 6.4.1 6.5.1 ESQ 10 ESQ 12	7.1.2 7.1.3 7.2.1 ESQ 14	8.1.3 8.2.1 8.3.5
3	Predict		2.1.5 2.3.2	3.1.1 3.3.3 3.5.2	4.1.1 4.2.3 4.3.1 4.4.1	5.1.4 5.2.2	6.1.3		8.3.5
3	Sketch		2.4.1 2.5.7	3.1.1	4.2.3 ESQ 10	5.1.2 5.1.3	6.1.1 6.3.4		ESQ 13
3	Suggest	1.2.1	2.1.6 2.3.2 2.3.3 2.5.5 2.5.7 ESQ 7	3.4.2	4.1.1 4.1.4 4.1.6 4.2.2 4.2.3 4.3.1 4.4.1 4.4.2	5.1.4 5.2.3 5.3.1 5.3.2	6.1.2 6.1.3 6.2.4 6.3.1 6.3.5 6.5.1	7.1.3 7.2.1	8.1.1 8.1.2 8.1.3 8.2.1 8.2.2 8.3.4 8.3.5

AO	Command term	9. Plant biology	10. Genetics and evolution	11. Animal physiology	A. Neurobiology and behaviour	B. Biotechnology and bioinformatics	C. Ecology and conservation	D. Human physiology
1	**Define**	9.1.1 9.1.2 9.2.1 9.3.2 9.4.3 9.4.4	10.1.1 10.2.3 10.2.4 10.3.1	11.1.1 11.3.2 11.4.2 11.4.4 11.4.5 ESQ 18	A.1.1 A.1.2 A.3.1 A.4.2 A.6.1 A.6.2 ESQ 16	B.1.2 B.3.3	C.1.4 C.3.1 C.4.2 C.5.1 C.6.1 C.6.2 ESQ 17	D.2.1 D.2.2 D.4.1 D.5.1 D.6.1 D.6.3 ESQ 13
1	**Draw**	9.4.4	10.1.2	11.3.3 11.4.3 ESQ 16 ESQ 17	A.4.1 ESQ 18		C.2.2 C.6.2 ESQ 17	
1	**Label**	9.4.4 ESQ 17	10.1.1 10.1.2	11.2.4 11.3.3 11.3.4 ESQ 16 ESQ 17	A.3.2 A.4.2 ESQ 18	B.1.1	C.2.2 C.5.1 C.6.2 ESQ 17	D.2.2 ESQ 14
1	**List**	9.3.1 ESQ 16	10.3.4	11.1.1	A.1.1 A.3.2 A.5.2	B.1.1 B.2.1 B.4.2	C.6.2 C.6.3	D.2.3 D.3.1 D.6.1
1	**Measure**	ESQ 17		11.2.4		B.1.2		
1	**State**	9.1.2 9.2.1 9.4.2 9.4.3 9.4.4	10.1.1 10.2.1 10.2.2 10.2.5 10.2.8 10.3.1 ESQ 14	11.1.1 11.3.1 11.3.3 11.3.4 11.4.2 11.4.4 11.4.5	A.2.1 A.3.2 A.4.4 A.4.5 A.6.2	B.1.1 B.2.3 B.3.2 B.3.3 B.4.2 B.4.4 B.5.2 ESQ 13	C.1.1 C.1.2 C.1.3 C.2.2 C.2.3 C.4.2 C.5.3 C.6.1 C.6.2	D.2.1 D.2.3 D.3.1 D.3.2 D.6.1 D.6.2 D.6.3
2	**Annotate**	ESQ 17	10.2.7	11.2.1 11.3.4 11.4.3	A.1.1			D.2.2
2	**Calculate**	9.2.3 ESQ 16 ESQ 17	10.1.1 10.1.2 10.2.8	11.2.4				D.1.1 D.1.2 D.1.5 D.3.1
2	**Describe**	9.1.1 9.2.1 9.2.2 9.3.1 9.3.2 9.4.2 9.4.3	10.1.1 10.3.1 10.3.3	11.1.2 11.2.1 11.2.3 11.3.4 11.4.4 ESQ 17	A.1.1 A.3.2 ESQ 18	B.3.2 B.3.3 B.4.4 B.5.3	C.1.1 C.3.4 C.4.1	D.6.1 D.6.2 ESQ 13 ESQ 14
2	**Distinguish**	9.2.2 9.3.1 9.4.3	10.3.3	11.1.1 11.2.1 11.2.4		B.1.1 B.2.1	C.3.4	D.1.1 D.3.1 D.6.1 D.6.2
2	**Estimate**	ESQ 16	11.1.1	11.2.1			C.5.1 ESQ 14	D.4.1

AO	Command term	9. Plant biology	10. Genetics and evolution	11. Animal physiology	A. Neurobiology and behaviour	B. Biotechnology and bioinformatics	C. Ecology and conservation	D. Human physiology
2	Identify	9.1.2 9.2.2 ESQ 2 ESQ 3 ESQ 4 ESQ 6 ESQ 7 ESQ 9 ESQ 12	10.1.1 10.2.3 10.2.6 10.2.7 ESQ 2 ESQ 3 ESQ 5 ESQ 6 ESQ 8	11.2.4 11.3.1 11.3.4 11.3.6 11.3.7 ESQ 2 ESQ 3 ESQ 6 ESQ 7 ESQ 8 ESQ 10 ESQ 13	A.1.1 A.2.1 A.2.3 A.3.1 A.3.2 A.4.1 A.4.2 A.4.3 A.5.1 A.5.2 ESQ 6 ESQ 8 ESQ 9 ESQ 14	B.1.1 B.1.2 B.2.1 B.2.2 B.3.1 B.3.3 B.4.1 B.4.2 B.5.1 B.5.3 ESQ 4 ESQ 6 ESQ 7 ESQ 8 ESQ 9	C.1.3 C.2.1 C.3.2 C.3.3 C.4.1 C.5.1 C.5.3 C.6.1 ESQ 2 ESQ 3 ESQ 9 ESQ 13	D.1.1 D.1.3 D.1.4 D.2.2 D.2.3 D.3.1 D.4.1 D.5.1 ESQ 3 ESQ 4 ESQ 8 ESQ 10 ESQ 11
2	Outline	9.1.1 9.1.2 9.2.1 9.2.2 9.2.2 9.3.1 9.3.2 9.4.1 9.4.4 ESQ 17	10.1.1 10.2.1 10.3.3	11.1.1 11.1.2 11.1.3 11.2.1 11.2.4 11.3.1 11.3.2 11.3.3 11.3.4 11.3.6 11.4.2 11.4.4 ESQ 16 ESQ 18	A.1.1 A.1.2 A.3.2 A.4.1 A.4.3 A.4.5 A.5.1 A.5.2 A.6.2 ESQ 16 ESQ 17	B.1.1 B.1.2 B.2.1 B.2.3 B.3.2 B.4.4 B.5.2 ESQ 13	C.1.1 C.2.1 C.3.1 C.3.2 C.3.4 C.4.1 C.4.2 C.5.1 C.5.2	D.1.1 D.1.3 D.2.1 D.2.2 D.3.1 D.3.2 D.4.1 D.4.2 D.5.1 D.6.1 D.6.3 ESQ 13 ESQ 14
3	Analyse	ESQ 16	10.2.3 10.2.6	11.1.1 11.1.2 11.4.1	A.2.1 A.2.2	B.4.2	C.3.1 C.3.4	D.3.2
3	Comment	9.3.1	10.2.1 10.2.8	11.1.1 11.3.1	A.1.1 A.3.3 A.5.1	B.2.1 B.4.2 B.5.1	C.4.1	D.2.1 D.3.2 D.5.1 D.6.1
3	Compare	9.1.1		11.4.4	A.2.2 A.3.3			D.6.3
3	Compare and contrast	ESQ 19	10.2.6	11.3.1 11.4.4 ESQ 16	A.5.2	B.5.2	C.2.1 C.4.2	D.3.1 ESQ 13
3	Construct	9.1.2 9.4.1 9.4.2 9.4.4	10.1.1 10.2.2 10.2.3 10.2.5 10.2.6 10.2.7 ESQ 14		A.1.1		C.4.1	D.3.1 D.6.3
3	Deduce	9.2.1 9.3.2 9.4.2	10.2.1 10.2.8 ESQ 13	11.1.1 11.2.1 11.2.3 11.2.4 11.3.1 11.3.4 11.4.5 ESQ 12	A.1.1 A.2.1 A.2.3 A.3.2 A.4.3 A.4.4 A.6.2	B.1.1 B.3.3 B.4.3	C.1.3 C.1.4 C.6.2 C.6.3 ESQ 5 ESQ 10	D.1.2 D.4.1 D.4.2 D.5.1 D.6.3

AO	Command term	9. Plant biology	10. Genetics and evolution	11. Animal physiology	A. Neurobiology and behaviour	B. Biotechnology and bioinformatics	C. Ecology and conservation	D. Human physiology
3	Design	9.1.1 9.2.3 9.3.1 9.4.4 ESQ 16		11.1.2 11.4.1			C.1.3 C.3.4 ESQ 16	D.1.1
3	Determine	9.4.3	10.1.2 10.2.1 10.2.2 10.2.3 10.2.4 10.2.5 10.2.6 10.2.7 10.3.2 ESQ 14	11.1.2 11.3.5	A.3.3 A.4.1 A.4.3 A.4.5 A.5.2 A.6.2	B.2.1 ESQ 5	C.1.1 C.1.3 C.2.1 C.2.3 C.3.2 C.5.2 C.5.3 ESQ 8	D.1.1 D.4.2 ESQ 9
3	Discuss	9.2.1 9.3.1	10.3.3	11.3.6	A.1.1 A.2.2 A.3.3	B.1.2	C.4.1 ESQ 16	D.1.1
3	Evaluate	9.2.3 9.3.1		11.3.4 ESQ 18	A.2.1		C.3.4 C.4.1	D.3.1
3	Explain	9.1.1 9.1.2 9.1.3 9.2.1 9.2.2 9.3.1 9.3.2 9.4.1 9.4.4 ESQ 18	10.1.1 10.1.2 10.3.1 10.3.3 10.3.4	11.1.1 11.2.1 11.2.2 11.3.1 11.3.2 11.3.5 11.4.2 ESQ 16 ESQ 18	A.2.3 A.3.1 A.4.1 A.4.3 A.5.1 A.6.1 A.6.2 ESQ 16 ESQ 17	B.2.1 B.3.2 B.4.3 B.5.2 B.5.3	C.1.1 C.1.4 C.2.1 C.3.1 C.4.1 C.5.2 C.5.3 ESQ 16 ESQ 17	D.1.1 D.1.2 D.1.3 D.3.1 D.3.2 D.5.1 D.6.3
3	Predict	9.1.1 9.1.3	10.3.4 ESQ 4	11.3.4	A.3.1 A.4.1 A.4.4 A.6.2	B.5.2	C.1.4 C.5.2	D.2.1
3	Sketch	9.1.3 9.3.2	10.1.1 10.2.6	11.4.3	A.4.2	B.1.1	C.2.1 C.5.1	
3	Suggest	9.1.1 9.2.1 9.2.2 9.2.3 9.3.1 9.4.1	10.2.1 10.2.6 10.2.7 10.3.1	11.1.2 11.1.3 11.3.4 11.3.7 11.4.1 11.4.4	A.1.1 A.1.2 A.2.2 A.2.3 A.3.1 A.5.1 A.6.1 A.6.2	B.1.2 B.2.1 B.3.2 B.3.3 B.4.3 B.5.2	C.1.3 C.1.4 C.2.1 C.3.1 C.3.2 C.4.1 C.6.1	D.1.3 D.1.5 D.3.1 D.4.1 D.4.2

Cell biology 1

Chapter outline

In this chapter you will:
- describe how the evolution of multicellular organisms allowed cell specialisation and cell replacement
- compare the complex cell structure of eukaryotes to that of prokaryotes
- outline how the structure of biological membranes makes them fluid and dynamic
- outline how membranes control the composition of cells by active and passive transport
- outline the unbroken chain of life from the first cells on Earth to all cells in organisms alive today
- describe how cell division is essential and controlled.

KEY TERMS AND DEFINITIONS

Cell cycle – the sequence of events that takes place from one cell division until the next; made up of interphase, mitosis and cytokinesis.

Endosymbiosis – theory that proposes that mitochondria and chloroplasts evolved from bacteria.

Eukaryotic – organism whose cell contains a membrane-bound nucleus.

Fluid mosaic model – the accepted model of the structure of a membrane that includes a phospholipid bilayer in which proteins are embedded or attached to the surface.

Prokaryotic – organism whose genetic material is not contained in a nucleus.

Exercise 1.1 – Trends in smoking

1 Use the information in Figure 1.1 to answer the following questions:
  a State the percentage prevalence of smokers aged 20–24 in 1974.
  b State the percentage prevalence of smokers aged 20–24 in 2012.
  c Use the previous answers to calculate the percentage decrease of smoking prevalence in males aged 20–24 between 1974 and 2012.
  d Outline the general trend that you observe in Figure 1.1 for the prevalence of smoking in males aged 20–24.
  e What would be the difference in your answer to part d if the command term was 'describe' instead of 'outline'?

Cigarette smoking prevalance, by age, males, Great Britain, 1974–2012

······ 16–19　　── 20–24　　── 25–34　　── 35–49　　── 50–59　　── 16–19

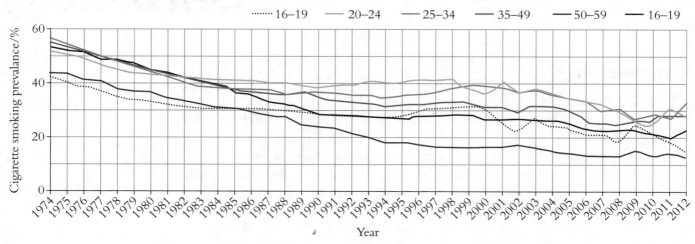

Figure 1.1 Trends in smoking in Great Britain.

2 Figure 1.2 shows a similar graph for the prevalence of both male and female smokers over time.

Cigarette smoking prevalance, adults aged 16 and over, Great Britain, 1974–2012

── males　　── females

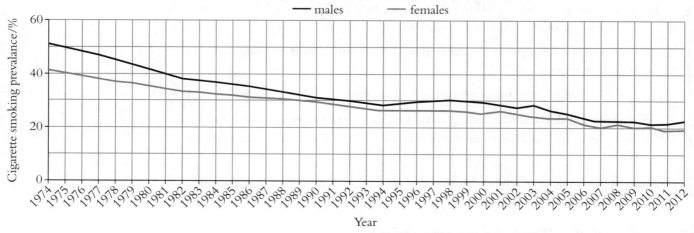

Figure 1.2 Trends in smoking prevalence for males and females over 16 in Great Britain.

a Compare the trend in smoking prevalence for males and females between 1974 and 2012.

b Explain why the prevalence of smoking has become similar in males and females.

3 You are responsible for the social media page of a company that promotes healthy living. Your editor has asked you write a tweet about why people should stop smoking. You only have 140 characters (not words) to use but must get your message across to the thousands of followers that will read it. Use your message to tell people why they should stop smoking cigarettes.

4 Read the following article about smoking before answering the questions that follow.

To vape, or not to vape?

Many people smoke electronic cigarettes (e-cigarettes) as these are deemed to be much safer than traditional tobacco-filled cigarettes. E-cigarettes are battery-operated devices that provide inhaled doses of a vaporised solution and liquid nicotine.

Manufacturers claim that the devices offer the following advantages:

- A safer alternative to tobacco cigarettes.
- Flavoured to taste better for customers.
- Help smokers to stop smoking and reduce the damaging effects of tar, nicotine and other carcinogenic ingredients.
- Fewer people, especially children, are now smoking tobacco cigarettes.

However, various authorities, such as the Food and Drug Administration (FDA) and the Centers for Disease Control and Prevention (CDC) have raised the following questions or statements.

- The products might not be safe to use.
- There are traces of nicotine and other toxic chemicals in the e-cigarettes.
- Use among children has doubled.
- The ingredients have not been sufficiently studied or regulated.
- The voltage of the device and the temperature of the vapour can affect level of emissions.
- New, probable carcinogens have been identified in vapour – propylene oxide and glycidol.

It is clear that manufacturers do not explicitly state that e-cigarettes are safer as they tend to imply this message. It is evidently successful as the industry is worth over three billion US dollars in America alone. Coupled with the recent decreasing trends in numbers of smokers, this can only be a good thing. Most e-cigarette companies are part of the same tobacco companies that they are trying to replace; is this unbiased enough for e-cigarette users to feel safe?

a Identify the evidence from this article that supports e-cigarettes as being safer than tobacco cigarettes.

b State the names of the authorities named in the article that offer a different viewpoint to the manufacturers.

c Glycidol is a potential carcinogen. Define *carcinogen*.

d Using the article above, discuss whether you think that students at your school should be allowed to smoke e-cigarettes.

5 The harvesting, production, and sale of tobacco is banned in Bhutan and the consumption of tobacco is largely prohibited in public places. The government of Bhutan has taken these steps as part of its drive for spiritual content and happiness (Gross National Happiness). Tobacco is recognised as being harmful to both spiritual and social health. Bhutan is the only country in the world with such wide-ranging control over tobacco. However, the penalties for infringement of these laws has been criticised as being draconian and overly harsh.

Using the information in the text above, and your own knowledge of the effects of smoking, evaluate whether Bhutan is right to enforce anti-tobacco laws.

Exercise 1.2 – Drawing and labelling cells

1 Look at the question and the answer provided below it (in the form of a diagram) before answering the following questions.

Draw a labelled diagram showing the ultrastructure of a *Paramecium* cell.

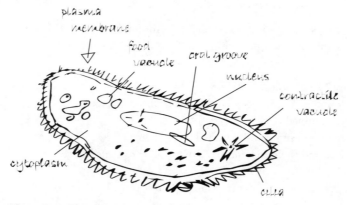

Figure 1.3 The ultrastructure of a *Paramecium* cell as drawn by a student.

a The student did **not** receive full marks for their drawing of the *Paramecium* cell. Suggest possible reasons why the student missed out on the full marks available.
b Identify the structure in Figure 1.3 that controls the water balance of the cell by contracting to expel its liquid contents.
c Look at the criteria in the table below. Some of these are guidance towards doing an excellent biological drawing. State the **four** criteria that are **not** relevant for an excellent biological drawing.

Straight label lines	Artistic quality ✗	Clearly written labels
Rough lines used for outlines ✗	Scale bar included where appropriate	Use of an arrowhead ✗
Lines touch the intended structure	Excellent use of colour ✗	Good use of the space allowed
No unnecessary shading	No unnecessary colouring	Clear lines drawn with pencil

Table 1.1

d Figure 1.4 shows a labelled drawing of a liver cell. Copy and annotate the drawing with the functions of each named structure.

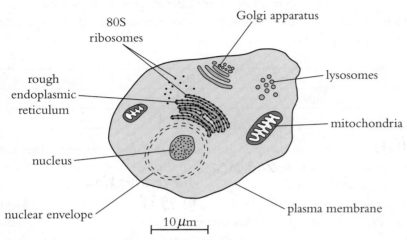

Figure 1.4 A labelled drawing of a liver cell.

e The liver cell is a eukaryotic cell. State **one** difference between an animal cell and a plant cell. → lack of cell wall

2 Figure 1.5 Shows a microscopic image of a mitochondrion.

Figure 1.5 A microscopic image of a mitochondrion.

a State the size shown by the scale bar.
b Use a ruler to measure the length of the mitochondrion at its longest points.
c Use a ruler to measure the length of the scale bar.
d Use the formula provided to calculate the actual length of the mitochondrion. Convert all units to be the same and show your working.

$$\frac{\text{scale}}{\text{length of scale bar}} = \frac{\text{actual length}}{\text{measured length of mitochondrion}}$$

e State the formula used for calculating the magnification of the image.
f Calculate the magnification of the microscope used to capture the image in Figure 1.5.
g Outline the role of the mitochondrion in eukaryotic cells.

Exercise 1.3 – Membrane structure and transport

1 Copy and complete the paragraph to show your understanding of how models of membrane structure lead to our current knowledge of membranes. All of the answers are included in the word grid below.

three	microscopy	bilayer	falsification
1925	mosaic	evidence	integral
tension	scientists	Danielli	

Many _scientists_ have been involved in refining our understanding of membrane structure. This happens as they use _evidence_ to support, and reject, theories as new data is gathered by developments in technology and _falsification_. The lipid bilayer was first proposed by Gorter and Grendel (_1925_) but it was Davson and _Danielli_ (1935) that developed this theory to show a model of a phospholipid _bilayer_ between two layers of globular protein. The Davson–Danielli model attempted to explain the phenomenon of surface _m_____. The Davson–Danielli model was usurped in 1972 when Singer and Nicholson developed their 'fluid _mosaic_' model. This model described _tension_ proteins throughout the membrane and is the basis for the model that you use today in your biology lessons. Freeze-etching was used to provide a _three_-dimensional view of the surface and detail of the membrane's structures and contributed to the _'_____ of the Davson–Danielli model.

2 Using the information in question 1, describe how falsification of theories allows scientists to develop new theories as they gather new evidence.

3 You may think of cholesterol as a bad thing, due to its association with heart disease and fatty foods. However, your membranes require cholesterol to function properly.
Which of the following statements about cholesterol is true?
A Cholesterol makes the membrane less flexible to give support.
B Cholesterol enables the membrane to remove hydrogen ions from saturated phospholipids.
C Cholesterol enables the membrane to maintain fluidity, even when there is a change in temperature.

4 Define the following words.
a Hypertonic.
b Hypotonic.
c Isotonic.

5 Carlos carries out an investigation to measure the change in mass of potato cylinders before and after being immersed in solutions of different sucrose concentrations. He records his results as below.

Test	Sucrose concentration (%)	Average percentage change in mass
A	0.0	2.5
B	10.0	−6.1
C	30.0	−17.5
D	50.0	−25.1
E	70.0	−25.5

Table 1.2

a State the sucrose concentrations that were hypertonic.
b State the sucrose concentration that was hypotonic.
c On graph paper, draw a line graph that shows how the sucrose concentration affected the average percentage change in the mass of the potato.
d Using the graph from part c, estimate the sucrose concentration that you would expect to be isotonic.
e Explain why the potato mass changed as it did for the range of sucrose concentrations.

Exercise 1.4 – Ultrastructure of cells

1 Eukaryotic and prokaryotic cells have a number of differences and similarities between them.
  a Copy and complete the table below to show whether the description of the ultrastructure is from a eukaryotic cell or a prokaryotic cell.

Structure	Description	Eukaryotic or prokaryotic?
Nucleus	Present, surrounded by nuclear envelope	
Mitochondria	Never present	
Chloroplasts	Never present	
Endoplasmic reticulum	Usually present	
Ribosomes	80S	
Chromosomes	Long strands of DNA, associated with histones	
Cell wall	Always present	

Table 1.3

  b Using all of the structures in the first column of the table in part a, outline the structure of a typical eukaryotic cell.

c   Mitochondria can be found in the cytoplasm of most eukaryotic cells and their primary function is to produce adenosine triphosphate (ATP) by extracting energy from nutrients. This ATP is crucial to a range of cellular functions and is critical to our survival. The process of extracting energy is aerobic respiration and requires oxygen.

    i   State the singular term for mitochondria.

    ii   Explain why the production of ATP is important for the survival of our cells.

d   State the main function of the eukaryotic organelles listed below.

    i   Plasma membrane.

    ii   Cytoplasm.

    iii Centrioles.

    iv Mitochondria.

    v   Chloroplast.

    vi Vacuole.

    vii 80S ribosomes.

    viii Nucleus.

    ix Rough endoplasmic reticulum.

    x   Golgi apparatus.

    xi Lysosomes.

    xii Cell wall.

e   Of the organelles above, which ones would typically be found in plant cells but **not** in animal cells?

Exercise 1.5 – Cell division

1   Interphase is the longest phase of the cell cycle and is made of three main stages: G1, S and G2.

a   State the terms that are represented by 'G' and 'S' during interphase.

b   Determine the stage of interphase that produces the proteins required for DNA synthesis.

c   State what happens to the amount of DNA in the S-phase of interphase?

d   State which part of interphase is when mitochondria are replicated?

2   Cyclins control the progression of cells through the cell cycle and were a serendipitous discovery by Tim Hunt. Cells can only enter the next stage of the cell cycle when each cyclin reaches a specific level. The cyclins bind to CDKs (cyclin-dependent kinases) and activate them. This, in turn, activates other proteins in the cell by attaching phosphate groups and they are then able to carry out their tasks.

a   Tim Hunt was awarded the Nobel Prize in 2001 for his discovery of cyclins. His discovery was one of serendipity and Dr Hunt has often spoken about this in his public speaking engagements. Define *serendipity*.

b Look at the graph in Figure 1.6.

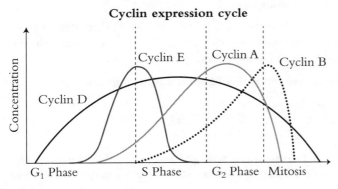

Figure 1.6 A simple cyclin graph.

   i Identify the cyclin that is required throughout the cell cycle.
   ii State which cyclin activates the G2 phase when it reaches its threshold level.
   iii Using Figure 1.6, describe how cyclins are important in the regulation of the cell cycle.

3 The stages of mitosis are outlined below. List them in the correct order:

anaphase, telophase, metaphase, prophase, cytokinesis

4 Klaus is observing cells under a microscope that are undergoing mitosis. He identifies six cells that that have chromosomes lined up on the equator of their cell. Klaus also observes three cells that have visible chromosomes due to the disintegration of the nuclear membrane. There are five cells that have separated sister chromatids. The other 31 cells do not show any signs of mitosis.
   a State the formula required to calculate the mitotic index of this particular population of cells.
   b Calculate the mitotic index for these cells.
   c State the stage of mitosis are the five cells with separated sister chromatids?
   d Klaus finds the following text in his notes: *a package of histones with DNA wrapped around them*. State the name of the structure that his notes must be describing.

Exercise 1.6 – Endosymbiotic theory

1 Read the following conversation between two students and answer the questions that follow.

   Paul: **Hi.**

   Riya: Hi, how are you?

   Paul: **Good, thanks. I'm revising endosymbiotic theory after Mr Hull mentioned it in class yesterday. He said that certain parts of eukaryotic cells were once independent prokaryotic cells.**

   Riya: Yes, I think he mentioned mitochondria.

Paul: **Well, I don't understand. How did mitochondria become part of eukaryotic cells if they didn't exist?**

Riya: Basically, some cells engulfed the mitochondria and were then able to make useful energy. It is really clever and allowed these cells to develop into cells capable of respiration, not to mention photosynthesis as well.

Paul: **Wow! Did someone see all of this happen under a microscope?**

Riya: Microscopes were nowhere near invented when all of this happened! We just happen to know that the cell that was able to perform respiration was an ancestor of the mitochondria… and scientists worked it out from there.

Paul: **Thanks, Riya. Now I understand how eukaryotes evolved through the incorporation of free-living organelles into larger prokaryotic cells and organelles.**

a State the parts of eukaryotic cells that were once suggested to be prokaryotic cells.

b State the role of the mitochondria in cells today.

c Outline why there was no evidence at the time that endosymbiosis happened.

d Which organelle, not mentioned in the conversation, is the site for photosynthesis?

e State an example of a prokaryotic cell.

? Exam-style questions

1 **The movement of molecules across a partially permeable membrane is not affected by which factor? [1]**
   A Concentration gradient of the particles diffusing
   B Surface area of the membrane
   C A selective membrane
   D Temperature

2 **The correct movement of water molecules in osmosis is: [1]**
   A From high solute concentration to low solute concentration
   B From low water concentration to high water concentration
   C From low solute concentration to high solute concentration
   D Between solutes of equal concentration

3 **Observe the following statements about cell theory.**
   I   Living organisms are composed of cells.
   II   Cells are the smallest units of life.
   III Cells come from pre-existing cells.

   Which combination of statements about cell theory is true from the statements above? [1]
   A I and III only
   B I and II only
   C I, II and III
   D None of the above

4   Outline what happens to the chromosomes in each stage of the cell cycle. [10]

5   Draw and label a diagram to show the structure of the fluid mosaic model of the plasma membrane. [8]

6   Design a reliable investigation to test the effect of solute concentration on the rate of osmosis, using potatoes in solution. [6]

1) D

2) A

3) C

4)

Interphase: DNA in chromosomes copies itself ready for mitosis + longest phase

Prophase: DNA in chromosomes and copies condenses + become more visible → membrane arnd nucleus disappears.

Metaphase: Chromosomes + copies line in middle of cell

Anaphase: "   ,, ,, pulled to diff. ends of cell.

Telophase: New membranes form arnd chromosomes at each end of cell

Cytokenisis: Cell membrane pinches in + divides into 2 daughter cells.

2 Molecular biology

KEY TERMS AND DEFINITIONS

Amino acid – building block of proteins.

Condensation reaction – removal of water to form a larger molecule.

Enzyme – biological catalyst, globular protein.

Monosaccharide – simple carbohydrate.

Polypeptide chain – chain of amino acids.

Polysaccharide – natural polymers of sugars joined by condensation reactions.

Proteome – the complete set of proteins in an individual's genome.

Exercise 2.1 – Water, carbohydrates and lipids

1 You are expected to be able to draw molecular diagrams of glucose, ribose, a saturated fatty acid, and a generalised fatty acid. Draw a molecular diagram of the molecules in parts a–d.

  a Alpha-D-glucose.

  b Beta-D-glucose.

  c Ribose.

  d $CH_3(CH_2)_{16}COOH$.

  e State the name of the molecule in part d.

2 Table 2.1 shows some of the chemical groups that you might be required to draw. Copy and complete the table to show the name, structure and simplified notation of each of the groups.

Name of group	Full molecular structure	Simplified notation
Hydroxyl	—O—H	
Carboxyl		—COOH
	H H—C— H (with H above and below C)	—CH$_3$

Table 2.1

3 Many years ago, people believed that organic compounds could only be created in real-life living things. They did not believe that molecules of living matter could be created in the laboratory as all compounds required a spark of life. This is the theory of vitalism. Friedrich Wöhler was able to produce urea by heating an inorganic compound known as ammonium cyanate. Wöhler had successfully created an organic compound from something inorganic.

   a State the name of the organic compound that Wöhler created.

   b Identify the theory that the work of Wöhler was able to disprove.

   c *Wöhler had a major role to play in the molecular biology that we learn about today.*
   Comment on this statement.

4 The polarity of water contributes to many of the important properties that make it such a special substance. Hans is playing sport outside and, as he runs more, he starts to sweat. He remembers what a good coolant water is from what his teacher told him in a biology class.

   a State the name of the bonds that must be broken to convert water from liquid to vapour.

   b Outline why water is such a good coolant.

   c Water has cohesive and adhesive properties. Compare and contrast the cohesive and adhesive properties of water.

   d The blood in the human body is a vital transport medium that carries many different molecules to where they need to be in the body. Not all of these metabolites are soluble. Copy the table below and state whether each metabolite is soluble or insoluble.

Metabolite	Solubility
Glucose	
Amino acids	
Cholesterol	
Lipids	
Oxygen	
Sodium chloride	

Table 2.2

5 For each of the groups shown below in parts a, b and c, state the name of **two** different carbohydrates.
   a Monosaccharides.
   b Disaccharides.
   c Polysaccharides.
   d Explain why glucose is such an important sugar in biology.
   e Glucose and fructose are known as reducing sugars. Cu^{2+} ions are reduced to Cu^+ ions when heated with a particular solution. This causes the solution to turn from blue to a different colour. Design an investigation that would test different substances for the presence of a reducing sugar.
   f If you were to carry out the investigation designed in part e, predict the colour change of two substances of varying concentrations of reducing sugar.
   g Describe how polysaccharides such as cellulose, glycogen and starch are used in plants and animals.
   h Outline how maltose is formed.

6 Lipids contain more energy per gram than carbohydrates or proteins, and are therefore lighter than carbohydrates that store an equivalent amount of energy. Lipids are less dense than water, which is why oil floats on water. Aquatic animals have larger fat stores and this helps them to float on water. Lipids are non-polar, insoluble molecules and have no effect on the net movement of water. Lipids are excellent insulators as fat beneath the skin reduces heat loss. Animals such as whales and polar bears benefit greatly from this.
   a State the **four** main properties of lipids as stated in the text above.
   b State the type of diffusion that is **not** affected by lipids.
   c Read this conversation between two scientists and answer the questions that follow.

   Asha: **Hi, Ada! What are you eating?**

   Ada: Hi, just a donut with extra frosting on top. It's pretty amazing.

   Asha: **No, that does not sound healthy at all. Donuts and frosting are full of artificial trans fats. It makes them last longer but it's so bad for you.**

   Ada: Really? If I put on weight, I will just exercise and it'll be OK.

   Asha: **Come on now, you must know about the health risks of these fats? They are linked to high cholesterol levels, coronary heart disease (CHD) and strokes.**

   Ada: *You're* talking nonsense, there have been patterns found between the intake of the fats and CHD but no-one has actually established a causal relationship.

   Asha: **What are you talking about? Eating trans fats makes you likely to suffer from CHD, I have read this in loads of places.**

   Ada: On the contrary, our friend Abdu, who lives in Kenya, tells me about his people. Apparently, they have a diet rich in saturated fats and hardly anyone suffers from CHD. Just because there is a pattern in some places, it doesn't prove what actually causes it. There are so many other factors that must be considered. You should definitely wait for more evidence before jumping to such conclusions. Now, let me enjoy my donut!

   i Artificial trans fats are formed when vegetable oil is hydrogenated. State what this process does to the oil.
   ii Suggest other foods that might also contain artificial trans fats.

iii State the sort of relationship that Ada is suggesting has **not** been found between the fats and CHD.

iv Ada and Asha cannot agree on this issue. Evaluate whether the health claims about lipids and CHD are true or not. When evaluating such claims, it is up to you to weigh up the strengths and limitations.

v Suggest the other reasons that might influence whether someone is likely to suffer from CHD.

vi *A clinical study that restricted people to a certain diet would be an excellent way of establishing a causal relationship between artificial trans fats and CHD.*
Comment on this statement and whether you agree with it or not.

Exercise 2.2 – Proteins

1 Copy the paragraph and state the missing terms required for this introductory paragraph about proteins.

_____ reactions between amino acid monomers form _____ chains, as the amino group of one amino acid is _____ bonded with the carboxyl group of the next amino acid. The synthesis of polypeptides is carried out by _____ in the cytoplasm and there are _____ different amino acids that make up the polypeptides.

2 State the type of bond mainly responsible for the following parts of protein formation.
a Primary structure.
b Secondary structure.
c Tertiary structure.

3 Every individual has a unique proteome. Define *proteome*.

4 Read the text about different proteins and their functions before answering the questions that follow.

Rubsico, insulin, hemoglobin, immunoglobin and rhodopsin are all spherical proteins that are often involved in the metabolism of a cell. Rubsico is involved in carbon fixation in chloroplasts but the other four proteins are more commonly associated with animal functions. Insulin regulates glucose uptake, immunoglobin helps to fight infections as part of the immune system, and hemoglobin transports oxygen. Rhodospin is found in the rod cells of the retina and is able to detect light of low intensity. Collagen and spider silk are long and thread-like proteins that are made of long polypeptide chains. The hydrophobic R group of these chains is exposed. Collagen gives tensile strength to parts of the body and spider silk is tough, extensible fibre spun by spiders to make their webs.

a State the proteins in the text that are globular proteins.
b State the proteins in the text that are fibrous proteins.
c List the proteins that have an application in plant cells.
d Distinguish between globular and fibrous proteins.
e Outline the application of collagen.
f Outline the application of insulin.
g Outline the application of immunoglobin.

5 Look at Figure 2.1.

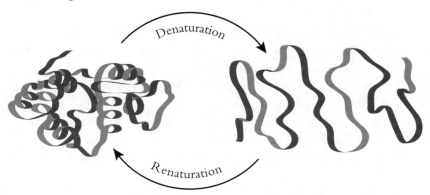

Figure 2.1 A protein that has been exposed to a strong alkaline solution.

a Describe how the solution causes proteins to become denatured. You should refer to the bonds between the amino acids in your answer.

b Explain how denaturation prevents the protein from carrying out its function.

6 The number of amino acid sequences can be calculated by multiplying the number of different types of amino acid (20) by the number of amino acids in the chain. For example, a dipeptide would have 20×20 amino acid sequences.

a Calculate the number of amino acid sequences in a tripeptide.

b Calculate the number of amino acid sequences in a polypeptide that contains six amino acids.

7 The proteome is the mapping of the entire set of proteins expressed by the genome of an organism. Many mouse proteins are homologous with their human counterparts, causing scientists to use the mouse brain as a model for studying and observing the human brain. The expression and distribution of proteins in the human brain can be mapped out and explored further.

Evaluate the use of studying the proteome of a mouse brain.

Exercise 2.3 – Enzymes

1 Look at Figure 2.2 and answer the questions that follow.

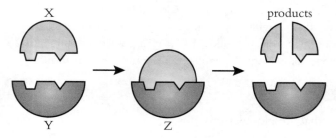

Figure 2.2 How enzymes work.

a Copy and label Figure 2.2 and add labels to state the names of X, Y and Z.

b Annotate your copy of Figure 2.2 to outline what is happening at each stage of the reaction.

c Identify the location of the active site of the enzyme and add a label to it.
d Define *enzyme*.

2 Figure 2.3 shows the effect of temperature on the reaction rate of an enzyme. Use Figure 2.3 to answer the questions that follow.

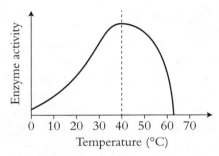

Figure 2.3 The effect of temperature on the reaction rate of an enzyme.

a State the optimum temperature of this enzyme.
b Explain why the enzyme activity decreases after that point.
c Design an investigation that allows you to measure the effect of different pH solutions on the hydrolysis of starch by amylase.
d Amalia carries out your method to investigate the effect of different pH solutions on the hydrolysis of starch by amylase. Predict the optimum pH of the amylase for the hydrolysis of starch.
e State the name of the disaccharide that the starch was broken down into.
f Most enzymes work best at a neutral pH but there are plenty of examples that do **not**. Suggest an example of an enzyme that works best in highly acidic conditions.

3 Enzymes have a wide range of uses in industry, ranging from washing detergents to juice extraction, to the production of antibodies and the softening of leather. Table 2.3 lists several uses of enzymes.

Enzyme	Industry	Uses
Protease, amylase, lipase	Detergents	Removing protein, lipid and starch stains
Chymosin	Cheese production	Coagulates milk proteins
Isomerase	Food	Fructose manufacture
Amylase	Baking	Converts starch to sugar
Glucose oxidase	Biosensors	Tests for glucose in samples of blood
Ligninase	Paper	Removes lignin from pulp
Invertase	Food	Smoothing agent in chocolates
Streptokinase	Medicine	Treatment of bruises
Protease	Leather	Removes hair and softens leather
Protease	Photography	Digests gelatin of old film

Table 2.3 The role of enzymes in industry.

a *The most important role of enzymes is in the food and drink industries.* Discuss this statement, using the information in Table 2.3, and your own knowledge of enzyme use in industry.

b Read the article about Liam and answer the questions that follow.

> ## LACTOSE-FREE MILK HELPS LOCAL BOY
>
> Liam (14) is lactose-intolerant and, as a result, he suffers from regular diarrhoea and flatulence. Liam is unable to break down lactose in the small intestine as he cannot produce the important enzyme that carries out this function, lactase. For years, Liam has suffered or not been able to have milk on his favourite cereals but hope is around the corner. Liam's local shop now stocks lactose-free milk, thanks to new enzyme technology. The technology uses lactase from bacteria that is purified and enclosed in capsules before milk is passed through a container that contains the immobilised lactase. Liam has been researching immobilised enzymes for a school project and provided us with the following quote; *'I am happy that I can have this milk because it tastes so much nicer and sweeter than the milk that used to make me ill. I am not the only person with this problem as I have read that people in other parts of the world do not produce lactase either. However, I am lucky because I have access to this lactose-free milk but not everyone is that lucky'*. Liam is referring to the lack of lactose-free milk in some countries, even though many people in the population do not produce lactase naturally. An example of this is India, where many people are lactose-intolerant but commercial production of lactose-free milk only began in 2015. It seems that Liam has benefited from enzyme production but there may be many people in the world who do not have the same benefits available to them.

    i State the name of the enzyme that Liam is unable to produce naturally.

    ii Outline the advantages of using immobilised enzymes.

    iii Lactose-free milk is not available in many developing countries even though some populations cannot produce lactase naturally. Suggest how this problem might be rectified.

    iv Liam states that his lactose-free milk tastes sweeter than normal milk. Explain why the lactose-free milk tastes sweeter.

c Chante carries out the following method to measure the rate of reaction using catalase.

> **1** 10 ml catalase is mixed with 30 ml hydrogen peroxide solution.
> **2** Oxygen, released via delivery tube, is collected by an inverted cylinder of water.
> **3** The amount of oxygen (cm^3) produced at 30-second intervals is observed and recorded.

    i Identify the independent variable in the investigation.

    ii Identify the dependent variable in the investigation.

    iii The collection of oxygen might not be reliable because oxygen might escape from the delivery apparatus. Suggest a method of measuring the oxygen produced that might be more reliable than the inverted cylinder method.

iv Chante records her results as shown in Table 2.4. Use these results to draw a graph to show the rate of reaction over time.

Time (s)	Oxygen collected (cm³)
30	7
60	12
90	17
120	20
150	23
180	24
210	25
240	26

Table 2.4

v Describe the pattern shown in the graph that you have drawn for the previous question.

Exercise 2.4 – DNA, RNA and transcription

1 a A nucleotide contains a nitrogenous base, a pentose sugar and a phosphate group. Sketch and label a simple diagram of a nucleotide.

b State the full names of DNA and RNA.

c Distinguish between a DNA and a RNA molecule. A table is often a good way of showing this information and ensures that you refer to both DNA and RNA in your answer.

d Compare and contrast the bonding between the base pairs of T and A, and G and C. Remember that a 'compare and contrast' question expects you to account for similarities AND differences, while referring to both examples in your answer.

e Scientists often use models to represent the real world and it was the collaborative modelling over many years that allowed scientists to understand DNA structure. Miescher was the first person to record the isolation of DNA in 1869 and Edwin Chargaff suggested that there would be pairing between the four bases. Watson and Crick continued to work on various models, using what others had previously observed. This included the vital X-ray diffraction shown by Rosalind Franklin, who was working with Maurice Wilkins. Watson and Crick used cardboard models and scrap metal to show the three-dimensional structure of DNA. It is this model that is accepted and used in science lessons around the world today. Although Franklin arguably made the key discovery, she did not realise this and it was Watson and Crick (and later, Wilkins) that were awarded the prestigious Nobel Prize for their discovery.

i *Franklin was most responsible for the discovery of the structure of DNA.* Comment on this statement, using the information from the text above to support your judgement.

ii Outline the important roles of competition and cooperation in the discovery of the structure of DNA.

2 The paragraph below describes the process of DNA replication but it can be made clearer, especially when answering an exam question by putting it into stages. Construct the process of DNA replication as a step-by-step process.

> DNA replication can be divided into distinct steps. The two strands require 'unzipping' and this is carried out by DNA helicase. DNA helicase moves along the double helix and unwinds the two strands by breaking the weak hydrogen bonds between the bases. This then exposes unpaired bases and this is the template for the formation of a complementary strand. Free bases will pair with their complementary base on the template strand (G with C, and T with A). DNA polymerase links the new nucleotides together and the DNA molecule will begin to supercoil to produce a new double helix of DNA.

3 Transcription is the first step in protein synthesis. Answer the following questions about transcription.
  a State the name of the enzyme that is responsible for transcribing a sequence of DNA bases onto the mRNA.
  b State the name of the strand that is the template for transcription.
  c State the name of the base that pairs with adenine.
  d There are four different bases that can make up the triplet code of an amino acid. Determine how many different possible triplet combinations there are.

4 Deduce the complementary base sequences for these mRNA sequences.
  a GUC CCU AGA UUG
  b CGA CCU CAC AAC
  c CCC GCU GGA GUG

5 a State the name of the organelle where the synthesis of polypeptides in translation takes place.
  b Define *codon*.
  c Outline the role of a 'stop codon'.

6 PCR is a technique that allows the rapid production of multiple copies of DNA, using *Taq* DNA polymerase. PCR is often used in forensic science to allow scientists to work with even the smallest amounts of DNA that have been found at crime scenes. Just one molecule of DNA can be multiplied until billions of copies are produced by the heating and cooling of a DNA sample.
  a State the full name of PCR.
  b State the name of the enzyme used in PCR.
  c If there is one copy of a gene, calculate how many copies will be produced after eight cycles of PCR.

Exercise 2.5 – Cellular respiration and photosynthesis

1 a Define *cellular respiration*.
  b State the word and chemical equations for aerobic respiration.

2 For each of the following stages of respiration, outline what happens.
  a Glycolysis.
  b Link reaction.

3 An overview of cellular respiration is shown in Figure 2.4.

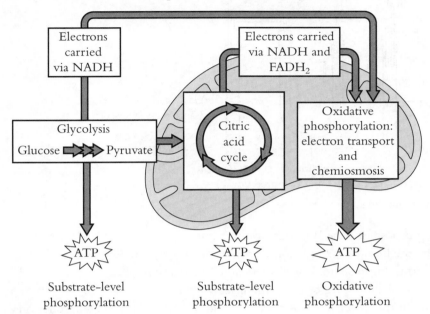

Figure 2.4 An overview of cellular respiration.

  a State the part of the cell that glycolysis takes place in.
  b State the part of the mitochondrion that the following take place in.
   i Kreb's cycle.
   ii Electron transport chain.
  c Explain why ATP is so important in meeting the needs of our body.

4 Anaerobic respiration is respiration without the presence of oxygen. It is useful in many different ways, both artificially and naturally.
  a Outline how humans have used anaerobic respiration in yeast and bacteria for their own benefit.
  b State the product that animals produce as a result of anaerobic respiration in cells.
  c State the products of anaerobic respiration in yeast.
  d Compare the amount of ATP produced in aerobic and anaerobic respiration.

5 Vega sets up the following investigation using a respirometer (Figure 2.5). She knows that this measures the rate of oxygen taken in by an organism, and this will give her an idea of the rate of respiration for that organism at that time.
  • Insect is placed into tube A with the tap closed.
  • Alkali solution (or soda lime pellets) at the bottom of tube A will absorb any carbon dioxide that is produced.
  • Tube B has the same set-up but without an insect inside.
  • The two tubes are connected by a manometer.
  • As the insect takes in oxygen for respiration in Tube A, the coloured liquid in the manometer will move in the direction of Tube A.
  • The amount of oxygen consumed in a particular time can be calculated.

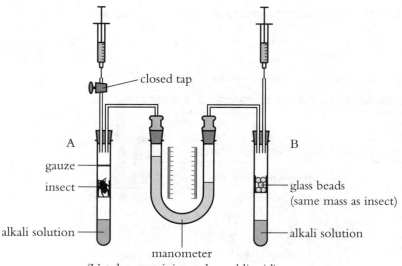

closed tap

A

gauze

insect

alkali solution

B

glass beads
(same mass as insect)

alkali solution

manometer
(U–tube containing coloured liquid)

Figure 2.5 A respirometer.

a Explain the purpose of Tube B in this investigation.
b Outline why the liquid in the manometer moves towards Tube A.
c Discuss the ethical implications of this research investigation.
d Suggest an ethical alternative to using the insect.
e Vega carries out the experiment using an ant and a beetle. The average respiration rate was calculated and recorded as follows. Analyse the results that Vega gathered.

Insect	Rate of respiration (mm^3 hr^{-1})
Ant	13.8
Beetle	28.3

Table 2.5

6 Photosynthesis converts the energy in sunlight into the chemical energy required for life. Carbon dioxide from the atmosphere and water taken in from the roots is combined in the presence of sunlight and chlorophyll to produce useful carbohydrates and oxygen.
  a State the word equation for photosynthesis.
  b State the chemical equation for photosynthesis.
  c Outline the two main stages of photosynthesis.
  d Photosynthesis requires energy. Outline how plants are able to use ATPase to make ATP in chloroplasts.
  e Compare and contrast the processes of respiration and photosynthesis.

7 Light and carbon dioxide are both limiting factors of photosynthesis.
  a Define *limiting factor*.
  b Look at Figure 2.6 and answer the questions that follow.

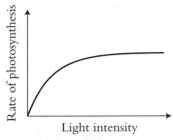

Figure 2.6 The effect of light intensity on the rate of photosynthesis.

  i Describe the effect of light on the rate of photosynthesis.
  ii Explain why the rate of photosynthesis is affected by light in this way.
  iii Suggest a reason for a low level of light intensity.
  iv Explain why the rate does **not** keep on increasing rapidly after a certain point.
  v Sketch a graph to show how carbon dioxide is a limiting factor of photosynthesis.
c The effect of temperature on the rate of photosynthesis has a very different shape to the graphs for light and carbon dioxide. This may also depend on the type of plant used as a plant from the Middle East would have a very different optimum temperature than a plant from the Finnish tundra.
  i Sketch a graph that shows a possible curve for the effect of temperature on two plants – one from the cold plains of the Finnish tundra and one from the desert in the Middle East.
  ii Suggest why the two plants have different optimum temperatures.
  iii Explain why the rate decreases after the optimum temperature for each plant.

? Exam-style questions

1 Which of the following is not a property of water? [1]
  A Cohesive
  B Capillary
  C Adhesive
  D Solvent

2 Identify the fatty acid shown in Figure 2.7. [1]

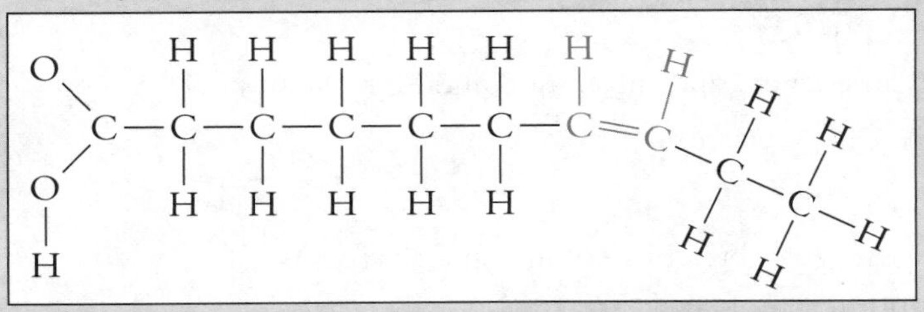

Figure 2.7 A fatty acid.

  A Unsaturated *cis* fatty acid
  B Unsaturated *trans* fatty acid
  C Saturated *cis* fatty acid
  D Saturated *trans* fatty acid

3 **What type of reaction takes place when a dipeptide is broken down into** two **amino acids? [1]**
   A Hydrolysis
   B Condensation
   C Polymerisation
   D Dipeptide bond

4 **Which of the following is** not **an advantage of lactose-free milk? [1]**
   A No harmful side effects
   B Faster rate of fermentation
   C Sweeter tasting milk
   D Prevents formation of lactase

5 **The universality of the genetic code allows gene transfer between species. This makes the production of which human hormone in bacteria possible? [1]**
   A Insulin
   B Diabetes
   C Adrenaline
   D DNA polymerase

6 **Which of the following is** not **a limiting factor in photosynthesis? [1]**
   A Light intensity
   B Carbon dioxide
   C Temperature
   D Oxygen

7 a State **three** factors that affect the activity of an enzyme. [3]
   b Describe how temperature affects the rate of activity of an enzyme. [3]
   c Most enzymes work best at a neutral pH. Suggest an enzyme that has an optimum pH of 2–3. [1]

8 **A DNA strand is comprised of individual nucleotides joined together.**
   a Draw a diagram to show how two nucleotides are joined together. [2]
   b Label your diagram to show the different parts of one of the nucleotides. [3]
   c Label your diagram to show the type of bond that joins the nucleotides together. [2]

9 a Define *enzyme*. [2]
   b Describe the induced fit model of an enzyme. [3]
   c Using diagrams, outline the reaction steps of an enzyme and substrate colliding to form new products. [4]

10 **Anaerobic respiration has many uses.**
   a Explain how respiration without oxygen in yeast gives bread its volume and shape. [3]
   b State the **two** products of anaerobic respiration in muscle cells. [2]
   c Compare how animals and plants get the glucose needed for respiration. [2]

11 **Discuss the uses of enzymes in industry, using at least two named examples in your answer. You should include any advantages of using the enzyme in this manner. [5]**

Genetics 3

Chapter outline

In this chapter you will:
- describe how every living organism inherits a blueprint for life from its parents
- outline how chromosomes carry genes in a linear sequence that is shared by members of a species
- describe how alleles segregate during meiosis allowing new combinations to be formed by the fusion of gametes
- explain how inheritance follows patterns
- outline the techniques developed for artificial manipulation of DNA, cells and organisms.

KEY TERMS AND DEFINITIONS

Alleles – different versions of a gene found at a locus of a chromosome.

Chromosome – long structure of DNA that carries genetic information of the cell.

DNA profiling – analysis of DNA from samples and compared to that of a known individual.

Inheritance – the passing of traits or characteristics from parent to offspring.

Meiosis – cell division that produces haploid number of chromosomes in daughter cell.

Exercise 3.1 – Genes

1 Sickle cell anemia is a blood disorder that affects the ability of the blood to carry oxygen properly. The effects for a person living with sickle cell anemia are constant, and often quite painful. People with sickle cell anemia have hemoglobin that is abnormally shaped due to one of a number of genetic reasons. Sufferers will experience great pain and damage to any of the following parts of the body: spleen, eyes, lungs, liver, penis, bones, skin, and many more. Symptoms include anemia, strokes, spleen dysfunction, pain crises, and acute chest syndrome.

  a Sketch a diagram to show what a sickle cell looks like when compared to a normal red blood cell.

  b Explain why a sickle cell is **not** able to carry as much oxygen as a normal red blood cell.

  c Outline the structure and function of hemoglobin.

  d Outline why sickle cell sufferers experience such terrible bouts of pain.

  e Describe how the shape of the sickle cell prevents it from getting around the body to deliver oxygen.

f A red blood cell typically lives for around 100 days but a sickle cell will only survive for 10 to 20 days. The body cannot make enough red blood cells. Predict the consequence for a body that is not making as many red blood cells.

g Outline the genetic reasons that cause sickle cell anemia.

h Sickle cell anemia is controlled by a single gene mutation. Malaria is a fatal disease caused by a parasite that invades red blood cells. Look at the following scenarios (A, B and C) and answer the questions that follow.

   A A person that is heterozygous for sickle cell anemia in a malarial country.

   B A person who is homozygous for sickle cell anemia in a malarial country.

   C A person with normal hemoglobin in a malarial country.

    i Identify the person that is most likely to contract malaria.

    ii Identify the person who has a high chance of suffering from sickle cell anemia.

    iii Identify the person(s) who has protection from malaria.

    iv Explain why the person(s) with protection from malaria does **not** suffer from sickle cell anemia.

    v The presence of **two** alleles that both benefit the body is known as which key term?

i Describe the structure of a DNA molecule.

j Identify the key words being described by the following definitions:

   i A section of DNA that codes for the formation of a polypeptide.

   ii A different form of a gene that occupies the same gene locus on a chromosome.

   iii The whole of the genetic information of an organism.

   iv A change in the base sequence of a gene.

   v Triplet of bases in the DNA molecule that codes for proteins.

2 a The Human Genome Project was able to sequence the entire base sequence of human genes. Copy and complete the table below to indicate the potential uses of the Human Genome Project.

Possible use	Useful application of the Human Genome Project? Yes/No
Physical mapping of all chromosomes	
Altering the chromosome number	
Screening of genetic diseases	
Better understanding of genetic diseases	
Allows for bacteria to be destroyed	
Development of drugs and cures for diseases	
Identifies the nucleotides that fit with certain cells	
Comparison with the genome of another species	

Table 3.1

b As well as sequencing the human genome, the Human Genome Project has been able to sequence the genome for hundreds of other organisms to compare them with the human genome. The table below shows the different species and their own number of genes.

Organism	Estimated number of genes	Number of chromosomes
Homo sapiens (humans)	25 000	46
Mus musculus (mouse)	25 000	40
Drosophilia melanogaster (fruit fly)	13 000	8
Escherichia coli (bacteria)	3000	1
H. influenza (bacteria)	1700	1
Arabidopsis thaliana (plant)	25 000	10

Table 3.2

   i Determine the organisms that have a similar number of genes to humans.

  ii *The mouse and humans are of similar evolutionary status.* Discuss this statement.

Exercise 3.2 – Chromosomes

1 Chromosomes carry the genetic code for each organism but prokaryotic and eukaryotic chromosomes have many differences. When distinguishing between the prokaryotic and eukaryotic chromosome structures, a table like the one below is a great way to make sure that you refer to all differences of each structure throughout the answer.

  a Copy the table and complete the headings to show which type of chromosome is being described (prokaryotic or eukaryotic).

Contains one circular chromosome	Linear DNA enclosed in nucleus
Contains small plasmids	No plasmids
Naked DNA **not** associated with proteins	DNA associated with histone proteins

Table 3.3

  b Identify the key terms being described by the following descriptions and definitions. You may choose the answer from the word box.

haploid	somatic cell	karyogram
homologous chromosomes	karyotype	diploid

    i Nucleus, or cell, that contains two copies of each chromosome.

   ii Nucleus, or cell, that contains one copy of each chromosome.

  iii A pair of chromosomes with the same structure and genes at the same locations.

   iv A body cell that is **not** a gamete.

    v A diagram or photograph of the chromosomes of an organism.

   vi The number and type of chromosomes present in a nucleus.

  c You are expected to be able to use karyograms to deduce sex and diagnose Down syndrome in humans. Down syndrome occurs when a person has a full or partial additional copy of chromosome 21 and this can be spotted on a typical karyogram. Down syndrome is the most common chromosomal condition and over 6000 babies are born with the condition each year in the United States of America.

    i State the chromosomes for a female and a male person.

ii Analyse the karyogram shown in Figure 3.1 and explain your reasons for the conclusions that you come to.

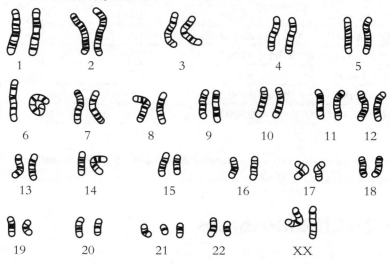

Figure 3.1 Karyogram of an individual.

iii Determine the sex of the individual shown in the karyogram in Figure 3.2.

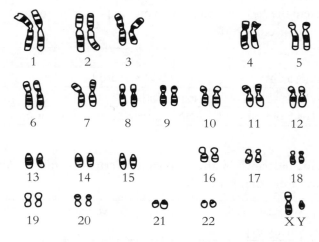

Figure 3.2 Karyogram of another individual.

2 John Cairns was able to measure the length of DNA molecules by using autoradiography. This involves the use of an X-ray film to visualise the 2-D structure of a substance that has been radioactively labelled. Cairns' method involved the labelling of part of a nucleotide. The length of DNA could be measured and was calculated to be approximately 1 mm.

a *Cairns could have just used powerful electron scanning microscopes if he were carrying out the same investigation today.* Comment on why this statement is **not** true, making sure that you refer to importance of technical innovation in your answer.

b Explain why the labelling of part of a nucleotide was beneficial to Cairns.

c Cairns' work showed the structure of *E. coli*. Describe the structure of the DNA that Cairns would have observed when looking at a prokaryote such as *E. coli*.

3 Use the table below to answer the question that follows.

Organism	Common name	Diploid chromosome number
Parascaris equorum	Equine roundworm	4
Aedes aegypti	Yellow fever mosquito	6
Drosophilia melanogaster	Fruit fly	8
Caenorhabditis elegans	Nematode	12
Sarcophilus harrisii	Tasmanian devil	14
Pisum sativum	Pea	14
Raphanus sativus	Radish	18
Zea mays	Maize	20
Xenopus tropicalis	Western clawed frog	20
Oryza sativa	Rice plant	24
Neovison vison	American mink	30
Panther leo	Lion	38
Xenopus laevis	African clawed frog	38
Castor canadensis	Beaver	40
Homo sapiens	Human	46
Pan troglodytes	Chimpanzee	48
Ananas comosus	Pineapple	50
Canis familiaris	Domestic dog	78
Paralithodes camtschaticus	Red king crab	208
Morus nigra	Black mulberry	308
Oxytricha trifallax	Ciliated protozoa	16,000 +

Table 3.4

a Compare the chromosome numbers of *Homo sapiens*, *Pan troglodytes*, *Canis familiaris*, *Oryza sativa* and *Parascaris equorum*.

b *There is a correlation between diploid chromosome number and the size of the organism.* Comment on this statement, using evidence from the table above.

Exercise 3.3 – Meiosis

1 Meiosis occurs in several stages and produces gametes. For each of the descriptions that follow, identify the stage being described, and sketch a diagram to show how the stage looks. Parts a–d are from the first division of meiosis, parts e–h are from the second division of meiosis.

a Spindle microtubules contract towards the poles, sister chromatids remain together but homologous pairs are separated.

b Chromosomes line up at the equator and the centromere attaches to the spindle microtubules.

c Chromosomes supercoil after replication, during interphase. The homologous pairs line up side by side, and genetic material may be exchanged at this point. The spindle microtubules will start to form and the nuclear envelope will break down.

d Spindles break down and a new nuclear envelope forms around each new nucleus. Cytokinesis happens after this and the cell is split into **two** daughter cells, each containing only **one** chromosome of each homologous pair. The second division of meiosis is now ready to begin.

e Nuclear envelope breaks down, chromosomes line up at the equator, spindle fibres attach to the centromere.

f Sister chromatids separate as centromere splits, spindle fibres pull the chromatids to the poles of the cell.

g Nuclear envelopes form around the nuclei and chromosomes uncoil, followed by cytokinesis resulting in **four** cells.

h New spindle fibres form, chromsomes re-coil and nuclear envelope starts to break down.

i List parts a–h to show the correct order of events that take place in meiosis.

j Identify the stage that is known as the reduction division.

k Explain how genetic variety is increased during metaphase I.

l Describe how crossing over takes place during prophase I.

m Outline the main event that occurs in the second division of meiosis.

n State the number of haploid nuclei that are formed during the second division of meiosis.

2 Sometimes, things may go slightly wrong during meiosis and DNA replication.

a Define *non-disjunction*.

b Explain the consequence of your answer to part a.

c As a result, some chromosomes may have an extra copy of a particular chromosome. State the key term that refers to this extra copy of a chromosome.

d Trisomy in chromosome 21 results in which human condition?

e Outline the health problems associated with trisomy 21.

f Figure 3.3 shows the relationship between the age of the mother and the chances that their unborn child will have chromosomal abnormalities. Analyse the patterns and relationships shown in the graph.

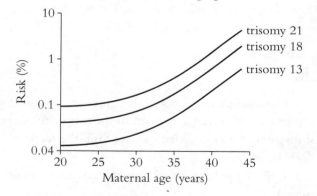

Figure 3.3 Maternal age-related risk for chromosomal abnormalities.

g *The graph in Figure 3.3 shows the causal relationship between maternal age and the chance of chromosomal abnormalities developing.* Discuss this statement.

h A 36-year-old woman is pregnant. Outline the diagnostic tests that she may undergo in order to screen for chromosomal abnormalities.

i The diagnostic screens for checking for chromosomal abnormalities carry a very small chance of the pregnancy ending prematurely. Discuss whether doctors should carry out these tests if there is a risk to the fetus.

3 Read the article about the discovery of the human chromosome number and answer the questions that follow.

> Calculating the number of human chromosomes has proven to be trickier than one might originally have thought. At the start of the 20th century it was not commonplace for humans to donate their bodies for medical science. Some rather unscrupulous biologists used to hang around for public executions in the hope of harvesting the genitalia of the condemned criminals. Some of the misconceptions of that time included the wide range of numbers for human chromosomes (between 20 and 50 at one point), as well as the crazy-sounding notion that white people would have more chromosomes than their other racial counterparts. In another gory twist of the tale of human chromosomal discovery, Theophilus Painter used the discards of castrated inmates at a lunatic asylum to work on. Painter was able to narrow the human chromosome number to either 46 or 48 chromosomes. The next chromosomal twist came from Painter's fear of not being taken seriously if he did not decide whether humans had 46 or 48 chromosomes. So, he did what most people do when they do not want to look uneducated; he guessed at 48 and this was the figure that remained as 'common knowledge' for nearly 30 years.

a Predict what happened that allowed scientists to realise that Painter was mistaken, and that it was actually 46 chromosomes in a human diploid cell.

b State the sex chromosomes that a human may have.

c State the key term that describes all other chromosomes that are **not** sex chromosomes.

d The number of combinations that can occur in a human gamete is 2^n, with n being the number of chromosome pairs.

   i Calculate the possible number of different combinations that are possible in a human gamete.

   ii Calculate the possible number of different combinations that would be possible in a human gamete, if Painter had been correct with his original estimate.

Exercise 3.4 – Inheritance

1 This section contains possibly the greatest number of specialist terms that you need to learn. For the following descriptions, deduce the key term being described.

a The alleles possessed by an organism, usually denoted by letters as part of a pair (Tt).

b The observable characteristics of an organism, such as the colour of eyes, or the height of a plant.

c An allele that is represented in the phenotype whether it is homozygous or heterozygous. Denoted by a capital letter (B).

d An allele that is only expressed in the phenotype when in a homozygous pair (bb). This allele is always expressed as a lower-case letter (b).

e Pairs of alleles that both affect the phenotype when present in a heterozygote. These alleles are represented by matching capital letters but different superscripts. For example, blood types A and B are shown as I^A and I^B.

f The specific location of a gene on a homologous chromosome.

g Two identical alleles at a gene locus and may be either recessive or dominant (ee) or (EE).

h Having two different alleles at a gene locus, usually one recessive and one dominant (Rr).

i The test to see if a dominant phenotype is heterozygous (Tt) or homozygous (TT). If the offspring show the recessive phenotype, then the parent must be heterozygous.

j An individual organism with one copy of a recessive allele that causes a genetic disease in individuals that are homozygous for that particular allele.

k Individuals of the same phenotype that will produce offspring with that phenotype, if mated with another individual with the same phenotype.

2 The story of Gregor Mendel is the ideal place to start learning about inheritance as he is often considered to be the 'Godfather' of genetics. Mendel carried out his work into inheritance in the mid-19th century but this was almost 100 years before the discovery of DNA. Mendel studied hundreds of pea plants and focused on certain characteristics. Careful observation, counting and recording of each generation of offspring allowed Mendel to identify the patterns of inheritance.

a Outline the characteristics that Mendel studied in his work on pea plants.

b Mendel's result can be seen in the table below. Calculate the ratio for the results that Mendel recorded.

Phenotype	Cross made	Numbers in F_2 generation	Ratio
Stem height	Tall v short	787 tall, 277 short	
Petal colour	Purple v white	704 purple, 244 white	
Seed shape	Smooth v wrinkled	5474 smooth, 1859 wrinkled	
Seed colour	Yellow v green	6022 yellow, 2001 green	

Table 3.5

c The results in the table above are for the F_2 generation. Outline what is meant by F_2 generation.

d Allele combinations can be determined by using genetic crosses. Brown fur in mice is dominant to white fur. A mouse that is heterozygous for brown fur is crossed with a white mouse. Follow the steps below to determine the possible genotypes and phenotypes of the offspring.

i State the parental phenotypes.

ii State the parental genotypes.

iii Determine the parental gametes.

iv Construct a Punnett square for the F1 generation.

v Calculate the probability that the offspring will have white fur.

e A plant that is heterozygous for smooth seed shape is crossed with another plant that is also heterozygous for smooth seed shape. Follow the steps below to determine the possible genotypes and phenotypes of the offspring.

   i   State the parental phenotypes.

   ii   State the parental genotypes.

   iii   Determine the parental gametes.

   iv   Construct a Punnett square for the F1 generation.

   v   Calculate the probability that the offspring will have smooth seed shapes.

f A man is heterozygous for brown eyes (Bb) and produces offspring with his wife, who is homozygous recessive for blue eyes. Follow the steps below to determine the possible genotypes and phenotypes of the offspring.

   i   State the parental phenotypes.

   ii   State the parental genotypes.

   iii   Determine the parental gametes.

   iv   Construct a Punnett square for the F1 generation.

   v   Calculate the probability that the offspring will have brown eyes.

g Huntington's disease is an inherited disorder that affects the nervous system of humans. It is caused by a dominant allele, which means that any carrier will express the disease, whether they are heterozygous or homozygous. Parent A is heterozygous for Huntington's and parent B is homozygous recessive. Follow the steps below to determine the possible genotypes and phenotypes of the offspring.

   i   State the parental phenotypes.

   ii   State the parental genotypes.

   iii   Determine the parental gametes.

   iv   Construct a Punnett square for the F1 generation.

   v   Calculate the probability that the offspring will have Huntington's disease.

h A plant with red flowers is crossed with a plant that has yellow flowers of the same species. All of the offspring have red flowers. Deduce which allele is dominant, and which is recessive.

i The allele for short fur (S) is dominant to the allele for long fur (s). Two heterozygous dogs produce offspring. Follow the steps below to determine the possible genotypes and phenotypes of the offspring.

   i   State the parental phenotypes.

   ii   State the parental genotypes.

   iii   Determine the parental gametes.

   iv   Construct a Punnett square for the F1 generation.

   v   Calculate the probability that the offspring will have short fur.

From the offspring, the two homozygous dogs mate and produce eight puppies. Follow the steps below to determine the possible genotypes and phenotypes of the offspring.

   vi   State the parental phenotypes.

   vii State the parental genotypes.

   viii Determine the parental gametes.

   ix   Construct a Punnett square for the F1 generation.

   x   Calculate the probability that the offspring will have short fur.

   xi   Calculate how many of the puppies will have short fur.

j Cystic fibrosis is carried by 1 in 25 of Caucasians and is caused by a recessive allele (f). Two parents, who are both carriers for the disease, produce offspring. Follow the steps below to determine the possible genotypes and phenotypes of the offspring.

    i State the parental phenotypes.

    ii State the parental genotypes.

    iii Determine the parental gametes.

    iv Construct a Punnett square for the F1 generation.

    v Calculate the probability that the offspring will have cystic fibrosis.

    vi Calculate the probability that the offspring will **not** have cystic fibrosis or be carriers.

    vii Calculate the probability that the offspring will be carriers of cystic fibrosis.

    viii One of the offspring that is a carrier of cystic fibrosis produces offspring with a person who does **not** carry, or have, the disease. Calculate, using a Punnett square, the chances of their offspring being a sufferer of cystic fibrosis.

    ix Suggest how parents can find out if they are carriers of cystic fibrosis.

k A rabbit with black fur produces offspring with a rabbit that has white fur. Black fur is dominant to white fur. The rabbits produce 12 offspring, half of whom have white fur. This question aims to find out whether the rabbit with black fur is heterozygous or homozygous for the allele for black fur.

    i State all of the possible parental phenotypes.

    ii State all of the possible parental genotypes.

    iii Determine the possible parental gametes.

    iv Construct a Punnett square for the F1 generation.

    v Determine whether the parent rabbit with black fur was homozygous or heterozygous for the allele for black fur.

l The genotypes for several blood groups are listed below. For each genotype, state the phenotype that will be expressed.

    i $I^A I^A$

    ii $I^A i$

    iii $I^B I^B$

    iv $I^B i$

    v $I^A I^B$

    vi ii

A man that is heterozygous for blood group A produces offspring with a female that is heterozygous for blood group B. Follow the steps below to determine the possible genotypes and phenotypes of the offspring.

    vii State the parental phenotypes.

    viii State the parental genotypes.

    ix Determine the parental gametes.

    x Construct a Punnett square for the F1 generation.

    xi Calculate the phenotypic ratio for the possible blood groups of the offspring.

m Sickle cell anemia is a co-dominant disease. State the phenotype (normal or sickle-shaped red blood cells) that would be expressed for the genotypes below.

    i $Hb^A Hb^A$

    ii $Hb^A Hb^S$

    iii $Hb^S Hb^S$

iv Outline which of the genotypes above are most likely to be affected by malaria.

A man with two alleles for normal hemoglobin production produces offspring with a woman who is a carrier. Follow the steps below to determine the possible genotypes and phenotypes of the offspring.

v State the parental phenotypes.

vi State the parental genotypes.

vii Determine the parental gametes.

viii Construct a Punnett square for the F1 generation.

ix Calculate the probability that the offspring will be carriers of sickle cell anemia.

Exercise 3.5 – Genetic modification and biotechnology

1 One of the problems of our increasing human population is how to feed everyone on the planet. With the United Nations predictions that the world population will reach 9 billion people by 2050, combined with issues of climate change, it is a real worry as to how people will get enough food. As the abiotic factors within various ecosystems change, many plants will not be able to grow due to the threat of floods and droughts. However, if scientists can continue to develop genetically modified crops, these new crops can develop resistance to the changing conditions.

A powerful method has been developed that allows for the rewriting of genes so that they can combat different diseases. An example of this is editing the genes that make wheat vulnerable to mildew so that these wheat plants are now resistant to mildew. Tomato plants have been altered so that they produce tomatoes throughout the year without having to wait for certain light and temperature conditions.

Biologists are also working on making plants more efficient at photosynthesis by transferring a mechanism that concentrates carbon dioxide where it is most needed. Malnourished people may also benefit, too. Nearly a quarter of a million people die from vitamin A deficiency each year, especially in those whose diet is mainly rice as they do not get enough of this important vitamin. Golden rice – a genetically modified crop – is a golden colour because of the large quantities of yellow dietary carotenoids that our bodies can easily convert into vitamin A.

a State some examples of abiotic factors that may affect an ecosystem.

b Comment on whether the editing of genes in plants is useful.

c Biologists are working on a method to transfer the features of one plant to another, in order to make the plant better at photosynthesis. List the following stages in the correct order to show the stages involved in gene transfer and genetic modification.

- Isolate the desired genes (using the appropriate enzymes) from the cells of the organism.
- Isolate a bacterial plasmid.
- Prepare the plasmid with restriction endonucleases.
- Merge the desired gene and the opened plasmid in a process called ligation (using DNA ligase).
- Transfer the recombinant plasmid back into the organism that desires the characteristic.

d Explain why the genetic modification of the tomato plant is beneficial to humans.

e Explain why golden rice is beneficial to humans in areas where diet is the main part of the local diet.

2 Read the conversation between two friends about genetically modified organisms and answer the questions that follow.

> **Michael:** **Hi, how are you?**
>
> Adina: Not bad, thanks, but I was learning today about genetically modified organisms in my IB Biology class. I really don't think they're a good idea and we should maybe be careful before we start something that we cannot stop.
>
> **Michael:** **Really? I think it's a great thing, it could benefit the human race, massively!**
>
> Adina: No! Animals get harmed and that's just cruel.
>
> **Michael:** **Come on, Adina! If we don't do something, there will not be enough food to feed our population. The world is growing so fast.**
>
> Adina: Well, what studies have you looked at? Have you seen any long-term proof that GM crops are harmless? How do you know that we are not being harmed and will get ill in later life?
>
> **Michael:** **It won't matter if we are all dying from the droughts and floods that the crops can't survive anyway. Something has to be done – the world is changing.**
>
> Adina: The world could become dangerous if food is completely controlled by a handful of people, or companies. Haven't you seen films where this happens?
>
> **Michael:** **Those films are made-up; I only deal with *real* science. These modifications can be applied to real things that make us healthier and live longer, like antibodies and vitamins.**
>
> Adina: Yes, but it can still cause more damage than good. Prices won't be affordable for everyone and that is not very fair, is it? Not to mention the reduction in biodiversity; if this is reduced then ecosystems might suffer.
>
> **Michael:** **Look, this argument could go on forever. Let's ask one of our friends and we will see who knows best.**

a Now you need to evaluate the arguments for and against genetically modified organisms and state your own opinion.

b One of the arguments is that genetically modified organisms will reduce the need for using pesticides. Explain why this is a positive aspect of genetically modified organisms.

c Predict what might happen if the genetically modified organisms escaped into the wild populations of that organism.

3 Reproductive clones can be produced by somatic cell transfer.

a Define *clone*.

b The first successful clone was Dolly the sheep, at the Roslin Institute in Edinburgh, UK. List the stages used to clone Dolly in the correct order, using the stages below.

- The unfertilised egg is fused with a somatic cell, using an electric current.
- Unfertilised egg is removed from another sheep.

- The embryo is transferred and implanted in the womb of a surrogate sheep.
- The nucleus of the unfertilised egg cell is removed.
- Embryo divides by mitosis.
- Somatic cell removed from donor.
- Cloned embryo grows until a lamb is born.

c Dolly was the only successful clone from 277 attempts, with many failures resulting in lost money, time and animals that suffered greatly before dying. Comment on whether it was acceptable to make so many attempts at cloning a mammal.

d *Humans should be cloned*. Discuss this statement.

? Exam-style questions

1 **Which of the following is the correct structure that makes up hemoglobin?** [1]
   A Two α-chains and two β-chains
   B One α-chain and two β-chains
   C Two α-chains and one β-chain
   D One α-chain and one β-chain

2 **Which of the following is a possible symptom of sickle cell anemia?** [1]
   A Jaundice
   B Kidney issues
   C Colour-blindness
   D Enlarged spleen

3 **Which of the following is** not **applicable to the genetic material of a prokaryote?** [1]
   A Contains nucleoid
   B DNA is naked
   C Contains just one circular chromosome
   D DNA associated with histones

4 **Identify the number of chromosomes from the list that a typical human haploid cell would contain.** [1]
   A 48
   B 46
   C 24
   D 23

5 **What is the key term that describes a diagram or photograph of the chromosomes from an organism?** [1]
   A Karyogram
   B Karyotype
   C Karyotic
   D Karyoka

6 **Identify the stage of meiosis shown in Figure 3.4. [1]**

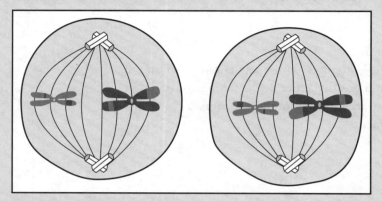

Figure 3.4 Stages of meiosis.

A Prophase II
B Metaphase II
C Anaphase II
D Telophase II

7 **Identify the correct order of stages in the second division of meiosis. [1]**
A prophase II → metaphase II → anaphase II → telophase II
B prophase I → metaphase I → anaphase I → telophase I
C metaphase II → prophase II → anaphase II → telophase II
D metaphase I → prophase I → anaphase I → telophase I

8 **Identify the key term that refers to the specific position of a gene on a homologous chromosome. [1]**
A Allele
B Gene
C Centromere
D Locus

9 **Which of the following best describes DNA profiling? [1]**
A Matching the alleles of an individual to their homologous chromosome
B Matching the DNA from a sample to a known individual
C Matching the protein group of an individual to a sample at a crime scene
D Matching the blood group of an animal to the parents

10 **Which of the following is an argument against the use of genetically modified crops? [1]**
A Could lead to a reduction in biodiversity for an ecosystem
B Reduces the needs for harmful pesticides
C Provides more food in areas that previously could not grow food
D Could lead to production of antibodies for humans

11 **A plant that is heterozygous dominant for red flowers is crossed with a plant that has white flowers. White flowers are a recessive trait in this particular species of plant. Calculate the likelihood that the offspring will have red flowers. [1]**

A 25%

B 50%

C 75%

D Not possible to tell from the information given

12 **Durance has the blood group A. Identify the possible genotype that Durance might have. [1]**

A $I^A I^A$ or $I^A i$

B $I^A I^A$ or $I^B I^B$

C $I^A I^A$ or $I^B i$

D ii or AB

13 a Outline the causes of Down syndrome. [5]

b The karyogram in Figure 3.5 shows a person that has Down syndrome.

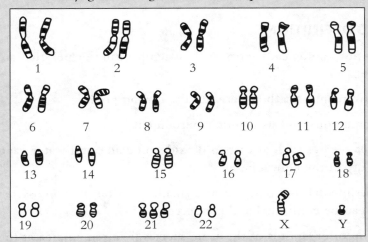

Figure 3.5 Karyotype of a person with Down syndrome.

  i Identify the evidence that this person has Down syndrome. [1]

  ii Determine the sex of the person in the karyogram. [1]

c Explain the causes of sickle cell anemia. [6]

14 a Describe the technique that could be used to transfer genes between species. [4]

b Outline the technique for the transfer of the insulin gene using *E. coli*. [6]

4 Ecology

Chapter outline

In this chapter you will:
- outline that the continued survival of living organisms including humans depends on sustainable communities
- explain that ecosystems require a continuous supply of energy to fuel life processes and to replace energy lost as heat
- explain that the continued availability of carbon in ecosystems depends on carbon cycling
- describe how the concentrations of gases in the atmosphere affect climates experienced at the Earth's surface
- evaluate claims that human activities are not causing climate change.

KEY TERMS AND DEFINITIONS

Abiotic factors – non-biological factors, such as temperature or pH, that are part of the environment.

Carbon flux – movement of carbon between the carbon pools.

Ecosystem – a community and its abiotic environment.

Greenhouses gases – gases such as carbon dioxide, methane, and water vapour that trap heat energy in the atmosphere.

Mesocosm – experimental tool that acts as a smaller version of an ecosystem in which conditions can be controlled and measured.

Population – group of organisms of the same species living in an area at the same time.

Precautionary principle – system in place to protect against potential damage in instances where scientific proof is not yet evident or absolute.

Exercise 4.1 – Species, communities and ecosystems

1 A lion and a panther are two different species, although they may have some similarities and may even live in the same area at the same time.
   a Define *species*.
   b Sometimes, it is possible for closely related species to interbreed. Suggest what the offspring might **not** be able to do.
   c Figure 4.1 shows a photograph of a *zonkey*. Using the name, *zonkey*, deduce the two species that have been interbred to produce this genetic hybrid.

Figure 4.1 A *zonkey*.

2 Before going further into this topic, it is essential that you are able to define the keywords for the topic.

   a You defined species in question 1; now you need to define the following terms.

     i Population.

     ii Community.

     iii Ecosystem.

     iv Abiotic factors.

     v Trophic level.

   b List the following levels of an ecosystem in order of smallest to largest: community, ecosystem, population, species.

   c Figure 4.2 shows a transect through a pond as an example of a freshwater ecosystem. In this, you can see rooted and floating plants (producers), a range of consumers in and out of the water, mud and detritus, and different habitats. Match the correct term from the box to the list of features in parts i–vi below.

population	abiotic factor
ecosystem	community
habitat	

     i The lake.

     ii All of the ducks of the lake.

     iii All of the plants and animals present.

     iv The mud of the lake.

     v The pH of the water.

     vi The organisms in the water.

Figure 4.2 Transect of a pond.

d Human population has increased massively in the past 50 years. Look at Table 4.1 below. You can see that the human population of these cities has grown since 1950.

City / Year	Population in 1950 (millions)	Population in 2007 (millions)	Percentage increase
New York	12.3	19.0	
Tokyo	11.3	35.7	

Table 4.1 Population of New York and Tokyo.

   i Calculate the percentage increase of each city between 1950 and 2007.

   ii State the name of the city that has had the greater population increase between 1950 and 2007.

3 Look at the food chain below and answer the questions that follow.

maize → locust → lizard → snake

a Identify the producer in this food chain.

b Explain why the producer in the food chain is considered to be autotrophic.

c The other organisms gain their organic compounds from feeding on other organisms. State the name of this mode of nutrition.

d Explain what the arrow in the food chain signifies.

e Distinguish between the modes of nutrition of the maize and the lizard.

4 Look at the food chain below and answer the questions that follow.

grass → locust → scorpion → baboon → leopard

a Copy and annotate the food chain above to show the producers and consumers at each trophic level.

b Detritivores are examples of heterotrophs that get their nutrients from detritus by internal digestion. Examples include dung beetles, fiddler crabs and earthworms. Outline some of the things making up detritus, which contain organic compounds that can be fed upon.

c Read the following description and identify the third type of consumer that is being described.

- Obtains nutrients from dead organisms.
- Uses external digestion.
- Secretes digestive enzymes to break down complex molecules.
- Absorbs the simple products of digestion.

   i the name of the consumer that is described above.

   ii Suggest a type of organism that is usually found within this group.

5 Abiotic factors such as carbon dioxide and oxygen levels, rainfall, pH, soil types, and temperature ranges are all examples of abiotic factors that interact with the many communities that form an ecosystem. The nutrients within the system can be reused and recycled.

   a Construct an overview of how nutrients are recycled, using the statements below.
- Plants and organisms die.
- Soil.
- Litter/vegetation.
- Plants and organisms.
- Nutrients taken up by plants.
- Nutrients released.

   b State the name of the consumer group responsible for decomposing litter and vegetation in order to release the nutrients into the soil.

   c Describe how nutrients from a dead organism may be taken up by a member of the same species.

   d Although nutrients can be recycled within an ecosystem, it is not the same for energy. All energy comes from the same source. State where all of the energy in the food chains originates from.

6 Figure 4.3 shows a typical mesocosm.

Figure 4.3 A typical mesocosm.

   a Sealed glass tanks are ideal for a mesocosm. Comment on why a sealed vessel is considered to be better than an open vessel.

   b Light energy can enter and leave the mesocosm. State what is **not** able to enter or leave the mesocosm.

   c State the names of the two common types of mesocosm used by scientists.

   d In order to respect the IB animal experimentation policy, you must ensure that no organisms used will suffer from pain or stress. Suggest how the levels of oxygen and carbon dioxide may be monitored in a mesocosm.

   e Distinguish between an aquatic mesocosm and a terrestrial mesocosm.

Exercise 4.2 – Energy flow

1 As mentioned in the previous section, food chains show the flow of energy from producers to consumers. Food chains rarely exist on their own as different organisms will feed on more than one organism. Multiple food chains may be interconnected to show these relationships as a food web.

a Figure 4.4 shows a food web. Answer the questions that follow.

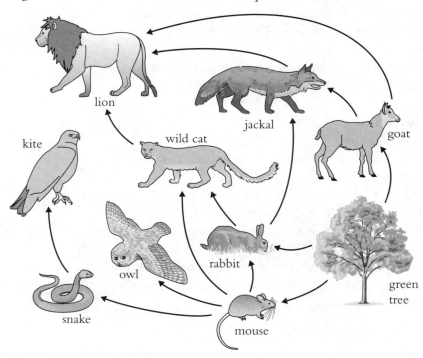

Figure 4.4 A food web.

  i Identify the producer in the food web.
  ii State the names of the **three** primary consumers of this food web.
  iii Construct a food chain from this food web that contains **four** organisms.
  iv Annotate your food chain to show the different trophic levels.

2 Figure 4.5 shows a typical marine food web. Use Figure 4.5 to answer the questions that follow.

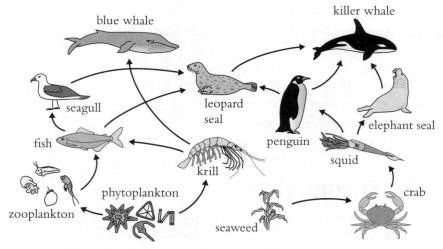

Figure 4.5 A marine food web.

a Draw and label a food chain to show the flow of energy from seaweed to penguin, to killer whale.

b Suggest what might happen to the populations of the organisms in parts i–iii below if all of the elephant seals died.
   i Killer whale.
   ii Squid.
   iii Crab.
   iv Explain why the crab population was affected.

3 Light energy from the Sun is taken in by producers to make organic molecules. The energy passed on by organisms in the food chain is used for ion transport across membranes, cell division, growth, and synthesis of nucleic acids. However, not all energy is passed on at each stage of the food chain. Some energy is lost as heat or as a waste product of respiration and other cellular processes, such as metabolism. Some parts of an organism are not fully digested and may be excreted. Some energy is lost to detritivores and saprotrophs in the soil.

   a From the text above, state the ways in which an organism might use the energy that it gains from feeding.
   b Identify **two** cellular processes that use up much of the energy in an organism.
   c Compare and contrast the role of producers and saprotrophs in the flow of energy.
   d *Food chains are rarely more than five stages because the animals get too big.* Discuss whether this statement is true or not.
   e Figure 4.6 shows a typical pyramid of energy for the following food chain:

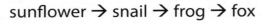

sunflower → snail → frog → fox

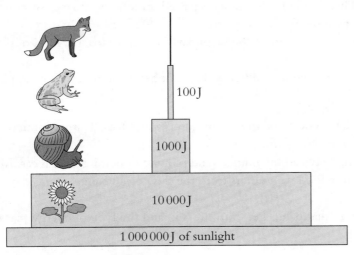

Figure 4.6 A pyramid of energy.

   i State the name of the producer in this food chain.
   ii State the name of the secondary consumer in this food chain.
   iii Estimate the likely energy in the level represented by the fox.
   iv Outline what happens to the rest of the energy from the frog.
   v If the fox were to be eaten by another predator, therefore extending the food chain, predict the amount of energy that would theoretically be passed on from the fox.
   vi The energy in this pyramid is shown in joules. A typical pyramid of energy refers to the energy per unit area per unit of time. Suggest a more appropriate unit for this energy pyramid.

f Figure 4.7 shows the energy pyramid for an ecosystem.

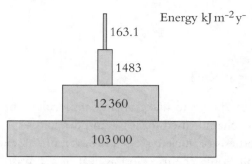

Figure 4.7 An energy pyramid for an ecosystem.

  i Calculate the percentage energy transfer between the secondary and tertiary consumers of the ecosystem.

  ii Analyse the shape of the food pyramid.

  iii Predict the amount of energy that might have been taken in from sunlight by the producer, if the producer had conserved 10% of the original energy.

g An organism consumes 4000 joules of energy. Of this, 1200 J is lost as heat energy during respiration and 1800 J is lost as urine and faeces.

  i Calculate the amount of energy that this organism has available to be passed on the next trophic level.

  ii Comment whether this amount of energy is likely to be passed on by the organism.

h A producer $(50\,000\,MJ\,m^{-2}\,yr^{-1})$ is consumed by a primary consumer $(7000\,MJ\,m^{-2}\,yr^{-1})$. Then 11% of this energy is passed on to a secondary consumer.

  i Sketch an energy pyramid for this scenario.

  ii Calculate the amount of energy at the secondary consumer trophic level of the food chain.

  iii Food chains are likely to contain different types of heterotrophs and autotrophs. Define *autotroph*.

4 Herbivores in an ecosystem tend to be greater in number and have a larger biomass than carnivores in the same ecosystem.

  a Explain the relationship between the number and biomass of herbivores and carnivores.

  b Explain how energy in a food web differs from the flow of nutrients.

  c Define *herbivore*.

  d State the type of energy that plants get from the Sun and the type of energy that they convert this to.

Exercise 4.3 – Carbon cycling

1 Carbon dioxide is a gas that typically accumulates at the lowest layers of the atmosphere as it is heavier than air. Autotrophs absorb carbon dioxide from the atmosphere for synthesis of carbon compounds, as well as releasing carbon dioxide during cellular respiration. Carbon dioxide is also soluble in water as a dissolved gas; or if it combines with the water it can form carbonic acid (H_2CO_3). Dissolved carbon dioxide may be absorbed by plants (autotrophs) that live in the water to make carbon compounds.

a State the process by which plants move carbon dioxide from the air into their leaves.

b Carbonic acid can disassociate to form hydrogen ions (H$^+$) and hydrogen carbonate ions (HCO$_3^-$).

   i State the effect that this has on the pH of water.

   ii Suggest how you might be able to monitor the pH levels of water in a mesocosm.

   iii Ahmed monitors the pH and light intensity of an aquarium that contains aquatic plants and animals. The aquarium was placed under natural light and monitored for several days. Predict and explain the expected trend in pH during a 5–day cycle.

c Figure 4.8 shows the carbon dioxide concentration measured at Mauna Loa in Hawaii. The concentration varies between the months of each year, hitting a peak in April but then decreasing until August before increasing again in the autumn and winter months.

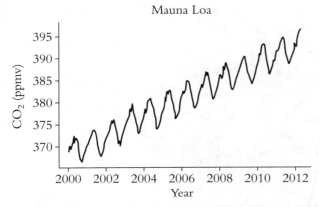

Figure 4.8 The carbon dioxide concentration as measured at Mauna Loa in Hawaii.

   i Describe the trend in carbon dioxide concentration between 2000 and 2012.

   ii Explain the trend in carbon dioxide concentration between 2000 and 2012.

   iii Deduce why the concentration of carbon dioxide decreases between the months of April and August.

   iv The Mauna Loa observatory has collected records of carbon dioxide concentrations for longer than anywhere else in the world. Evaluate the importance of Mauna Loa in making accurate, quantitative measurements about the concentration of carbon dioxide in the atmosphere.

d Read the following article about the peatlands of Ireland and answer the questions that follow.

> The Irish peatlands make up approximately 17% of the country's land area and there is an estimated 4.4 billion tonnes of carbon dioxide contained within the peatlands. Total carbon dioxide emissions for Ireland currently stand at 69 million tonnes. This important terrestrial carbon pool must be protected to prevent the water levels dropping, which will release massive amounts of carbon dioxide. Peat has many uses, from firewood to agriculture and horticulture.

   i Identify how peat is used in the home.

   ii Outline how peat is formed.

   iii Determine how much greater the carbon pool of the peatlands is compared to the total Irish carbon emissions.

e The shells of molluscs and the exoskeletons of hard corals contain calcium carbonate ($CaCO_3$). This calcium carbonate will dissolve in alkaline conditions and form limestone rock. 10% of the sedimentary rock on Earth contains limestone and 12% of that limestone is made up of carbon. This means that there are huge stores of carbon locked away in places such as the white cliffs of Dover in the UK.

    i State the names of the organisms mentioned that contain lots of carbon.

    ii Outline the conditions needed for the formation of limestone from the bodies and exoskeletons of your previous answer.

    iii Predict what might happen if the pH of seawater becomes acidic.

2 Carbon is one of the chemical elements of nutrients that are constantly recycled within an ecosystem. Figure 4.9 shows the carbon pools and carbon fluxes of a typical carbon cycle.

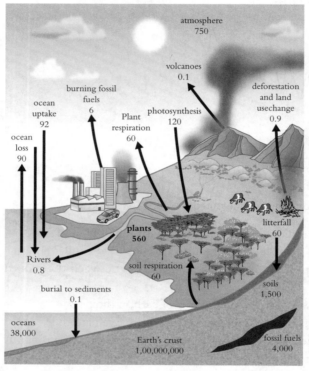

Figure 4.9 A typical carbon cycle (Units: Pools – Pg; Fluxes – Pg/year).

a Define *carbon pool*.

b List the carbon pools in Figure 4.9.

c Define *carbon flux*.

d List **three** carbon fluxes shown in Figure 4.9.

e Estimate the total carbon fluxes in Figure 4.9.

f Discuss the following statement, using evidence from Figure 4.9 to support your argument: *Human activity has a significant impact upon the carbon cycle.* You are expected to use evidence from Figure 4.9 to support your answer, as well as other arguments, calculations and factors that support your hypotheses.

3 Mauna Loa Observatory (MLO) in Hawaii has collected and monitored data related to atmospheric change since the 1950s – longer than anywhere else in the world. The remote location of MLO means that the air is generally undisturbed and there is little impact from human activity and vegetation on the atmospheric readings.

Carbon dioxide levels in the 1960s were around 320 parts per million (ppm) and have been steadily increasing ever since. When shown on a graph, it is not a continual increase as there are seasonal fluctuations; carbon dioxide readings are naturally higher in the winter and lower in the summer. MLO measured a record-high reading for carbon dioxide concentration of 400.8 parts per million.

One of the largest jumps in atmospheric carbon dioxide was in 1998 during a particularly strong El Niño – which is often responsible for causing forest fires and deforestation. The increase in carbon dioxide levels means that more and more carbon dioxide enters the oceans. The historical average pH of the ocean is 8.16 but recent data has shown that is now closer to 8.06. The logarithmic nature of the pH scale means that this small change is actually quite significant. Without further action to reduce this, the oceans will continue to become more acidic and may reach levels of close to 8.0, or even 7.3 if worst-case scenario predictions are true. The effect on marine life that relies on minerals to construct their exoskeletons will be catastrophic, and it is unlikely that organisms would adapt quickly enough to such an aggressive change in their environmental conditions.

a MLO has recorded data for far longer than any other observatory in the world. Evaluate if this makes MLO a reliable authority on climate change and the human impact upon this.

b Explain why carbon dioxide readings are higher in the winter than in the summer at MLO.

c Analyse why 1989 led to such a large increase in carbon dioxide readings in the atmosphere.

d Using the information from the text above:
   i Calculate the percentage increase in carbon dioxide emissions since the early 1960s.
   ii Outline the role of fossil fuels in the increase of carbon dioxide levels.

e Explain why organisms such as corals and clams would be affected by the absorption of carbon dioxide into the oceans.

f Design an investigation that could be carried out in the school laboratory to observe the effect of increased carbon dioxide levels in oceans on natural life.

g Explain how the destruction of the rainforests affects the concentration of carbon dioxide in the atmosphere.

Exercise 4.4 – Climate change

1 Use Table 4.2 to answer the questions that follow about greenhouse gases and their effect on climate change.

Greenhouse gas	Chemical formula	Pre-1950 concentrations	2010 concentrations	Increase
Carbon dioxide	CO_2	278 ppm	365 ppm	
Methane	CH_4	700 ppb	1745 ppb	
Nitrous oxide	N_2O	270 ppb	314 ppb	
Hydrofluorocarbons	HFC-23	0	14 ppt	
Perfluorocarbons	CF_4	0	80 ppt	
Sulfur hexafluoride	SF_6	0	4.2 ppt	

Table 4.2

a Calculate the increase for the concentration of each of the greenhouse gases between the pre-1950 and 2010 recordings.

b Sulfur hexafluoride is an insulator used in the electronic industry. Outline why there has been an increase in sulfur hexafluoride since the 1950s.

c Hydrofluorocarbons, perfluorocarbons and sulfur hexafluoride all had zero concentrations before the 1950s but have since increased. These gases are produced in the manufacture, and use of, electronic components, magnesium, aluminium, refrigeration and liquid coolants.

   i Distinguish between the pre-1950 readings for these gases and the pre-1950 readings for carbon dioxide, methane and nitrous oxides.

   ii Suggest why there is such a difference between the readings for the previous question.

d Carbon dioxide is a prominent greenhouse gas, more so than methane which is released in far smaller quantities than carbon dioxide. However, methane and nitrous oxides are able to trap a lot more heat energy than carbon dioxide.

   i Outline how methane and nitrous oxides are produced and released into the atmosphere.

   ii Predict which gas, methane or carbon dioxide, will cause the Earth to warm up the faster. Explain your reasons for your answer.

   iii The difference between these greenhouse gases and their effect is explained in the way that they trap heat. Rearrange the following steps to show the sequence of events that leads to global warming.

- Greenhouse gases re-emit the absorbed light back towards the Earth.
- This causes the overall temperature of the Earth to increase.
- Short-wavelength radiation from the Sun reaches the Earth's surface.
- Long-wavelength radiation (light) is absorbed by greenhouse gases.
- Short-wave radiation is absorbed by the Earth but is re-emitted as longer wavelength heat energy (infrared radiation).

2 There is much evidence reported in scientific research and the media about how environmental change is caused, or triggered, by the production of the greenhouse gases. **Sea levels are rising** and threatening low-lying islands and major cities that have been built around rivers and coastlines, such as London and New York. Mountain ranges are suffering from **glacier retreats** as glacier ice at the top of these mountains is lost, and this affects the water supply for people that live in these areas. Mount Kilimanjaro is a famous example of a rapidly-retreating glacier at its tropical summit. It is widely reported in the media that the **polar ice cap** of the Arctic has shrunk by around 20% in the past 40 years and is contributing to dramatic rises in sea levels. These events can lead to **changing weather patterns** as hurricanes and typhoons become stronger; less oxygen and carbon dioxide is dissolved in the oceans and ocean currents are greatly slowed down. Combustion of fossil fuels contributes towards these changes as humans burn more fossil fuels for use in:

- cars, lorries and airplanes
- producing electricity
- powering factories and homes.

a Design a plan that could be delivered to the government of a country that is in danger of suffering from some of the effects mentioned in the text. Your plan should include suggestions for how global warming may be combated, prevented, or reduced.

b Consider the following text and answer the questions that follow.

Earth's climate used to change quite dramatically well before the Industrial Revolution, for reasons **not** related to human activity at all. The fluctuations and changes in sunlight that reaches our planet have been as a result of 'wobbles' in its orbit. Volcanic activity has caused periods of global warming as huge volumes of gas are released quickly into the atmosphere. Even today, natural events often cause changes in atmospheric conditions and it is difficult to distinguish between those and the effects caused by human activity. This makes it very difficult to prove that global warming is caused by humans alone. It is generally accepted that much less than 1% of the gases in the atmosphere are greenhouse gases caused by humans – so is it possible that such a small concentration can have such a huge effect? Scientists have also shown that Earth has previously been much hotter on many occasions (such as during the Paleocene-Eocene Thermal Maximum – PETM – around 56 million years ago) and that we are merely in a period of warming that is part of the natural cycle of the Earth's existence. This is also supposed of CO_2 levels as there is further evidence that the concentrations of carbon dioxide have been as high as 5000 ppm in the late Ordovician around 440 million years ago. Compare this to the panic and hysteria that reaching 400 ppm has caused in recent months. The Intergovernmental Panel on Climate Change (IPCC) produced a report that led to current thinking about rising sea levels and changing weather patterns. The IPCC is made up of 60 scientists but you would expect this number to be seven or eight times greater for a thorough scientific vetting and peer review. Reviews of the report have been generally favourable and carried out by supporters of the findings – is this the way that we conduct our science in the 21st century?

i Evaluate the evidence from the whole of question 2 (including parts a and b) as to whether humans have contributed to global warming or not.

ii Suggest why it is important that other evidence is taken into account, and that the findings are reviewed by many scientists of different backgrounds and beliefs.

iii The precautionary principle is made up of **four** key components. Outline the components of the precautionary principle.

iv Explain why it is important that humans keep to the precautionary principle when reviewing human impact on climate change.

? Exam-style questions

1   **Which of the statements below, A–D, are true of a species? [1]**
    I   Group of organisms
    II Can produce offspring
    III Can produce fertile offspring
    IV Live in the same area
    A I only
    B I and II
    C I and III
    D I, III and IV

2   *Cyanobacteria* is capable of making its own complex organic molecules from carbon dioxide and other simple compounds. Which of the following does *Cyanobacteria* belong to? [1]

   A Heterotrophs

   B Autotrophs

   C Herbivores

   D Population

3   **Which of the following statements is** not **true of a food chain?** [1]

   A Shows how energy is passed along in a habitat

   B Usually begins with a plant

   C Usually ends with an animal

   D Shows interconnections between food chains

4   **Fungi and bacteria obtain their food by external digestion of dead organisms. Which of the following groups do fungi and bacteria belong to?** [1]

   A Heterotrophs

   B Detritivores

   C Producers

   D Saprotrophs

5   **Not all energy is consumed between organisms in a food chain. Which of the following is** not **a reason for this?** [1]

   A Not all parts of the organism are consumed

   B Some material is released as faeces

   C Energy is 'lost' during respiration

   D Consumers do not need very much energy

6   **What is the alternative name that hydrogen carbonate ions are also known as?** [1]

   A Bicarbonate ions

   B Carbon dioxide ions

   C Carbohydrates

   D CHO_2

7   **Identify the carbon pool from the list below.** [1]

   A Respiration

   B Photosynthesis

   C Deforestation

   D Fossil fuels

8   **Which of the following is** not **a gas that contributes to global warming?** [1]

   A Oxygen

   B Methane

   C Carbon dioxide

   D Hydrofluorocarbons

9   In a cross between two heterozygous peas, a 3:1 yellow:green ratio is expected. Kalim tests this experimentally to see whether the results differ significantly from this expected ratio.

   a   i   State the probability of the offspring being yellow. [1]
       ii Select the best null hypothesis (H_o) from the choices given: [1]
           • The results will match the expected results of Kalim.
           • 75% of peas will be yellow.
           • There is a significant difference between observed and expected results.
           • There is no significant difference between observed and expected results.
       iii Kalim observes the following results; there were 35 yellow peas and 15 green peas. Calculate the expected number of each pea colour (E) for the results collected by Kalim. [1]
       iv Using the formula $(O-E)^2$, calculate the value for yellow peas and green peas. [2]
       v   Now, divide the value for part iv by the value for E and add them together to provide a value for X^2. [1]
       vi The critical value for Kalim's experiment is 3.84 (based on degrees of freedom being $2 - 1 = 1$). State whether Kalim should accept the null hypothesis or not. [2]

   b   Kalim gathers information about blood type for his fellow students in his year group. His research shows that the expected distribution of blood types for his school are:
       A: 38%   O: 48%
       B: 10%   AB: 4%

       Kalim's data collection of his peers is as follows:
       A: 32   O: 50
       B: 25   AB: 14

       i   Calculate the value of X^2. [5]
       ii State the number of degrees of freedom. [1]
       iii Using the table below, state the critical value for $p = 0.05$. [1]

Degrees of freedom (n–1)	p = 0.1	p = 0.05	p = 0.01
1	2.71	3.84	6.63
2	4.61	6.00	9.21
3	6.25	7.81	11.34

       iv Determine if Kalim should accept the null hypothesis. [1]

10 a   Draw a labelled diagram of the carbon cycle to show how carbon pools and carbon fluxes interact with each other. [8]
    b   Draw and label a food chain and explain why food chains rarely extend beyond four or five organisms. [3]
    c   Sketch a pyramid of energy for your food chain. [3]
    d   State the amount of energy typically passed on to each trophic level in a food chain. [1]
    e   Explain what happens to the rest of the energy that is **not** passed on in the food chain. [3]

5 Evolution and biodiversity

Chapter outline

In this chapter you will:

- explain how different types of evolution occur, and the evidence that supports this
- outline how, and why, selective breeding takes place
- explain how natural selection can only occur if there is variation among members of the same species
- outline named examples of natural selection, from finches on Daphne Major to antibiotic-resistant bacteria
- outline the binomial system of names for species that is universal among biologists
- outline that a clade is a group of organisms that have evolved from a common ancestor.

KEY TERMS AND DEFINITIONS

Binomial system – system used to name organisms using the genus and species.

Cladistics – the system of classifying organisms according to their shared characteristics and based on ancestry.

Evolution – the cumulative change in the heritable characteristics of a population.

Heritable characteristics – traits passed on to offspring.

Homologous structures – structures that are similar due to common ancestry.

Natural selection – when organisms adapt to their environment in order to survive and reproduce.

Exercise 5.1 – Evidence for evolution

1 Read the passage of text about evolution and answer the questions that follow.

Evolution is one of the most contested scientific theories but, as scientists gather more and more evidence, it becomes very difficult to argue against evolution. Going right back to 1859, and the publication of Darwin's *On the Origin of Species,* it is amazing to think that Darwin could have been so accurate with his predictions and ideas. 'International-mindedness' is brilliantly highlighted in the topic of evolution, as the acknowledgement that ALL humans and organisms are derived from ONE common ancestor is humbling and compelling.

'Survival of the fittest' is commonly discussed as organisms adapt to their environment and those that are most able to survive and reproduce will pass on those heritable characteristics to their offspring. Darwin proposed that a black bear could be related to a whale, and although he was originally ridiculed, he was vindicated in later years as his ideas were shown to be correct but with different examples. The story of the whale is a brilliant example of natural selection as the movement from land mammal to water developed key features that allowed the whale to survive, such as the blowhole, flippers and streamlined bodies.

It was not just Darwin that was able to theorise about evolution and how animals adapted to their environment. Biologists such as Lamarck and Wallace also contributed to our understanding of evolution.

It is too easy to dismiss a lack of evidence as lack of proof, but this is why scientists continue to collaborate and work towards common goals. It took nearly 130 years for scientists to start finding evidence that would support what Darwin had proposed. The remains of *Ambulocetus natans* were found and this organism was clearly adapted for swimming although it still retained the ability to walk on land. The literal translation of this name – *Ambulocetus natans* – is 'swimming-walking whale'. Other fossil records have supported the theory of evolution and natural selection.

a Define *heritable characteristics*.
b According to evolution, outline what needs to change over a period of time.
c State the evidence that is observed by scientists to create evolutionary links with organisms that are millions of years old.
d Identify the **three** key features that are beneficial to the survival of a whale.
e *Ambulocetus natans* was able to walk on land. Deduce what evidence in the fossil record could be observed to make this assumption/observation.
f Creationists might suggest that evolution **cannot** be true because X, Y and Z cannot be proven. Comment why it is important that scientists continue to gather evidence and observations.
g According to the text, state the number of common ancestors that humans are derived from originally.

2 Read through the example of selective breeding below and answer the questions that follow. Selective breeding is carried out by humans to develop only organisms with the most desirable characteristics.
• A cow in a particular herd is able to produce more milk than the rest of the herd.
• A bull whose offspring have excellent milking quantities.
• From their offspring, the cows that produce the most milk are selected.
• Only those offspring are allowed to reproduce, as measured by progeny testing.
• The process is repeated.

a Suggest how the original cows, and the cows produced in the third or fourth generation, might be different from each other.
b Identify the desirable characteristic that is being selectively bred in this example.
c Outline any other example of selective breeding that you have learnt about.
d Imagine that you are a tomato farmer. Design a plan that would allow you to grow only the best-tasting tomatoes on your farm.

3 Look at Figure 5.1 and answer the questions that follow about homologous structures.

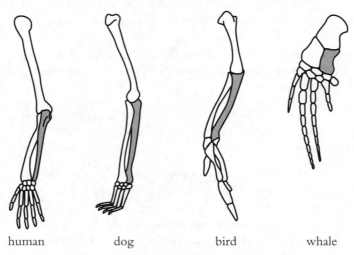

human   dog   bird   whale

Figure 5.1 Homologous structures.

a State the bones in Figure 5.1 that appear to provide evidence of common ancestry.

b Define *homologous structure*.

c Distinguish between the shaded bones of the whale and the dog in Figure 5.1.

d Compare and contrast the shaded bones of the organisms in Figure 5.1.

e Suggest what the evidence in Figure 5.1 shows about the common ancestry of these organisms.

f Identify the form of evolution that is shown in Figure 5.1.

g Some species develop structures that are similar between different species but have different bone structure in ancestry. State the type of evolution that these analogous structures are examples of.

4 A natural disaster or event, such as a volcano erupting, an earthquake or a flood, causes the population of a species to separate. The two new populations end up in different environmental conditions and after several generations they become genetically different.

a i State the name of the process that has occurred in the text above.

ii Define *species*.

iii Define *population*.

iv Predict what would happen if the two 'new' species attempted to breed with each other.

b Darwin did much of his work on the Galapagos Islands as speciation events occur more commonly on archipelagoes.

i Explain what an *archipelago* is.

ii State the name of the birds that Darwin studied on the Galapagos Islands.

iii Suggest why the nature of an archipelago enables such obvious speciation, as noted by Darwin.

5 One of the most famous examples of industrial melanism is the peppered moth found in the UK, *Biston betularia*. The change in environment for this moth led to adaptation and increased survival of those that were the 'fittest'.

a Describe how the peppered moth usually avoids detection by prey.

b Outline which event of the 19th century led to a change in colour of tree bark in some areas.

c State the **two** types of peppered moth that make up the peppered moth population.

d Determine which of these two varieties was able to survive in the more industrial areas.

e Explain why this type of peppered moth was most likely to survive in industrial areas.

f Imagine you are able to blog about the events of the 19th century. Write a mini-blog that summarises how the dark peppered moth was able to become more prominent. You may need to research key dates and population information to support your article.

Exercise 5.2 – Natural selection

1 As covered in Exercise 5.1, a species is a group of organisms that can produce fertile offspring. The organisms of each species have a number of genes from which the ones best suited to the environment may be chosen. There may be genes which are not as obviously shown, but these may be useful if, and when, there are changes in the environment for that species. This genetic variation is vital to the process of natural selection.

a Define *gene pool*.

b Explain why a larger gene pool increases the chances of survival of a particular species.

c Genetic variation may be caused by a number of different methods, including mutations, meiosis (independent assortment) and sexual reproduction. Outline how each of the methods in parts i–iii below cause genetic variation.

   i Mutations.

   ii Meiosis.

   iii Sexual reproduction.

   iv Suggest which organisms are **not** capable of genetic variation by sexual reproduction.

d Polar bears possess special hair structures that help to insulate them from the extreme temperatures of the Arctic. Describe how natural selection may have contributed to polar bears having this characteristic.

2 Organisms will produce far more offspring than actually survive to become mature individuals. Organisms will have to compete for the natural resources around them, such as shelter and food, in order to survive. This is why only the 'fittest' are able to survive and go on to reproduce. The offspring of these individuals will inherit the 'fit' genes and the adaptations will be passed on to the next generation. Read the article about natural selection and answer the questions that follow.

Natural Selection in Animals of the Earth

Charles Darwin (1809–1882) was a British explorer and scientist that almost everybody has heard of in the world of science. However, it was not all success for Darwin as he failed to complete his university studies. This led to him getting an unpaid role on board the *HMS Beagle*, which set off on a five-year expedition around the world. Darwin used this trip to observe natural selection in action, and to make observations that would still hold

Figure 5.2 Charles Darwin.

true nearly 200 years later. He claimed that many organisms would die, and that the ones with best adaptations would survive and pass on these adaptations to their offspring. It really is a remarkable story and Darwin would be a very happy man today, seeing the volume of evidence that supports his findings.

Had he lived today, Darwin would have learnt how giraffes with long necks survive a drought better than giraffes with short necks. He would have been astounded to find out that some lizards with long legs were able to escape floods and find food higher up than their short-legged peers. Not only would Darwin marvel at the wonder that is nylon (not produced until well after his death), but the knowledge that some bacteria that would evolve to eat nylon as a survival method would amaze him. It is amazing that some bacteria have evolved to eat something that was only 'invented' 75 years ago! Even humans have adapted to survive by being better at spear-throwing, or by developing resistance to malaria in Africa.

Darwin's journey took him to the Galapagos Islands in the Pacific Ocean, in 1835. He studied wildlife on the islands and noted that there were 14 species of finches across the many islands. These finches had different sized beaks that had clearly adapted to meet their needs in obtaining food. Small beaks were better at cracking smaller seeds and large beaks better for larger seeds. Some finches had evolved to cope with different environmental conditions and their beaks had become longer and narrower. This enabled them to obtain more seeds under different conditions and to be better at eating the larger seeds. It was the work of other scientists in later years, such as Peter and Rosemary Grant, that provided evidence to support the early theories of Charles Darwin.

a *Only the 'fittest' survive.* Comment on what you think happens to those that are not considered to be 'fit'.

b Define *natural selection*.

c i Suggest why giraffes with longer necks would be better suited to surviving a drought.

ii List the examples of natural selection stated in the article.

iii Outline **one** of the examples from the article that is an example of natural selection.

iv *Being better at spear-throwing does **not** help humans to survive today.* Discuss this sentence.

d The Galapagos Islands are many different islands, separated by water channels. State the name usually given to a group of islands scattered in this way.

e The El Niño of the early 1980s caused a massive rainfall over the Galapagos Islands. Predict what effect this had on the population of finches on the islands. Give reasons for your answer.

3 You are expected to be able to outline the evolution of antibiotic resistance in bacteria. Over the past 40 years, many antibiotics have become less effective in fighting bacteria. Bacteria, such as Methicillin–Resistant *Staphylococcus aureus* (MRSA), have become particularly powerful in their resistance to antibiotics. Answer the following questions to help develop your understanding of this evolution.

a Bacterial generation times are extremely rapid and can occur within hours. Deduce why this helps bacteria to develop resistance to antibiotics so quickly.

b An antibiotic might destroy certain bacteria. Explain why the bacteria **not** destroyed by the antibiotics may cause resistance to develop.

c Overuse of antibiotics creates breeding grounds for resistant bacteria. Suggest **one** example of where you might expect to see a high volume of antibiotics.

d Explain how doctors can protect against resistance to antibiotics by mixing up the types of antibiotic used.

Exercise 5.3 – Classification of biodiversity

1 Let us take the Atlas lion as an example for this exercise. Under the binomial system, first established by Linnaeus, the Atlas lion is classified as follows:

- Genus: *Panthera*
- Order: Carnivora
- Species: *leo*
- Phylum: Chordata
- Kingdom: Animalia
- Family: Felidae
- Class: Mammalia

a Put this list of classification for the Atlas lion into the correct order, from the largest group to the smallest.

b Outline the rules that are usually followed when writing the name of a species under the binomial system.

c State the binomial name of the Atlas lion.

d Suggest another organism that would be in the same class as the Atlas lion, but from a different family.

e Suggest another organism that would be in the same class as the dog, but from the same family.

f Explain why it is important that we follow the binomial system laid out by Linnaeus.

g The wild horse (*Equus ferus*) is a mammal that belongs to the order Perissodactyla. The family name of the horse is Equidae, a group that also includes other mammals such as donkeys and zebras.

  i Using the information above, complete the classification of the wild horse.
- Kingdom: ………………..
- Phylum: ………………..
- Class: ………………..
- Order: ………………..
- Family: ………………..
- Genus: ………………..
- Species: ………………..

  ii State the binomial name of the wild horse.

h Figure 5.3 shows a pygmy marmoset (*Cebuella pygmaea*), an incredibly small monkey that originates from the rainforests of South America. This mammal is sometimes known as a finger monkey; it can easily hold onto the finger of a human as it is so small. Being a monkey, it is obviously a primate (order) and is a member of the Callitrichidae family.

Figure 5.3 A pygmy marmoset.

  i Using the information above, complete the classification of the pygmy marmoset.
- Kingdom: ………………..
- Phylum: ………………..
- Class: ………………..
- Order: ………………..
- Family: ………………..
- Genus: ………………..
- Species: ………………..

  ii State the binomial name of the pygmy marmoset.

  iii The pygmy marmoset belongs to the phylum Chordata. State what this tells you about the pygmy marmoset.

i You have completed the classification information for several organisms. Now, research your own favourite animal or plant and specify their classification.
- Kingdom: ………………..
- ………………..
- ………………..
- ………………..
- ………………..
- Species: ………………..

2 DNA sequencing during the past 40 years has led scientists to divide all living things into three different domains.

   a State the names of the **three** domains that all living things can be classified into.

   b Scientists, such as Carl Woese, divide the three domains based on their characteristics. Copy and complete Table 5.1 to outline the main features of the three main domains.

Characteristic	Eubacteria		
Histones		Present	
Introns	Absent		Present
Cell membrane		L-form of glycerol	
Cell wall	Made of	Not made of	

Table 5.1

   c Figure 5.4 shows how the different domains are arranged by Carl Woese.

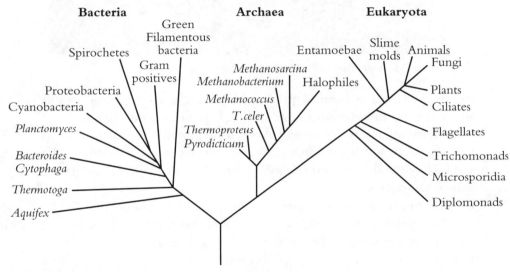

Figure 5.4 The domains as arranged by Carl Woese.

   i The middle branch of this phylogenetic tree includes organisms such as *Thermoproteus* and halophiles. These are organisms that used to be classified as prokaryotes but, as they show distinct structural differences to 'true' bacteria, they are classified separately. Suggest the conditions in which you might typically expect to find *Thermoproteus* and halophiles, based on their name.

   ii State the domain that *Thermoproteus* and halophiles belong to.

   iii Identify the group from the phylogenetic tree that you, a human, best fit into.

   iv The branch on the left-hand side of the tree includes cyanobacteria and Gram positives. Outline the main features of these organisms that place them into this particular domain.

   v *There should be a fourth domain for viruses.* Analyse this statement.

3 This question outlines the main features of some of the Eukaryota kingdoms: Animalia, Plantae, Fungi and Protoctista. You are expected to be able to recognise and differentiate between the features of different groups within these kingdoms.

a For each of the descriptions that follow, state the name of the phylum that each plant belongs to. In some cases, there is a photograph or picture to assist you.

   i Have stems, leaves and roots that are well adapted to terrestrial conditions.

Figure 5.5 A member of the Plantae kingdom.

   ii Best adapted to damp environments on land, have small stems with radial leaves.

   iii Cone-bearing trees that grow straight with branches to the side.

   iv Flowering plants that consist of two main groups – monocots and dicots.

   v For part i, outline the features that enabled you to identify the name of this phylum.

b For each of the descriptions that follow, state the name of the phylum that each animal belongs to.

   i Do **not** have a nervous system, made up of small colonies of cells.

   ii Includes slugs and snails, usually have soft bodies that includes a muscular foot.

   iii Possess metameric segmentation in their soft bodies.

   iv Body cavity is a gut, have stinging cells on the tentacles.

   v Usually known as flatworms and do **not** have an anus.

   vi Includes crustaceans, arachnids and insects that have jointed limbs.

   vii Compare and contrast the phyla named in parts iii and iv of this question.

   viii Deduce the characteristic that these six phyla have in common.

   ix State the name of the phylum that is **not** described in this question, but would include organisms such as the horse and the cat.

   x State the name of the group within the phylum Arthropods that contains the most species.

c For each of the descriptions that follow, state the name of the class that each animal belongs to. You must also include the name of **one** species (common name or binomial is accepted) for each class.

   i Have gills and live in water.

   ii Moist skin, breed in water, respiration occurs at the skin.

   iii Have hair or fur, have four pentadactyl limbs, endothermic, internal fertilisation.

   iv Have wings, are endothermic, and lay eggs to produce offspring.

   v There have been four different classes described so far. State the name of the fifth class and describe the main features that might describe an organism that belongs to this class.

4 Dichotomy means to divide things into **two** different groups. Scientists (and students) use dichotomous keys to quickly identify different organisms. Quite simply, you select the best option from a choice of two options until you identify the correct organism, based upon its observable features.

a Figure 5.6 shows a variety of different leaves. Use the dichotomous key that follows to identify the species that each leaf belongs to.

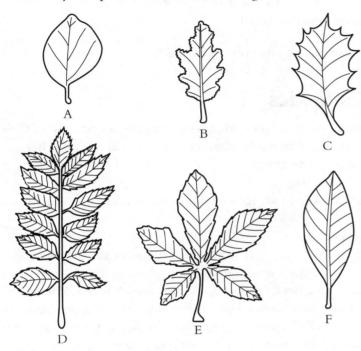

Figure 5.6 A variety of different leaves.

1	Has a smooth outline	Go to 2
	Has a jagged outline	Go to 3
2	Similar length and width	*quince*
	Twice as long as it is wide	*yulania*
3	Leaf divided into more than two distinct parts	Go to 4
	Leaf not divided into more than two distinct parts	Go to 5
4	Leaf divided into five parts	*chinensis*
	Leaf divided into ten or more parts	*dipetala*
5	Leaf has pointed spines along edge	*byronia*
	Leaf has rounded lobes along its edge	*alba*

b You find the organisms in Figure 5.7 on a field trip.

i Create a dichotomous key of your own to show how you may identify the species of each organism.

Figure 5.7 Which invertebrates are these?

ii State the name of each of the organisms in Figure 5.7.

Exercise 5.4 – Cladistics

1 Cladistics is the study of evolutionary relationships between species. Analysis of DNA allows scientists to trace different species back to their common ancestors, helping us to classify organisms into appropriate groups.

a Define *clade*.

b Outline how scientists are able to identify whether a species belongs to a particular clade.

c Outline what a cladogram shows.

d Assuming that all living organisms evolved from one common ancestor, discuss whether it is possible to produce one giant cladogram to show this.

e In a cladogram, explain what can be determined at the branch points of the tree.

f Traits can be analogous or homologous. Distinguish between analagous structures and homologous structures. Copy and complete the table below to show whether the statement describes analogous structures or homologous structures.

- Occur due to convergent evolution.
- Similar in basic structure.
- Similar in position.
- Used for similar function.
- Occur due to divergent evolution.
- Have different functions.
- For example, the pentadactyl limbs of some vertebrates.
- Differ in basic structure.
- Superficial resemblances.
- For example, the wings of birds and insects.

Analogous structures	Homologous structures

Table 5.2

g Based on your knowledge of DNA and proteins, determine which is the more accurate for cladistics: amino acid sequencing or base sequencing of a gene.

2 This section will help you to analyse cladograms to deduce evolutionary relationships. Although you may have seen these command terms many times so far, here is a reminder of what is expected when you analyse and deduce in IB Biology.

Analyse – break down in order to bring out the essential elements or structure.

Deduce – reach a conclusion from the information given.

Therefore, analysis of a cladogram requires you to break down the information available so that you are able to reach some sort of conclusion.

Figure 5.8 shows a typical cladogram.

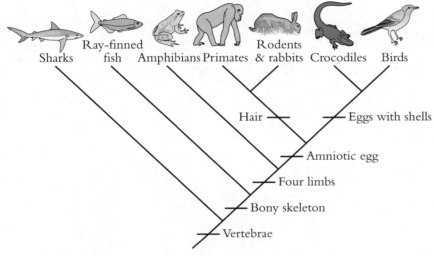

Figure 5.8 A typical cladogram.

a Outline the basic assumptions that must be made when analysing a cladogram.

b State the name of the organism that birds are most closely related to in Figure 5.8.

c Suppose that the time between amphibians and primates diverging is 20 million years.

   i Estimate the length of time between the divergence of primates and crocodiles, and crocodiles and birds.

   ii Explain the reasoning behind your answer to part i.

3 Conservatism in science is often likely when new data or theories come to light. This is never more true than the rewriting of our ancestral history due to developments in DNA and protein technologies. Carl Woese, as discussed in a previous section, famously created a new domain and a complete rethink of evolutionary relationships by analysing RNA from bacteria and eukaryotes. Woese was often mocked by fellow scientists, some of whom were very famous and prominent, such as Luria and Mayr. It took a further 20 years of evidence and data collection for the work of Woese to be accepted, but there are still many scientists today who have not yet accepted the new theories.

a *To what extent is conservatism in science desirable?* Evaluate this statement based on the work and theories of Carl Woese.

b Reclassification of the figwort family is a classic example of cladistics evidence supporting, and proving, new theories. The figwort family contains more than 275 genera with over 5000 different species. It was originally believed that all of these species were one clade but DNA analysis of chloroplasts showed that there were actually five different clades. The morphology of the clades was so similar that it was very difficult to distinguish between them, until the DNA evidence arrived. Now, there are only approximately 200 different species of figwort – a remarkable and dramatic difference from what we used to believe.

i Define *morphology*.

ii Calculate the percentage difference in number of figwort species after the reclassification due to DNA analysis of chloroplasts.

iii Explain why it was **not** possible to differentiate between the original 5000 species of figworts.

? Exam-style questions

1 **Which of the statements below, A–D, correctly describes an example of selective breeding? [1]**

   I Breeding race horses for speed
   II Breeding dogs for hunting
   III Breeding humans for black hair
   IV Breeding dogs for pets

   A I only
   B I and II
   C I and III
   D I, III and IV

2 **Humans and dolphins have similar bones in their arms and flippers, respectively. This is an example of which type of evolution? [1]**

   A Adaptive radiation
   B Convergent radiation
   C Natural selection
   D Natural variation

3 **What is the name of the island where Darwin observed the natural selection of finches? [1]**

   A Galapagos Islands
   B Archipelagoes
   C Daphne Major
   D Daphne Minor

4 **Industrial melanism was observed in *Biston betularia* in the UK. What is the common name of the *Biston betularia*? [1]**

   A Peppered moth
   B Finches
   C Lichen
   D Dark moth

5   **Which of the following are causes of variation? [1]**
    A Mutation
    B Meiosis
    C Sexual reproduction
    D All of the above

6   **Which of the following is a major reason to explain why antibiotic resistance has spread so rapidly? [1]**
    A Bacterial generation times are very short
    B Antibiotics are rarely used
    C Fewer people are getting sick
    D Bacteria are getting cleverer

7   **Which of the following is not a rule from the binomial system for naming species? [1]**
    A Genus begins with upper case letter.
    B Genus begins with lower case letter when on its own.
    C Species begins with lower case letter.
    D Name is written in italics or underlined.

8   **Which of the following is a characteristic of archaea? [1]**
    A Introns always absent
    B Absent cell wall
    C Cell wall not made of peptidoglycan
    D Lipid membrane contains a D-form of glycerol.

9   a Define *clade*. [1]
    b Distinguish between analogous and homologous structures. [1]
    c Compare convergent and divergent evolution. [3]
    d Outline how adaptive radiation occurs. [3]

10 **Analyse the relationships between the organisms of the cladogram shown in Figure 5.9. [4]**

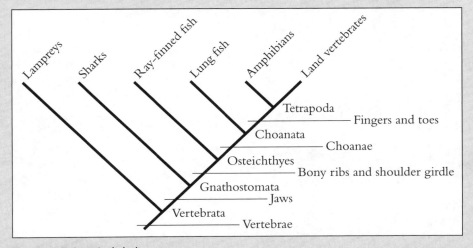

Figure 5.9 A typical cladogram.

11 Antibiotic resistance has increased in recent years. Figure 5.10 shows how resistance to a particular antibiotic changed during the 1990s in American hospitals.

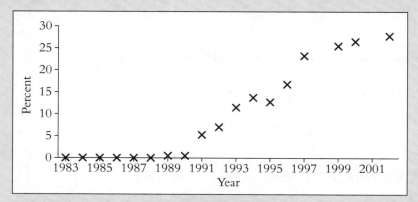

Figure 5.10 Antibiotic resistance in American hospitals.

a Describe the trend in antibiotic resistance in Figure 5.9. [2]
b Outline how the bacteria evolved to be resistant as an example of natural selection. [4]
c Explain why antibiotic resistance spreads so rapidly in hospitals. [3]

12 Distinguish between the phyla Angiospermophytes and Filicinophytes. [3]

13 Mark discovers two new organisms that are animals with a backbone. Construct a dichotomous key to show how he might identify each of the organisms as being one of the five main classes of Vertebrata. [6]

Human physiology 6

Chapter outline

In this chapter you will:
- explain how the digestive system is able to move, digest and absorb food
- outline how the blood system continuously transports substances to cells and simultaneously collects waste products
- outline the structures and processes of the human body that resist the continuous threat of invasion by pathogens
- outline how the respiratory system is adapted for efficient ventilation and gas exchange
- explain how neurons transmit the message and synapses modulate the message
- explain how hormones are used when a signal needs to be delivered to a wider distribution.

KEY TERMS AND DEFINITIONS

Circulatory system – circulates blood around the body; blood is pumped by the heart through this double circulatory system.

Digestion system – responsible for the breaking down of large, insoluble macromolecules into smaller, soluble monomers for absorption.

Homeostasis – maintaining a constant internal environment.

Immune system – provides resistance and protection against infections, toxins and pathogens.

Nervous system – the network of neurons, synapses and fibres that transmit nerve impulses around the body.

Respiratory system – group of organs that work together to ensure that oxygen and carbon dioxide are exchanged and delivered to where they are needed.

Exercise 6.1 – Digestive system

1 Figure 6.1 shows the outline of the human body. The organs (and associated tubes) in this word box all make up the human digestive system.

• Salivary glands	• Large intestine	• Stomach
• Oesophagus	• Small intestine	• Liver
• Gall bladder	• Anus	• Pancreas
• Mouth	• Rectum	

a Copy the outline in Figure 6.1 draw and label each organ to show the structure of the digestive system. Remember that the location, size and shape of each organ must be as accurate as possible.

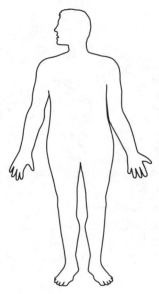

Figure 6.1 Outline of the human body.

b Peristalsis is the contraction and relaxation of certain muscles in the alimentary canal. Identify the organ of the digestive system where peristalsis begins.

c Starches begin to break down in the mouth as they are mixed with saliva. State the name of the enzyme that is responsible for breaking down starches.

d *The stomach is often considered to be one of the final barriers to infection.* Analyse this statement, using your knowledge of the role of the stomach in digestion.

e The **five** main stages of holozoic nutrition are shown in Table 6.1. Copy and complete the table to show an outline of what happens during each stage.

Stage	Outline of what happens
Ingestion	
Digestion	
Absorption	
Assimilation	
Egestion	

Table 6.1

f Describe the role of the following parts of the digestive system.
  i Pancreas.
  ii Liver.

g The small intestine is divided into **three** main parts.
  i State the names of the three main parts of the small intestine.
  ii The small intestine makes up most of the alimentary canal. State the estimated length of the small intestine in the average human.

iii Explain how the circular and longitudinal muscles of the small intestine continue the process of digestion.

iv State the name of the process that moves molecules from the alimentary canal and into the blood.

v Sketch a drawing to show how the surface area of the small intestine is increased.

2 Enzymes are amazingly diverse molecules that enable you to have clean clothes, soft leather jackets, enjoy your luxury chocolates, and allow you to keep healthy. Digestive enzymes help to deliver vital nutrients and molecules to cells in the body where they are needed. Larger, insoluble macromolecules need to be broken down into smaller, soluble monomers in order for them to be absorbed into the bloodstream and assimilated around the body to where they are needed. Enzymes work best at certain pH levels and this varies for different organs of the human body. Amylase, pepsin and lipase are examples of the digestive enzymes that you need to know about. Cellulose remains undigested during this process.

a Explain why digestion is essential for the body.

b State the substrate that is broken down by the following enzymes.
   i Amylase.
   ii Pepsin.
   iii Lipase.

c State the product formed after the enzyme has carried out its role.
   i Amylase.
   ii Pepsin.
   iii Lipase.

d State the optimum pH of the following enzymes based on their main source of secretion.
   i Amylase.
   ii Pepsin.
   iii Lipase.

e Explain why insoluble molecules need to be broken down.

f For the following enzymes, construct a table to show the substrate that is broken down and the product that each one of the enzymes produces.
   • Maltase.
   • Lactase.
   • Dipeptidase.

g The stomach contains enzymes that work best at very low pH and it also contains hydrochloric acid.
   i Outline why the stomach is very acidic.
   ii Suggest why the stomach does **not** digest itself, given that it contains such a strong acid and many enzymes.
   iii State the name of the semi-liquid that is produced by the stomach as it mixes up the food contents.

3 Copy and complete the following table to deduce which feature of the small intestine is being described.

Feature	Function
a	Increase the surface area for absorption
b	Provide active transport for nutrients to cross the membrane
c	Increased surface area for uptake of small molecules into the bloodstream
d	Absorbs digested fats (triglycerides)
e	Lubricates movement of food

Table 6.2

4 Draw a diagram of a villus to show all of the features described in question 3.

5 All of the food molecules and nutrients are absorbed into the blood, via the capillaries of the villus. Fatty acids move into the epithelial cells before being transported out by exocytosis into the lacteal. There are three other modes of absorption that enable molecules to move out of the intestine. For each one of those, identify the type of transport that is being described in parts a, b and c.

 a Small, hydrophobic molecules pass through the membrane.

 b Hydrophilic monomers are moved via protein channels.

 c This is important when concentrations are low and ATP will be needed to make the transport happen.

 d State the name of a hydrophilic molecule that **cannot** pass through the phospholipid bilayer.

 e Distinguish between the absorption of fats and the absorption of carbohydrates.

6 This question looks at the use of dialysis tubing to model absorption of digested food in the intestine. Dialysis tubing is also known as Visking tubing and is semi-permeable because it is covered in microscopic pores that allow very small molecules to pass through them. It is possible to use dialysis tubing to imitate the small intestine, when placed into a medium such as water. Your task is to design a suitable investigation to show this model, and evaluate it afterwards. Answer the questions that follow to achieve this.

 a Design an investigation to show how a piece of carbohydrate food is able to pass through the semi-permeable membrane. You have access to the following materials (be warned, you do not need all of them so planning is important here):

 • 1% starch solution
 • 1% amylase solution
 • 1% lipase solution
 • distilled water
 • bottled water
 • 250 ml glass beakers
 • 50 ml glass beakers
 • pipettes
 • syringes
 • test tubes
 • boiling tubes

- measuring cylinder
- dialysis tubing
- elastic band

b Predict what you would expect to happen in this investigation.

c Suggest how you could test your hypothesis to prove that it was correct.

d Evaluate how suitable this investigation is as a model of the small intestine.

e Define *absorption*.

Exercise 6.2 – Circulatory system

1 Theories about the 'nature of science' are regarded as being uncertain. William Harvey overturned theories developed by the ancient Greek philosopher Galen on movement of blood in the body.

Claudius Galen (CE131–201) was a Greek physician who intensely pursued, and enjoyed, his investigations of the human body. He enjoyed sharing his work via books and his work on the circulatory system was generally accepted for nearly 1500 years. Galen believed that the liver was at the centre of the circulatory system and that the liver made the blood for the veins. However, Harvey was able to refute this with his research, and this underpins our current understanding of how blood moves around the human body. Harvey was able to show that the heart pumped the blood via the arteries and veins (which had valves to prevent backflow). In a similar fashion to many other scientific predictions, Harvey even suggested that the arteries and veins must be connected by tiny vessels – even though he could not yet prove this.

a Compare the basic ideas that Galen and Harvey suggested about the focus of the circulatory system.

b Discuss the contribution of Galen to our understanding of the circulatory system today.

c Comment on whether you think Harvey or Galen made the more important contribution.

d Comment on Harvey's supposition that arteries and veins were somehow connected by tiny blood vessels.

2 A table such as Table 6.3 is excellent for questions that include command terms such as distinguish, compare, and compare and contrast. It ensures that you refer to both (or more) parts of the question without losing marks. This is a common error that should be avoided.

a Copy and complete the table below to compare and contrast the differences between the inner layers of arteries, veins and capillaries.

Description of layer	Name of layer	Artery	Vein	Capillary
	Tunica intima	Thick layer	Absent	
Middle layer made up of muscle cells, collagen and elastic fibres.				Thin layer
This is the outer layer, is very tough and made of collagen fibres to protect the vessel.				

Table 6.3

b Distinguish between the structure of an artery and a vein.

3 When you cut your arm, there is some blood loss. This blood contains lots of nutrients and oxygen that your body requires to be healthy. It is important that platelets are able to help in clotting the blood and forming a 'scab' to prevent pathogens from entering the body. The oxygen is transported in erythrocytes that do **not** have a nucleus, and these also transport carbon dioxide away from cells. The carbon dioxide may also be carried away in plasma and it is this component of blood that holds a range of different substances. These include various food nutrients, excretory products such as urea, heat energy, dissolved proteins, hormones, and enzymes. Lymphocytes and phagocytes have a major role to play as part of the immune system as they produce antibodies, and digest bacteria, respectively.

a List the main **four** main components of blood.

b List the main components that can be found in the plasma of the blood.

c Lymphocytes and phagocytes are examples of which major component of blood?

d Explain why it is an advantage for red blood cells to **not** have a nucleus.

e Determine why it is important for the blood to clot after a cut in the skin.

f The blood is made up of approximately 55% plasma and 45% cells. Of that 55% plasma, approximately 90% is water.

   i If a person had 5 litres of blood, calculate how much of that blood you would expect to be made up of dissolved substances.

   ii Explain why it is important that digestion breaks down larger, insoluble macromolecules.

g Outline the journey of oxygen and carbon dioxide in the blood.

h Construct a table to show the main components of blood and their primary role.

4 Figure 6.2 shows the double circulatory system of the human body. Use this to answer the questions that follow.

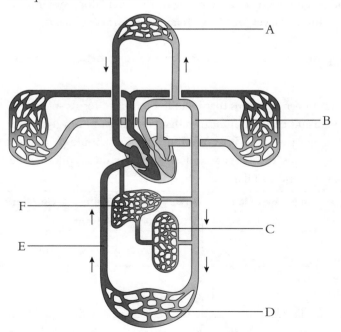

Figure 6.2 The double circulatory system of the human body.

a State the names of the different parts of the body, organs and blood vessels that are shown on Figure 6.2.

b Sketch and label a diagram of the heart to show how deoxygenated blood becomes oxygenated, before being pumped around the body. Your diagram should have the following components labelled.
- Left and right atria
- Left and right ventricles
- Superior and inferior vena cava
- Aorta
- Pulmonary artery and pulmonary vein
- Interventricular septum
- Valves
- Oxygenated blood
- Deoxygenated blood

c Distinguish between the pulmonary circulation and the systemic circulation.

5 a Rearrange the following stages of the heartbeat to show the correct order in which they occur.
- The signal is passed to the AV node at the bottom of the right atrium.
- The muscles of the ventricles contract (ventricular systole).
- Sinoatrial node produces electrical signal across the walls of the atria.
- The signal passed from the AV node to the base of the ventricles via the Purkinje fibres that are known as the bundles of His.
- Atrial systole occurs as both atrial walls contract at the same time.

b State the full name of the AV node.

c Identify the cause of atrial systole.

d Deduce which node acts as the pacemaker of the heart.

6 Cardiac output can be calculated using the stroke volume and pulse rate.

a State the formula that you can use to calculate cardiac output.

b If Lucy's stroke volume is 67 ml and her heart rate is 80 beats per minute, calculate the cardiac output of Lucy.

7 Atherosclerosis damages arteries and can causes blockages, depriving tissue of oxygen. Without this oxygen, tissue and cells will die. If this happens in the coronary arteries, it may mean that the heart will not be able to pump blood as well as it needs to. This is called a 'heart attack' or myocardial infarction.

a Outline what an atheroma is and how it leads to the blockage of an artery.

b Outline the role of the coronary arteries.

c Read the following article about causes of cardiovascular disease and answer the questions that follow.

> If you are eating lots of products that contain high levels of saturated and trans fats, then you may be putting yourself at the risk of heart disease. These foods include cakes, cookies, icing and margarines and they can cause plaque to build up in the arteries, called atheromas. Atheromas are caused by high blood concentrations of LDLs and are more likely if you have a diet high in trans fats. Smoking and stress are also contributors to the buildup of plaque in the arteries, as well as diabetes which can increase blood glucose concentration.

    i State the name of a food that is high in trans fats and is **not** listed in the leaflet above.

    ii LDLs are mentioned in the leaflet. State what an LDL is.

    iii List the main causes stated in the leaflet that can cause fatty deposits in the arteries.

Exercise 6.3 – Immune system

1 The spread and containment of diseases such as bird flu require international coordination and communication. The World Health Organization (WHO) plays a key role in this communication to ensure that an outbreak of a disease does not spread rapidly to other countries. The WHO has developed essential International Health Regulations and this legally binding document is applicable in all countries.

The role of the WHO was important in the containment of bird flu as information could be quickly communicated about the spread and containment of this disease.

a Suggest why diseases are able to spread so easily between different countries.

b The recent outbreak of Ebola spread from Africa to Europe and the USA. Ebola is spread throughout the human population by human-to-human transmission through broken skin. The disease has an average fatality rate of around 50% and was believed to have originated in central Africa. Prevention of further transmission is critical and the WHO has provided guidelines for countries on how they should do this. Outline how you might expect the WHO to respond to such a crisis.

c Explain how broken skin and mucous membranes lead to further transmission of the disease.

d The skin is the primary defence against such diseases.

    i Describe how the skin is such an effective barrier to disease.

    ii Outline the cascade reactions that take place in blood clotting and would seal a wound or cut in the skin.

    iii Thrombin catalyses the conversion of fibrinogen to fibrin. Deduce what type of molecule thrombin is.

e Suggest how health-care workers should protect themselves from contacting the Ebola virus.

f *The WHO should focus on producing more antibiotics to combat viruses like Ebola. That way, more people might survive, rather than just telling people how to stop it.* Analyse this statement, using your knowledge of how antibiotics work on pathogens.

2 Florey and Chain carried out experiments to test penicillin (discovered serendipitously by Alexander Fleming, of course) on bacterial infections in mice. They infected eight mice with hemolytic streptococcus, half of which also received timed doses of penicillin. Within a day, the four mice that did **not** receive penicillin were dead, whereas the other mice were alive. Further tests on humans helped to establish recommended dosages for such treatment, especially given that one patient who was getting better eventually died because Florey had run out of the penicillin.

a *Florey and Chain's experiments proved beyond doubt that the penicillin was the key factor in the survival of the mice.* Evaluate this statement.

b Comment on whether the work on Florey and Chain would be permitted today. Provide reasons for your response.

c Define *pathogen*.

d List examples of pathogens.

3 Lymphocytes secrete antibodies that formulate the body's immune response to pathogens. The steps of how lymphocytes deliver this immune response are outlined below.

   a List the steps in the correct order.
   - Lymphocytes recognise antigens on the outside of the pathogens and bind to them.
   - Some lymphocytes remain in the body as memory cells.
   - Antibodies are secreted into the bloodstream.
   - Antibodies destroy antigens and anything they are attached to.
   - Pathogens invade the human body.

   b Explain how memory cells protect against future invasions by pathogens.

   c Outline the ways in which the antibodies will use antigens to destroy pathogens.

4 Phagocytic leucocytes carry out phagocytosis on bacterial cells that have invaded the body.

   a Sketch a diagram to show how phagocytosis occurs in the following stages.
   - **i** White blood cell detects bacteria nearby.
   - **ii** Bacteria become attached to the phagocyte.
   - **iii** Bacteria become engulfed by the phagocyte.

   b Outline how lysosomes in the phagocyte help to destroy the bacteria.

5 HIV was first identified in the early 1980s as the cause of a very serious disease. That disease was Acquired Immune Deficiency Syndrome (AIDS) and is one of the biggest killers in the world. Over 36 million people are currently living with HIV and around 2 million of these are children. Over 35 million people have died from HIV-related causes. HIV is a retrovirus because the flow of genetic information from DNA to mRNA is reversed, allowing the virus copy its own code into the cells of the host.

   a State the full name of HIV.

   b There are many different symptoms of HIV in its early stages, including: high fever, headaches, loss of appetite, low blood pressure, high heart rate, nausea, joint pain. Outline any other symptoms of HIV that may also be present.

   c The best protection and treatment of HIV is prevention. List the possible methods of transmission that must be prevented to stop the disease spreading further.

   d In 2015, it was estimated that 36.7 million people were living with HIV but around 40% of these people were unaware that they were living with the disease.
   - **i** Estimate how many people are supposed to be living with HIV but do **not** know that they have it.
   - **ii** Suggest how the number of people having the disease without knowledge might affect the future transmission of HIV.

Exercise 6.4 – Respiratory system

1 Read the text below.

> The World Health Organization is also heavily involved in trying to reduce the number of people affected by tobacco. Their reach spreads across the world and by having a multi-targeted strategy they have been able to start reducing the number of new smokers in some countries. Tobacco kills around 6 million people each year, both from direct smoking and passive inhalation of the smoke of other people. 80% of the billion smokers in the world live in low-to-middle income countries. There are more than 4000 known chemicals in tobacco smoke, many of which are known to cause cancer. Second-hand smoke is just as dangerous and causes more than 600 000 deaths per year, some of whom are children. Some countries and governments have taken steps to ban smoking in certain places, with Bhutan having an almost complete ban on smoking in any public spaces. Some higher-income countries provide help to those that are trying to quit because smoking is so addictive and smokers find it very tough to give up. Media campaigns and the usage of graphic pictorial warnings are contributing to the increased quitting of smokers. Tobacco advertising is banned on many television stations and sponsorship by tobacco companies at sports events is almost unheard of. Some countries have very high taxation on tobacco products as research has shown that tax increases lead to a decrease in tobacco consumption. Only 10% of the world's population are subject to taxes of 75% or more of the retail price.

a Explain why the World Health Organization is committed to reducing the number of smokers in the world.

b State the names of some of the chemicals found in tobacco smoke.

c Carbon monoxide is able to diffuse into red blood cells and bind to hemoglobin. Describe the effect this might have on a smoker.

d **Not** all lung cancers are caused by smoking.

  i   List some of the other causes of lung cancer that you know.

  ii Mutations can lead to the formation of tumours. Define *tumour*.

  iii Define *carcinogen*.

e Tobacco contains nicotine and it is this substance that contributes to the addictive nature of cigarettes. Eventually, tobacco smokers require more and more nicotine to satisfy their cravings. Explain how nicotine causes this effect, despite it being a substance that gives pleasure.

f Emphysema is linked to smoking and this has quite an effect on the respiratory system in humans. The walls of the alveoli lose their elasticity and this makes ventilation more difficult. The walls of the lung are destroyed over time as more hydrolytic enzymes are produced but not enough of the enzyme inhibitors. Eventually, the walls of the alveoli break down and become one large sac instead of lots of smaller ones.

  i   Explain how the formation of larger air sacs causes problems for the patient.

  ii The alveoli are crucial to efficient gas exchange. Copy and complete the table below to show how the features of the alveoli are beneficial to gas exchange.

Feature	Benefit/efficiency
Surface area	Huge surface area for gaseous exchange
Wall of alveoli	
	Maintains concentration of oxygen and carbon dioxide
	Oxygen dissolves here ready for diffusion

Table 6.4

   iii Outline the physiological effects on a human that suffers from emphysema.

   iv Ventilation (inspiration and expiration) is more difficult in emphysema sufferers. Outline the main stages of inspiration in humans.

   v Distinguish between the composition of inspired air and expired air.

   vi Epidemiological studies are often used to study the incidence of lung cancer and emphysema and have been able to establish a causal relationship between the diseases and smoking of tobacco. Define *epidemiology*.

   vii Design an investigation that would enable you to monitor the ventilation of humans at rest and after mild and vigorous exercise.

Exercise 6.5 – Nervous system

1 Cooperation and collaboration between groups of scientists contributes to research into memory and learning. This is perfectly embodied by Suzana Herculano-Houzel, a Brazilian neuroscientist at the Vanderbilt University, who has published tens of publications with other scientists related to her field of neuroanatomy. Suzana has written about the size of many different brains, as well as carrying out research to determine the number of neurons that the average human brain consists of (it is 86 billion – despite what popular internet search engines will tell you!). These neurons transmit the electrical impulses that send messages around your body – whether it be for your survival, to be emotive, or even to decide if it is ethical to take that last chocolate in the box. Who would have thought that so much biology occurred in the nervous system, carrying messages to and from brain, crossing synapses and initiating action impulses? The delivery of acetylcholine 'mimickers' to the brain from cigarettes is one of the most addictive elements of tobacco and it only takes 17 seconds or so for this to stimulation to happen. Nicotine also causes the release of dopamine, another neurotransmitter that is associated with feelings of pleasure and well-being. The speed is remarkable and this area of biology is fast-growing and developing, as our understanding of neurotransmitters and synapses has led to the development of numerous pharmaceuticals for the treatment of mental disorders.

  a The text above states that there are 86 billion neurons in the average human brain.

   i Use your favourite internet search engine and state the commonly-believed number of neurons in the human brain. (Disclaimer: when the internet catches up with this, it should hopefully say 86 billion!).

   ii Suggest a reason why there may be differences in these figures.

   iii Define *neuron*.

   iv The myelination of nerve fibres in the neurons allows for salutatory conduction. Outline how the myelination of nerve fibres encourages this to happen.

b Synapses are the junctions between neurons.
   i State another example of a synaptic junction.
   ii In order for a neurotransmitter to be released, outline what needs to happen at the pre-synaptic neuron.
   iii State the primary function of a neurotransmitter.
   iv Acetylcholine is made up of **two** main parts. These parts make up the name acetylcholine. Deduce the two main components of acetylcholine.
   v State the name of the enzyme that breaks acetylcholine down into its constituent parts.
   vi The text above mentions the role of nicotine in mimicking the action of some neurotransmitters. Explain why this contributes to the addictive nature of tobacco.

Exercise 6.6 – Homeostasis

1 There are many different things that must be kept between certain levels in order for the body to continue to function. Homeostasis is responsible for this. For example, glucagon and insulin are secreted by α and β cells of the pancreas to control blood glucose concentration.
   a Define *homeostasis*.
   b Insulin is produced by β cells; deduce which cells of the pancreas must produce glucagon.
   c Describe the effect of insulin on blood glucose concentration.
   d Describe the effect of glucagon on blood glucose concentration.
   e There are two types of diabetes: type I and type II. People who suffer from diabetes have blood glucose levels that are too high.
   i Compare and contrast the causes of type I and type II diabetes.
   ii Distinguish between the treatments for type I and type II diabetes.

2 William Harvey would have been a huge fan of developments in scientific research. His own research into reproduction was hampered by a lack of suitable equipment. It was only 17 years after his death that the piece of equipment that he would have needed was invented. Most people believed the idea that a man's seed developed into an egg before becoming an embryo, as originally theorised by Aristotle. Harvey regularly dissected and observed deer but could find no evidence of this supposed embryo; however, he was not able to develop his theory fully enough to prove his suspicions that a female egg was involved. Harvey relied on a magnifying glass for his observations.
   a Describe how developments in technology and equipment would have enabled Harvey to find what he was looking for.
   b Describe how the fusion of **two** gametes in sexual reproduction develops into an embryo.
   c Identify the endocrine gland that produces spermatozoa and testosterone.
   d List the names of the hormones that are part of the female reproductive system.
   e In vitro fertilisation (IVF) is carried out for a number of reasons and to provide children for couples who cannot conceive.
   i List some of the reasons why couples might require IVF.
   ii There are some ethical and religious considerations with IVF. Evaluate whether IVF should be allowed to take place.

? Exam-style questions

1   Which of the statements below, A–D, correctly describes products broken down by digestive enzymes? [1]
   I   Starch
   II Glucose
   III Amylase
   IV Proteins
   A   I only
   B   I and II
   C   I and III
   D   I and IV

2   Fat droplets are absorbed into the lymphatic system. Identify the correct step of holozoic nutrition that this part of. [1]
   A   Ingestion
   B   Digestion
   C   Absorption
   D   Assimilation

3   Identify the digestive enzyme that works best at a pH of 2.0. [1]
   A   Amylase
   B   Pepsin
   C   Lipase
   D   Carbohydrase

4   Identify the layer of the small intestine that is composed of connective tissue, blood vessels, nerves and glands. [1]
   A   Sub-mucosa
   B   Mucosa
   C   Lumen
   D   Serosa

5   Identify the branch of the lymphatic system that triglycerides pass into for transport to the cells of the body. [1]
   A   Lacteal
   B   Mucus
   C   Villi
   D   Capillary

6   Which of the following factors is able to speed up the rate of diffusion in gaseous exchange? [1]
   A   Increased surface area
   B   Concentration gradient
   C   Short diffusion pathway
   D   All of the above

7 **Which of the following would not be suitable for the measurement of ventilation in humans? [1]**

   A Recording spirometer

   B Chest belt

   C Pressure monitor

   D EKG machine

8 **Identify the main difference between spermatozoa and ova. [1]**

   A Spermatozoa have a greater number of chromosomes

   B Ova have a greater number of chromosomes

   C Spermatozoa have a larger surface area to volume ratio

   D Spermatozoa contain a cellulose wall

9 **Blood is made up of four main components.**

   a State the names of the four main components of blood. [2]

   b Outline the role of the leucocytes. [2]

   c Describe how platelets help to protect the body from disease and pathogens. [3]

10 **a** Copy the table below and state the missing source, optimum pH, substrate and products of the digestive enzymes. [3]

Enzyme	Source	Optimum pH	Substrate	Products
Amylase	Salivary glands			Maltose
	Gastric glands		Protein	
Lipase		7		Fatty acids and glycerol

Table 6.5

   b Explain the importance of enzymes in digestion. [3]

   c Explain how the structure of villi are adapted for absorption. [3]

11 **a** Distinguish between type I and type II diabetes. [4]

   b Type II diabetes is caused by the lifestyle of the patient. Comment on this statement. [5]

   c Figure 6.3 shows how the prevalence of diabetes differs for different age groups.

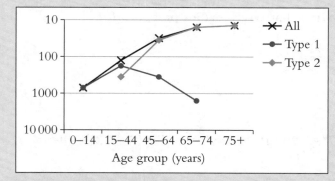

Figure 6.3 The prevalence of diabetes for different age groups.

    i Describe the pattern of data shown in Figure 6.3 for the prevalence of diabetes across different age groups. [2]

    ii Analyse the data in the graph and say if this supports your understanding of the onset of type I and type II diabetes. [4]

12 **a** Explain how the atria and ventricles contribute to the pumping of blood around the body. [4]

   b Arteries carry blood away from the heart at high pressure.

    i Draw and label an artery to show the main layers. [3]

    ii Annotate your diagram to show how the artery is able to carry out its function. [4]

   c Draw and label a diagram of the heart. [8]

7 (HL) Nucleic acids

KEY TERMS AND DEFINITIONS

DNA replication – double-stranded DNA is copied semi-conservatively to produce two identical DNA molecules.

Transcription – first part of gene expression where a section of DNA is copied into mRNA by RNA polymerase.

Translation – decoding of mRNA at a ribosome to produce an amino acid sequence.

Exercise 7.1 – DNA structure and replication

1 Read the text about the investigation of DNA structure carried out by Rosalind Franklin and Maurice Wilkins. Then answer the questions that follow.

Rosalind Franklin was a research associate at John Randall's laboratory at the same time as Maurice Wilkins worked at King's College, London. Both Franklin and Wilkins were working on X-ray diffraction but it was Franklin who developed a better camera for the X-ray diffraction detectors. Franklin was able to get high-resolution photos of crystallised DNA fibers. Franklin had some professional friction with Wilkins and they did not always agree. Wilkins shared Franklin's data with Watson and Crick (Cambridge University). Her data confirmed the 3-D structure that Watson and Crick had theorised for DNA. This was enough for them to work out the distance between base pairs and DNA repeats. So, although she did not realise it at the time, Franklin contributed to the discovery of DNA structure as her results were shared with Watson and Crick, who were able to confirm their own 3-D theory for the structure of DNA. Franklin's X-ray diffraction patterns showed the helical shape, the angle of the helix and the length of one turn of DNA (this was 3.4 nm).

Amazingly, it was Wilkins, Watson and Crick who were awarded the Nobel Prize for their work as they published their findings in *Nature*. Franklin's work was nothing more than a supporting article in the very same journal. Sadly, Franklin died at the age of 37 without truly receiving the recognition for her contribution to one of the most important scientific discoveries of the 20th century.

a State the full name of DNA.

b Identify the evidence that Franklin uncovered in her X-ray diffraction investigations.

c State the name of the length of DNA that is coiled around histones and is responsible for the supercoiling of DNA.

d Draw and label a single unit of DNA.

e The work of Watson and Crick helped to explain the complementary base pairing of DNA. Using examples, outline the bonding patterns that allow different base pairs to pair together.

f Franklin was able to analyse the DNA crystals.

    i Define the term *analyse.*

    ii Using your knowledge of this command term, comment on how Franklin analysed the X-ray diffraction photographs.

g *Franklin would not have been able to discover the structure of DNA without the help of Wilkins, Watson and Crick.* Discuss this statement.

h Describe how the double helix of DNA remains stable.

i Identify the feature of DNA structure that suggests a mechanism for replication.

2 Read the following imaginary web forum posts from the 1950s and answer the questions that follow.

1951:
Martha Chase
Hershey and I are THIS close to providing proof that Avery was correct (she did this in 1945!)
Alfred Hershey
We can solve this together......collaboration is key
Martha Chase
definitely – our work, using the DNA of a virus should help. That will show that the protein does not carry the genes

---

1952:
Martha Chase
totally convinced that DNA is the genetic material, not proteins as everyone keeps telling me

---

later, in 1952:
Alfred Hershey
and I are using a T2 bacteriophage to infect E.coli to show that the genes are in the DNA, not the proteins.
Alfred Hershey
great idea of yours to use the radioactive phosphorus to inject into the nonradioactive bacteria!

---

and then:
Martha Chase
it worked! the bacteriophages labelled with sulfur showed almost no radioactivity!

---

a State the names of the two geneticists who found the evidence that DNA is the genetic material.

b Deduce the year that the two scientists made their discovery.

c Identify the common assumption about how genetic material was carried before the work of Avery, Hershey and Chase.

d Outline how Hershey and Chase were able to show that the DNA, not the protein, was responsible for passing on the genetic material.

e Explain why DNA replication is considered to be semi-conservative.

f Compare and contrast how DNA replication occurs on the leading strand and the lagging strand.

g DNA replication is carried out by a complex system of enzymes. Outline the role of each of the important enzymes as follows:

    i DNA gyrase

    ii Helicase

      iii DNA primase

      iv DNA polymerase I

      v DNA polymerase III

  h Explain what is meant by antiparallel strands of DNA.

3 The Human Genome Project is a massive research project that maps out all of the 3 million or so bases that make up the 20 000+ genes of human beings. Scientists were surprised to find out that only 1.5% of our genome was made up of protein-coding sequences of DNA. Approximately 70% of our genes appeared to have no real use and so these genes were referred to as 'junk' DNA. This 'junk' DNA simply had no obvious function but the term 'junk' has come to mean 'of little value' so people sometimes believe that the non-coding part of DNA must be useless. This cannot be the case because some of the junk *does* have a function.

  a Estimate what percentage of the human genome contains non-coding sequences of DNA.

  b The Human Genome Project was a collaborative project between scientists from many different countries and backgrounds. Evaluate the use of such collaboration in scientific discovery.

  c If 1.5% of our genes are protein-coding sequences and 70% are 'junk', outline what the rest of our genes are responsible for regulating.

  d State the name of the 'junk' region described in each of the questions below:

    i Non-coding sequences of nucleotides that are removed during post-transcriptional modification.

    ii Located at the ends of chromosomes and protect the linear DNA inside from being damaged by each round of replication.

    iii Code for RNA molecules, folding to form tRNA molecules for use in translation.

    iv Highly important in DNA profiling as they are short sequences of bases that are repeated several times.

  e Professor Sir Alec Jeffreys of Leicester University, UK, is a respected name in the world of genetics as his work on inherited variation in human DNA led him to invent DNA fingerprinting. He began by using the technology to solve immigration and paternity cases. But it was the use in a murder case local to Alec Jeffreys (he was not a Sir nor a professor at the time, of course) that pushed DNA fingerprinting into the public spotlight. Read the article about the famous murder case and answer the questions that follow.

Genetic Profile Puts Killer Away
30 January 1988

The shocking murder of two young girls in Enderby, Leicestershire, has finally been solved with the help of a team of scientists from Leicester University, led by Alec Jeffreys.

The work of Mr Jeffreys had proven an original suspect to be innocent despite his confession. However, Mr Jeffreys and his team kept their composure and continued to work towards finding the DNA of the real killer. In January of last year, police began testing all men between the ages of 17 and 34 to find who the killer was. Only by chance did the killer get caught, as he had managed to evade capture by using his friend's blood sample to avoid detection. Once the killer had been arrested, his DNA was shown to match samples found at the crime scene and he was convicted and sentenced to life in prison.

The science behind the DNA profiling used to capture the killer involves counting the number of repeated regions of DNA. These regions vary from person to person, creating a unique 'fingerprint' for each individual. This is done by the following stages:

- DNA is extracted.
- Enzymes cut the DNA into fragments.
- Fragments are then separated.
- Fragments are treated with a radioactive probe which shows on an X-ray film and looks like a bar code (Figure 7.1).

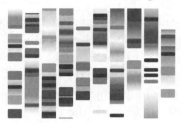

Figure 7.1 A DNA profile.

i Suggest from where DNA may be extracted in humans.

ii State the type of enzymes that are typically used to cut the DNA into fragments.

iii Outline how the DNA fragments are separated.

iv Look at Figure 7.2 below. Using your knowledge of DNA profiling, suggest which sample is a likely match for the sample from the crime scene.

DNA samples from:

crime   suspect   suspect   suspect
scene   #1   #2   #3

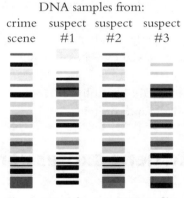

Figure 7.2 A forensic DNA profile comparison.

v Explain why you chose the suspect for the previous question.

vi Outline possible uses of DNA fingerprinting and DNA profiling.

4 Switzerland is the base of the Convention on International Trade in Endangered Species of Wild Fauna and Flora (CITES). One of the major issues that they are investigating is the illegal trade of meat from endangered animals. Of course, when the meat has been carved up it is not possible to identify where it might have come from. Some meat may originate from areas affected badly by HIV, Ebola and *E. coli*.

a Suggest why it is a problem that officers at customs and border control cannot identify the origin of meat coming into a particular country.

b Explain why DNA analysis is a potentially useful tool for customs and border officials in the identification of illegal meat.

c The profiling of such DNA uses tandem repeats. State the percentage of DNA sequences that you would expect to be highly repetitive in the human genome.

d Describe how DNA experts would use tandem repeats to analyse the DNA samples of meat tested at border controls. Your answer should include the following terms: STR sequences, DNA sample, polymerase chain reaction, gel electrophoresis.

e Outline the role of enzymes in the separation of DNA.

f State the name of the gel commonly used in gel electrophoresis.

g Explain why fragments of DNA are able to separate during gel electrophoresis.

h *The testing of meat at customs and borders control should be a priority for governments.* Discuss this statement.

i The role of enzymes in DNA replication has already been outlined in a previous question. The clues below indicate how some enzymes are involved in DNA replication. Use the clues to identify the name of the enzyme. The first one has been done for you to show how the clues might help you to identify the enzyme.

   i This is the sort of enzyme that you might expect to unwind at the end of a difficult day. (Answer: Helicase as this unwinds and separates the DNA.)

   ii Without this enzyme, DNA polymerase III would have no idea where to start.

   iii This enzyme is repelled by the replication fork when Okazaki is in town.

   iv Sometimes, helicase will be too tense so the relaxing powers of this enzyme are required.

   v Why don't they give me a proper cool name like the rest of my friends?

   vi The covalent catalyst for Okazaki + Okazaki.

   vii If this enzyme had a voice, it might shout 'Hey, primers! You are no longer needed and so I am replacing you'.

j Use the descriptions below to identify the types of non-coding DNA that are being described.

   i Sequences involved in transcription, such as promoters and enhancers.

   ii Non-coding sequences within genes that are removed by RNA splicing.

   iii Repetitive DNA at the end of a chromosome.

   iv Short tandem repeat sequences that are used for DNA profiling.

   v Codes for RNA molecules that are not translated into proteins.

Exercise 7.2 – Transcription and gene expression

1 Transcription occurs in three main stages.

a State the name of the stages of transcription that are described below.

   i RNA polymerase binds to the DNA and the double helix unwinds.

   ii The mRNA becomes longer as nucleotides are added to the 3' OH group.

   iii When mRNA synthesis is complete, the DNA, the RNA polymerase and the mRNA disassociate from each other.

b Define the following key terms related to transcription and gene expression.

   i Transcription

   ii Antisense strand

   iii Sense strand

   iv Exon

   v Splicing

   vi Spliceosome

c Identify the key terms from their description below.
  i Short sequence of non-coding DNA that acts as a binding point for RNA polymerase.
  ii Protein-DNA complexes that help to regulate eukaryotic transcription.
  iii The study of heritable changes in organisms not caused by changes in the DNA base sequences.
  iv Reversible reaction where a methyl group (–CH3) is added to a cytosine.

d DNA methylation can be passed on to future generations, as shown in the numerous case studies available. This type of transgenerational inheritance is observable in recent studies on tobacco smoke. There has been a direct impact on gene expression profiles and it is suggested that these epigenetic modifications can be passed from generation to generation. The effect of environment as the trigger of heritable changes in epigenetic factors is easily seen in studies of identical twins. As you know, identical twins will share the same DNA profile but, occasionally, twins can be subjected to a variance in environmental factors. Even when twins share the same environmental factors, it mystified scientists as to how they would have such different lives and would rarely die of the same diseases. Surely, if their genetic profile was identical and they had the same upbringing, then they would have the same characteristics and suffer the same diseases? Twins that have different tolerances for pain have been shown to have differences in their methylation states. This difference in methylation state has crucially been discovered in results for diabetes and cancer.

Some people who were starved during the Second World War had children and grandchildren that were smaller and appeared malnourished. This is evidence of epigenetic change. Other examples include the colour of fur in the calico cat as epigenetic changes cause each cat to have a unique fur colouration, and the increased likelihood of psychotic episodes in survivors of starvation in China.

  i DNA methylation inactivates a gene. Suggest how a gene that has been methylated may be turned back on.
  ii List some of the main causes of DNA methylation in humans.
  iii Only one of a pair of twins develops cancer. Deduce why only one twin developed cancer yet the other twin did not.
  iv Look at the DNA profiles of two twins, taken at the age of 3 and again at the age of 50 (Figure 7.3). The arrows on the 50-year-old profile indicate areas of DNA methylation.

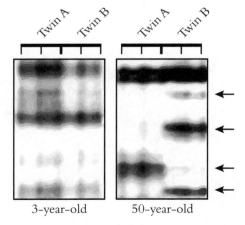

Figure 7.3 DNA methylation patterns.

Analyse the changes shown in the DNA methylation patterns of Figure 7.3.

e Changes in human development are influenced by both nature and nurture. The debate regarding the relative importance of an individual's innate qualities versus those acquired through experiences is a popular discussion in the scientific world.

   i Explain what is meant by *nature* and *nurture*.

   ii Discuss whether nature or nurture affects the phenotypic features of an organism.

f Which hand do you write with? The mystery of why some people are left-handed or right-handed is one of the most fascinating areas of genetic research. Recent studies have suggested that epigenetics might have a role in explaining why 10% of the world's population is left-handed. Researchers have shown that gene activity in the spinal cord while the child is in the womb might influence which hand that child will favour. It has been observed that some unborn children prefer to move their right or left hand in the womb. This was achieved by analysis of DNA methylation patterns in the spinal cord during the eight-to-twelve-week stage of pregnancy, before the motor cortex is connected to the spinal cord.

   According to the text in this question, determine what percentage of people are right-handed in the world.

g State the effect that direct methylation of DNA has on gene expression.

h State the name of the component that is attached to DNA during DNA methylation.

i Suggest possible factors that might occur during the lifetime of a human that may contribute to DNA methylation patterns.

j Explain why identical twins may not develop the same disease.

2 Identical twins share the same DNA but often experience different environments, particularly as the twins get older. Scientists can study twins and try to find out which genetic, or environmental, factors are responsible for the onset of different diseases and conditions. A comparison of traits between identical twins and fraternal twins (Figure 7.4) can help to further identify the influence of genetic factors. Use Figure 7.4 to answer the questions that follow.

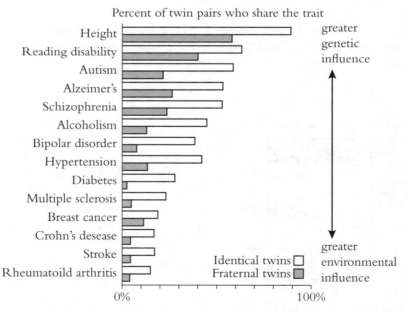

Figure 7.4 Comparison of identical and fraternal twins.

a Estimate the percentage of identical twins where both twins suffer from a reading disability.

b Estimate the percentage of identical twins where both twins suffer from a bipolar disorder.

c Estimate the percentage of identical twins where both twins suffer from diabetes.

d Estimate the percentage of identical twins where both twins suffer from breast cancer.

e Suggest what can be determined when a high percentage of identical twins share a particular condition.

f Explain why a high percentage of twins sharing a condition or diseases might be caused by genetic factors.

g *Height is determined by genetic factors.* Evaluate this statement.

Exercise 7.3 – Translation

1 State the number of amino acids that are involved in protein synthesis.

2 The four main stages of translation are outlined below.
  a List the correct sequence of stages.
    A the components of translation are assembled – the mRNA, the small subunit of a ribosome, an activated tRNA molecule and a large ribosomal subunit.
    B the ribosome moves along the mRNA strand in the 5' to 3' direction, one codon at a time.
    C stop codon signals end of translocation; the polypeptide chain and the mRNA are released from the ribosome, which separates into its subunits.
    D peptide bonds are formed by condensation reaction between two amino acids that are next to each other.
  b State the names of the three tRNA binding sites.
  c Outline the roles of the three tRNA binding sites.
  d The ribosome is separated into subunits during the termination stage. State the two subunits that the ribosome separates into.
  e Distinguish between transcription and translation.
  f A group of ribosomes is clustered together along an mRNA strand. This molecule is able to increase the efficiency of protein synthesis by working together on building the same protein. Deduce the name of the molecule described here.

3 Protein structure highlights the specific nature of how these complex molecules are fitted together. The function of the protein is reliant on its structure.
  a Describe the primary structure of a protein.
  b State the type of bonds formed by condensation reactions that join amino acids together.
  c The polypeptide chain becomes folded or twisted into a particular shape. Weak hydrogen bonds hold the structures in place. Distinguish between the two types of structure formed as part of the secondary structure of proteins.
  d The tertiary structure requires further folding of the polypeptide.
    i Identify the part of the amino acids that stabilises this 3-D structure.
    ii List some of the bonds that help to maintain the tertiary structure of a protein.
    iii *The tertiary structure of a protein is the most important part of the protein structure.* Comment on this statement.

e The following proteins have a quaternary structure. State the number of polypeptide chains that each one of them has.

 i Collagen

 ii Hemoglobin

 iii Antibiodies

 iv Myosin

f Define the term *conjugated protein*.

g Hemoglobin is made up of two alpha chains and two beta chains. State the name of the prosthetic group that helps the protein in the transportation of oxygen.

h Fibrous is a word that means long and narrow. Globular means of a spherical shape. Distinguish between the structure of fibrous and globular proteins.

i For each of the following proteins, state whether they are fibrous proteins or globular proteins.

 i Pepsin

 ii Myoglobin

 iii Collagen

 iv Keratin

 v Silk

 vi Enzymes

 vii Catalase

 viii Antibodies

 ix Hemoglobin

4 The use of computers in recent years has enabled scientists to make advances in bioinformatics applications. Since the term was first invented by Hogeweg and Hesper in 1970, the range of applications has grown further and wider than Hogeweg and Hesper could ever have imagined. These applications include (but are not limited to):

- DNA sequencing (Human Genome Project)
- mapping of the human proteome
- genome annotation
- comparative genomics
- gene and protein expression (analysis and regulation)
- protein localisation
- computational evolutionary biology.

The data gathered in the Human Genome Project was analysed using the Tiger Assembler, a vital algorithm in calculating the number of genes in the human genome. Genome annotation is possible because of the ability of the software of computers to recognise the start and stop codons of genes. The evolutionary relationships explored in Chapter 5 are a result of comparative genomics – allowing biologists to map the similarities of different organisms.

a State three bioinformatics applications that have been advanced by the use of computers.

b Define the term *proteome*.

c Outline the role of a start codon.

d Comment on the importance of bioinformatics in scientific research.

5 The differences between fibrous and globular proteins are shown in the table below.

  a Copy Table 7.1. Then use the word box to complete the boxes for the different rows and headings.

fibrous	globular	shape	durability
solubility	examples	sequence	

Long and narrow	Round
Repetitive amino acid sequence	Non-repetitive amino acid sequence
Less sensitive to changes in temperature and pH	More sensitive to changes in temperature and pH
Collagen, elastin, keratin, actin, myosin	Hemoglobin, insulin, immunoglobin
Insoluble in water	Soluble in water

Table 7.1

  b Identify the following proteins by the clues provided.

    i Responsible for transporting oxygen within red blood cells and is constructed of four polypeptide subunits.

    ii Fibrous protein that is a component of hair and skin.

    iii Integral membrane protein that forms channels for the passage of water molecules.

? Exam-style questions

1 **Which of the statements below, A–D, correctly describes what can be found in a nucleosome? [1]**
    I   H1 histone
    II DNA
    III Prokaryotic DNA
    IV Core of 8 histones
    A I only
    B I and II
    C I and III
    D I, II and IV

2 **What is the approximate length of the DNA in a typical eukaryotic nucleosome? [1]**
    A 50 base pairs
    B 100 base pairs
    C 150 base pairs
    D 200 base pairs

3 **How many bonds are there between adenine and thymine in a DNA molecule? [1]**
    A 2 hydrogen bonds
    B 3 hydrogen bonds
    C 2 peptide bonds
    D 3 peptide bonds

4 Identify the enzyme that is not required for DNA replication. [1]

   A DNA primase

   B DNA ligase

   C DNA polymerase I

   D DNA catalase

5 Identify the structure shown in Figure 7.5. [1]

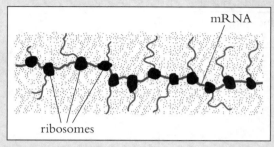

Figure 7.5

   A Polysome

   B Globular protein

   C Amino acid

   D Eukaryotic cell

6 The human genome has approximately 3 billion base pairs in each haploid set of chromosomes. Estimate the number of base pairs that would be replicated during the S phase of the cell cycle. [1]

   A 6 billion

   B 3 billion

   C 1.5 billion

   D 9 billion

7 Which of the following is the direction of replication in the leading strand of DNA? [1]

   A 5' to 3'

   B 3' to 5'

   C 5'

   D against the lagging strand

8 Identify the purine bases from the list below. [1]

   A Guanine and adenine

   B Guanine and thymine

   C Guanine and cytosine

   D Adenine and thymine

9 Identify the number of tandem repeats in this DNA sequence. [1]

GTACTAAGAGTAGTCCTACTACTACTACTACTATGATGCAGT

   A 4

   B 5

   C 6

   D 7

10 Rosalind Franklin was working on which process that enabled her to analyse DNA crystals? [1]

    A X-ray diffraction

    B DNA sequencing

    C X-ray crystallisation

    D The discovery of DNA

11 Which of the following is not a stage of transcription? [1]

    A Initiation

    B Translation

    C Elongation

    D Termination

12 *A short DNA sequence that acts as a binding point for RNA polymerase.* Identify the piece of DNA that is described in this sentence. [1]

    A Promoter

    B Intron

    C Stop codon

    D Repressor

13 Identify the sentence that best describes the primary structure of a protein. [1]

    A The sequence and number of amino acids

    B The formation of alpha helices and beta pleated sheets

    C The further folding of the polypeptide stabilised by interactions between R groups

    D The folding together of the alpha helices and beta sheets

14 **a** Draw and label a diagram to show three DNA nucleotides linked together in two strands. [6]

    b Outline the method behind DNA profiling. [5]

    c Explain why DNA profiling is important. [5]

    d Figure 7.6 shows the results of a paternity case.

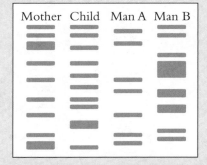

Figure 7.6 DNA results of a paternity case.

      i Deduce which man is the father of the child. [1]

      ii Annotate the diagram to show which bands match the child and man A. [1]

      iii Explain your reasoning for the answer to part i. [3]

    e Outline the process that could have been used to amplify the original DNA sample if larger quantities had been needed. [3]

15 Recent research into epigenetics suggests a link between poor diet in pregnant women and ADHD (Attention Deficit Hyperactivity Disorder). The studies have shown that a diet of high-fat and high-sugar may alter epigenetic markers in the child's DNA.

   a Define the term *epigenetics*. [3]
   b Outline the main factors that can contribute to DNA methylation. [2]
   c Annotate Figure 7.7 below to show the location of the methyl group in the methylated cytosine. [1]

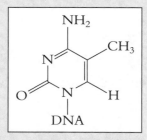

Figure 7.7 Chemical structure of methylated cytosine.

16 a Describe the structure of proteins. [8]
    b Distinguish between fibrous and globular proteins, using examples. [5]

HL Metabolism, cell respiration 8 and photosynthesis

Chapter outline

In this chapter you will:
- describe how metabolic reactions are regulated in response to the cell's needs
- explain how energy is converted to a usable form in cell respiration
- explain the processes involved in converting light energy into chemical energy.

KEY TERMS AND DEFINITIONS

Metabolic pathway – chain or cycle of linked events catalysed by enzymes.

Photosynthesis – the process by which light energy is absorbed and stored as chemical energy in organic compounds.

Respiration – the controlled breakdown of food molecules to release energy.

Exercise 8.1 – Metabolism

1 A huge project by an international group of researchers has enabled them to map out all reactions involved in human metabolism, much in the same way that scientists have collaborated to map out the human genome and the human proteome. The most recent effort, completed in 2013, contains information about 7439 reactions, 2626 metabolites (substance required for metabolic processes), and 2140 genes that are involved in human metabolism. Each part of metabolism is just a tiny part of our overall knowledge, making it even more important that scientists work together for the greater good. Without these efforts, and developing technology, it would take decades to sift through the mountains of data that is gathered during research into the human metabolism. New drugs can be designed for a range of treatments for diseases that are currently without cure, such as rheumatoid arthritis.

   a It is estimated that there are 20 000 protein-coding genes in the genome. Calculate the percentage of genes mapped in the project so far that are related to human metabolism.

   b Researchers can use the map to look closely at how diseases develop. Suggest how doctors might be able to use such a map of the human metabolism.

   c *Each part of the metabolism is just a tiny part of our overall knowledge.*

   i Discuss this statement, including the importance of such projects.

   ii Comment on the role of advances in computing and technology in helping projects such as this be successful.

2 Metabolic reactions are made up of anabolic and catabolic reactions that are responsible for building products up or breaking products down.
 a Outline what happens in catabolic reactions.
 b Outline what happens in anabolic reactions.
 c State whether the following reactions are anabolic or catabolic.
   i Amino acids forming dipeptides.
   ii Decomposition of hydrogen peroxide into water and oxygen.
   iii The breaking down of glucose to produce carbon dioxide and water.
   iv Glycerol reacting with fatty acids.
   v Carbon dioxide and water producing glucose and oxygen in photosynthesis.
 d Metabolic pathways are a series of linked reactions within a cell and are usually catalysed by enzymes. Sometimes the pathway is linear and other times it is cyclic. Enzymes lower the activation energy in order to speed up the reactions.
   i Copy and annotate the diagram below to remind yourself of how enzymes convert substrates into products. Use the terms in the word box to assist you – not all of them are required.

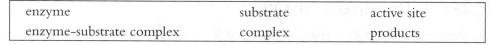

enzyme	substrate	active site
enzyme–substrate complex	complex	products

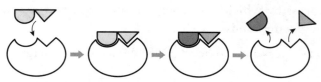

Figure 8.1 How enzymes work.

   ii Define the term *activation energy*.
   iii The graph in Figure 8.2 shows the effect of an enzyme on the activation energy of a reaction. Suggest possible labels for the axes in Figure 8.2.

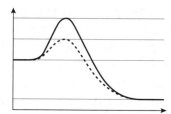

Figure 8.2 The effect of an enzyme on the activation energy of a reaction.

   iv Describe the effect of the enzyme in Figure 8.2 on the activation energy of the reaction.

3 The word 'inhibitor' means to slow something down, or to stop something from happening. So, an enzyme inhibitor does exactly that by stopping certain reactions from happening.

a State the names of the two types of enzyme inhibitors.

b Compare and contrast how the two types of inhibitor affect the active site.

c Copy and annotate the diagrams in Figure 8.3 to explain how each type of inhibitor functions.

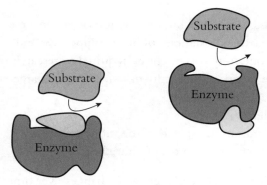

Figure 8.3 Inhibition of an enzyme.

d Figure 8.4 shows how the two types of inhibitor affect the rate of reaction.

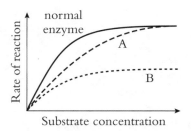

Figure 8.4 The effect of inhibitors on enzyme activity.

i Identify the type of inhibitor for curve A.

ii Identify the type of inhibitor for curve B.

iii Explain why the two types of inhibitor shown in Figure 8.4 have different rates of reaction.

e Have you ever started to eat an apple, left it and then come back to find it has turned brown inside? This is because oxygen in the air converts natural chemicals into melanin, causing the brown colour that you see. There is an enzyme that causes the browning reaction. It is possible to damage the enzyme through cooking or by altering the pH of the enzyme with citric juices.

i Suggest why the cooking of the apple prevents it from browning.

ii Suggest why citric juices are also able to prevent browning of the apple.

iii Design an investigation to observe the effect of inhibiting the enzymes involved in the browning of apples.

4 Malaria is a disease caused by the pathogen *Plasmodium falciparum*, and requires a human and a mosquito host. The parasite is able to develop as a result of coordination between particular enzymes. New anti-malarial drugs are required to target these enzymes and inhibit them.

a Determine the genus that causes malaria.

b Suggest the sort of database that might be able to help with targeting enzymes that control malaria.

c Use of a particular database that studied 310 000 different chemicals yielded 19 chemicals that may act as inhibitors. Calculate the percentage of chemicals that might be useful from this particular database.

d Outline how scientists could potentially use these 19 inhibitors to target the spread of malaria.

e Describe how a non-competitive inhibitor would limit the action of the enzyme.

f As part of your lessons, you will have studied examples of both competitive and non-competitive inhibitors. For this question, you might be required to research the examples given before answering the question. The influenza virus may be targeted by an inhibitor called Relenza.

   i State which type of inhibitor Relenza is.

   ii Describe how Relenza is able to prevent the spread of the influenza virus.

   iii Describe the action of a non-competitive inhibitor of your choice.

5 Figure 8.5 shows how the rate of reaction of a particular enzyme changes over time at different temperatures.

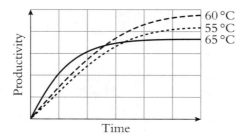

Figure 8.5 The effect of temperature on the rate of reaction of an unnamed enzyme.

a Describe the effect of temperature on the enzyme shown in Figure 8.5.

b Explain why the enzyme at 65 °C reaches a lower rate of reaction than the other enzymes.

c Determine which of the temperatures lowers the activation energy the fastest.

d Determine the optimum temperature that this enzyme works best at.

e Some enzymes operate best at different values of pH. For example, enzymes in the stomach might work best at around pH2.

   i State the name of an enzyme that you might expect to find in a human stomach.

   ii Teodora carries out investigations to test the activity of different enzymes under different values for pH. Her results are outline in Table 8.1. Construct a graph to show the enzyme activity of the enzymes.

pH	Enzyme activity (%)		
	A	B	C
0	10	5	
1		15	
2	85	25	
3		35	
4	10	45	
5		65	
6		75	5
7	0	85	10

pH	Enzyme activity (%)		
	A	B	C
8		75	
9	0	65	
10		55	45
11		45	
12		30	85
13		20	40
14		5	5

Table 8.1

iii Determine which enzyme operates best in acidic conditions.

iv Determine which enzyme works best in human blood.

v State the optimum pH of enzyme C.

Exercise 8.2 – Cell respiration

1 Cell respiration involves both oxidation and reduction reactions.

  a Define the term *redox reaction*.

  b The movement of electrons, hydrogen or oxygen result in either oxidation reactions or reduction reactions. Copy Table 8.2. Distinguish between each type of reaction in the table.

Oxidation	Reduction

Table 8.2

  c Look at the reaction below and answer the questions that follow.

$$C_6H_{12}O_6 + 6O_2 \rightarrow 6CO_2 + 6H_2O + ENERGY$$

    i Identify the reaction shown.

    ii State whether the glucose is oxidised or reduced in this reaction.

    iii Explain your answer to part ii.

    iv Suggest why this reaction is considered to be a redox reaction.

    v Remind yourself of the important examination tip by completing the OILRIG mnemonic.

  d i Define the term *cellular respiration*.

    ii State the name of the molecule that the released energy is stored as.

    iii The four main parts of the respiration pathway are shown below. List them in the correct order.

      - The link reaction
      - Electron transfer chain
      - Krebs cycle
      - Glycolysis

  e Glycolysis literally means 'the breaking down of glucose'. Answer the questions that follow about glycolysis.

    i Identify the part of the cell where glycolysis takes place.

    ii Glycolysis takes place in the absence of oxygen. State the key term that describes this type of reaction.

    iii The first stage of glycolysis requires phosphate groups to be added from ATP to produce a hexose bisphosphate molecule. State the name of this process.

    iv The hexose bisphosphate is then split into two triose phosphates. State the name of this stage of glycolysis.

    v An oxidation reaction is the third stage of glycolysis. Outline what happens at this stage.

    vi The phosphate groups from the triose bisphosphates are transferred onto ADP, forming two molecules of ATP and a pyruvate molecule. State the name of this stage of glycolysis.

vii The names of the four stages in questions iii–vi can be recalled using a mnemonic for **PLOA**. An example would be **P**aul **L**ikes **O**utdoor **A**erobics. Design your own mnemonic to recall the four stages of glycolysis.

viii Determine the net products of the glycolysis reaction.

ix Explain why the net production of ATP is only 2 × ATP.

2 Figure 8.6 shows a longitudinal section of a mitochondrion.

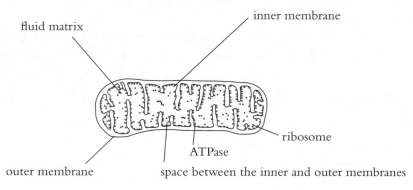

Figure 8.6 Longitudinal section of a mitochondrion.

a Copy the diagram. Then annotate the diagram of the mitochondrion to outline the importance of each structure.

b State the stages of respiration that occur in the mitochondrial matrix.

c State the key term being described for each process listed below.

    i   Removal of carbon dioxide.

    ii   Sometimes known as the citric acid cycle.

    iii Enzyme that converts pyruvate to acetyl CoA.

    iv Six-carbon compound formed when acetyl combines with a four-carbon compound.

    v   The removal of hydrogen atoms.

    vi The abbreviation of adenosine triphosphate.

    vii Use the answers to parts i–v to complete the gaps in the description of the link reaction and Krebs cycle below. Copy and complete the description.

        The _____ reaction converts _____ to acetyl CoA, using coenzyme A. At the same time, a _____ atom is removed as carbon dioxide in a _____ reaction. Pyruvate is oxidised by the removal of _____, forming NADH + H+. Acetyl CoA enters the _____ and coenzyme A is removed. _____ is formed as the acetyl part of acetyl CoA combines with a four-carbon compound. The acetyl groups are _____ to release four pairs of hydrogen atoms and _____ to form two molecules of carbon dioxide. One molecule of _____ is formed by the phosphorylation of ADP with P_i. There are two hydrogen carriers – NAD^+ and FAD^+ – and these have a _____ removed during oxidation reactions. The cycle can then begin again.

viii Determine the number of each product formed by the link reaction and the Krebs cycle.

_____ molecules of NADH + H$^+$

_____ molecules of FADH$_2$

_____ molecules of ATP

_____ molecules of CO$_2$

d Figure 8.7 shows an overview of the link reaction and the Krebs cycle. You are expected to analyse the diagrams of the pathways of aerobic respiration to deduce where decarboxylation and oxidation reactions occur.

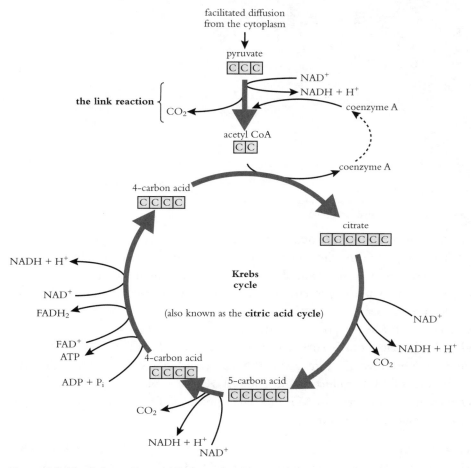

Figure 8.7 The link reaction and Krebs cycle.

i Analyse Figure 8.7 to deduce where the decarboxylation reactions are occurring.

ii Analyse Figure 8.7 to deduce where the oxidation reactions are occurring.

iii Deduce the number of carbon atoms fed into the Krebs cycle by the link reaction.

3 This question looks at the final stage of respiration, the electron transport chain, oxidative phosphorylation and chemiosmosis.

a Outline the role of the electron carriers in the electron transport chain.

b Describe how cristae are formed from the inner membrane of the mitochondrion.

c ATP formed in the mitochondria uses energy released by the oxidation of glucose during respiration. State the name of the process described.

d Figure 8.8 is required to answer the questions that follow.

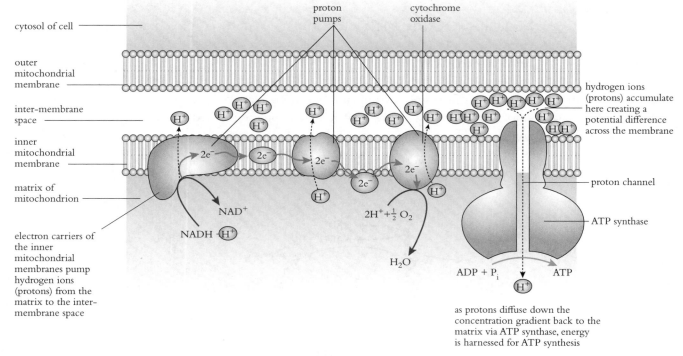

cytosol of cell

outer mitochondrial membrane

inter-membrane space

inner mitochondrial membrane

matrix of mitochondrion

electron carriers of the inner mitochondrial membranes pump hydrogen ions (protons) from the matrix to the inter-membrane space

proton pumps

cytochrome oxidase

hydrogen ions (protons) accumulate here creating a potential difference across the membrane

proton channel

ATP synthase

$2H^+ + \frac{1}{2} O_2$

H_2O

$ADP + P_i$ ATP

as protons diffuse down the concentration gradient back to the matrix via ATP synthase, energy is harnessed for ATP synthesis

Figure 8.8 Electron transport chain.

    i Determine the number of key electron carriers shown in Figure 8.8.

    ii State the part of the mitochondrion where electron carriers are held.

    iii Suggest why protons accumulate in the inter-membrane space.

    iv Determine where the electrons come from that are transferred onto the first electron carrier.

    v Describe the process of chemiosmosis.

    vi State the name of the enzyme that joins ADP and P_i to form ATP.

    vii If three protons flow through ATP synthase and one ATP is formed, calculate the number of ATP produced from one $NADH + H^+$ pump.

  e Determine the net yield of ATP molecules produced from each molecule of glucose broken down in respiration.

4 It is not always easy for scientists to accept new theories or a paradigm shift. Even when falsification of an existing theory occurs, it can still lead to ridicule and non-acceptance by peers. This was certainly the case for Peter Mitchell and his chemiosmosis theory (1961). His theory explained how the mitochondria converted ADP to ATP in the membrane but was contradictory to classical biology and actually made the scientific community quite angry. They believed that there was some sort of high-energy intermediate compound involved. Mitchell, and his colleague Dr Jennifer Moyle, continued with their work independently and it was nearly 20 years before his work was accepted and awarded with a Nobel Prize (1978). Mitchell's chemiosmotic hypothesis proved to be the foundation for our understanding of oxidative phosphorylation and was only accepted when ATP synthase was discovered.

  a Outline how the energy for ATP synthesis is supplied.

  b Describe what happens during oxidative phosphorylation.

  c Comment on why Peter Mitchell found it difficult to have his theories accepted as a lone innovator in science.

5 The ATP that is produced in cells has a vast array of uses in organisms and can be used to provide the energy for a number of cellular reactions. The assembly of various macromolecules requires a substantial amount of energy, as do the processes of exocytosis and endocytosis. The messages that are sent to your brain as you process different stimuli, the growth and repair of cells, and the contraction of muscles all require energy from ATP.

a Identify the examples of active transport that are described in the text.

b Suggest a macromolecule that could be assembled by a cell and requires energy for the biosynthesis of the molecule.

c The growth and repair of cells is carried out by which type of cell division?

d State the name of the electrical impulses that are sent as part of nerve transmission between cells.

e List the different uses of energy from ATP that are in the text above.

6 Electron tomography is used to produce images of active mitochondria. This allows the internal three-dimensional structure of the mitochondria to be shown clearly. The process involves the use of persistent imaging with a transmission electron microscope. As the images are captured, the sample is tilted at different angles to produce a range of images that can be computationally reconstructed as a three-dimensional image. This image is known as a tomogram.

a Suggest why a light microscope in the school laboratory cannot be used to carry out electron topography.

b Outline how samples are prepared for electron tomography.

c The inner workings of a typical mitochondrion have been observed using this technique. Describe how the inner membranes of a mitochondrion are arranged.

d Figure 8.9 shows a typical image of a mitochondrion produced by electron tomography.

  i Identify structures A to E in Figure 8.9 to show the main structures of a typical mitochondrion.

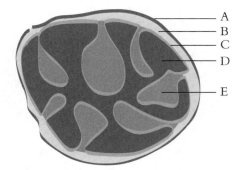

Figure 8.9 Mitochondrion model produced by electron topography.

  ii The diameter of the mitochondrion can be calculated using the image size of the tomograph. Describe how you would be able to calculate the size of the actual mitochondrion and the information that you would require to do so.

  iii The image in a tomograph shows that the length of a particular mitochondrion is 190 mm. The electron transmission microscope that was used captured the image using a magnification of ×10 000. Calculate the actual size of the mitochondrion captured in the tomograph.

Exercise 8.3 – Photosynthesis

1 The Global Artificial Photosynthesis (GAP) project is another example of scientists working to benefit the community. The aim is to create an artificial 'leaf' within the next decade. An electronic version of the leaf that creates oxygen and water has already been invented and will be developed for use. As fossil fuels and energy resources become more and more scarce, the scientific community is racing to find long-term energy and food production solutions.

Projects such as GAP, JCAP (Joint Center for Artificial Photosynthesis in America), and the Solar H network (in Europe) are aiming to produce cheap, localised conversion of sunlight, water and carbon dioxide. The projects aim for this energy to be used as fuel for cooking and heating and it may even be able to assist with crop production in areas where little photosynthesis is able to take place. These projects have the potential to reduce carbon emissions; and even more impressively, to reduce the current CO_2 levels in the atmosphere. Some say it may even lead to a reduction in geopolitical tensions as disagreements regarding fossil fuels, food scarcity and fuel usage would be largely negated.

   a Current projects in America and Europe work independently to achieve artificial photosynthesis. Evaluate whether these projects should remain independent or become part of a larger, collaborative effort.

   b Outline the benefits if artificial photosynthesis were to be achieved.

   c Define the term *photosynthesis*.

   d List some of the organisms that are capable of photosynthesis.

   e State the two main parts of photosynthesis.

   f Identify the part of a leaf where both of these two reactions take place.

   g Identify which part of the chloroplast each reaction takes place in.

      i Light-dependent reaction.

      ii Light-independent reaction.

   h *The light-dependent reaction is the only one of the reactions that can take place when there is sufficient sunlight.* Comment on this statement.

   i State the chemical equation for photosynthesis.

2 Answer the following questions about the stages of the light-dependent reaction of photosynthesis.

   a Outline what happens in photoactivation.

   b Photosystem II has to replace the lost electrons. Describe how this happens.

   c Define the term *photolysis*.

   d Identify where the excited electrons travel to along the electron transport chain.

   e Between photosystem I and photosystem II, ATP is formed in a similar fashion to that in the mitochondria.

      i State the name of the ATP formation that occurs in photosynthesis.

      ii Compare and contrast the chemiosmotic process in chloroplasts and in mitochondria.

   f The electrons at the higher energy level are combined with protons in $NADP^+$. Deduce the molecule produced by this reaction.

   g State the names of the two products that are formed during the light-dependent reaction.

   h Distinguish between $NADP^+$ in photosynthesis and NAD^+ in respiration.

3 State the names of the two processes described below.

  a Production of ATP, using energy from electrons that are flowing from photosystem II through photosystem I and on to $NADP^+$.

  b The alternative pathway taken when there is no acceptor available to take the electrons from photosystem I. This pathway is via photosystem II where they re-join the electron transport chain.

4 The light-independent reaction takes place in the stroma. Answer the following questions about the main stages of the light-independent reaction.

  a Make a sketch of the diagram below. Then label the empty boxes of the Calvin cycle shown in Figure 8.10.

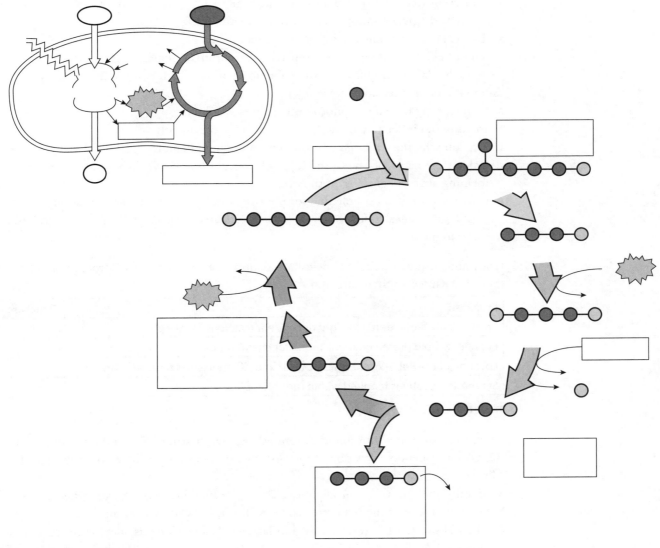

Figure 8.10 The Calvin cycle.

  b Describe the process of carbon fixation.

  c Outline the role of Rubisco in the process of carbon fixation.

  d The ATP and NADPH + H^+ from the light-dependent reaction convert glycerate 3-phosphate (3-PGA) into triose phosphate. Deduce the role of the ATP molecule in this stage.

e Only five of the six molecules of triose phosphate are needed to reform the ribulose bisphosphate. Suggest what happens to the one other molecule of triose phosphate that is not needed.

f State the number of turns of the Calvin cycle required to produce two triose phosphate molecules.

5 Melvin Calvin carried out experiments to elucidate the carboxylation of RuBP. Calvin used $^{14}CO_2$ as the starting material for photosynthesis in *Chlorella*. $^{14}CO_2$ is a radioactive isotope of carbon and had only been recently discovered at the time of Calvin's use. Calvin's experiment was carried out as follows.

- *Chlorella* was exposed to light using a flat, round disc that looked like a lollipop.
- Photosynthesis occurred at a steady rate while $^{14}CO_2$ was added for different periods of time (ranging from one second to a few minutes).
- The *Chlorella* was killed with boiling ethanol.
- The labelled compounds were separated by chromatography.

As a result, Calvin and his team were able to identify which compounds contained different amounts of radioactivity.

a Suggest why the rate of photosynthesis was stabilised.

b Identify the independent variable in Calvin's experiment.

c Explain why the *Chlorella* was killed with boiling ethanol.

d Predict the name of one of the sugar phosphates that Calvin would expect to see forming at the beginning of the cycle.

e Calvin's work was possible due to improvements in apparatus. *The availability of $^{14}CO_2$, and autoradiography were essential to Calvin winning the 1961 Nobel Prize.* Discuss this statement.

6 Copy and complete Table 8.3 below to identify the structures of chloroplasts and how they are adapted to their function.

Function	Structure
Provide large surface area for light dependent reactions to take place	
Provides a rapid proton gradient/pump for chemiosmosis.	
Location of the Rubisco, enzymes, NADPH and ATP molecules for the Calvin cycle	
Synthesises proteins required within the chloroplast	

Table 8.3

7 Chemiosmosis is the movement of ions across a semipermeable membrane to generate ATP. Andre Jagendorf was one of the first scientists to support the earlier theories of Mitchell.

a Identify the ions that typically move across the membrane in photosynthesis.

b State the name of the structure where ATP is produced by chemiosmosis.

c The pH of the ADP solution used in Jagendorf's experiments affected the ATP yield. Suggest a possible reason for this.

d The pH of the acid in the experiments is changed from pH3.9 to pH4.9.

   i Predict what will happen to the rate of chemiosmosis as a result of this.

   ii Explain why the ATP yield is affected by changing the pH.

e This experiment is typically performed in darkness. Suggest a reason for carrying out the investigation in darkness.

? Exam-style questions

1   Which of the statements below, A–D, describes the minimum energy required for a reaction to occur? [1]
    I   Activation energy
    II   Coenzyme A
    III Prokaryotic DNA
    IV   Reactants and products
    A   I only
    B   I and II
    C   I and III
    D   I, II and II

2   What usually remains the same during competitive inhibition of an enzyme? [1]
    A V_{max}
    B V_{min}
    C $V_{max} - V_{min}$
    D   Substrate production

3   Which of the following is not true of a non-competitive inhibitor? [1]
    A   Bears little/no similarity to the substrate
    B   Substrate concentration does not decrease the impact of the inhibitor
    C   Substrate concentration does decrease the impact of the inhibitor
    D   Binds to the enzyme at a different location than the active site

4   Identify the correct loss/gain of the different components for an oxidation reaction. [1]

	Oxygen	Hydrogen	Electrons
A	Gained	Lost	Lost
B	Gained	Gained	Gained
C	Lost	Lost	Gained
D	Gained	Gained	Lost

5   What is added during phosphorylation? [1]
    A   Phosphate ion
    B   Phosphorus
    C   Phosphate group
    D   Phosphorylate

6   Glycolysis is a metabolic pathway that yields ATP and reduced $NADH + H^+$. How many molecules of ATP and reduced $NADH + H^+$ are produced by glycolysis? [1]
    A   2 ATP and 4 reduced $NADH + H^+$
    B   2 ATP and 2 reduced $NADH + H^+$
    C   4 ATP and 2 reduced $NADH + H^+$
    D   4 ATP and 4 reduced $NADH + H^+$

7 The conversion of pyruvate to Acetyl CoA involves which reactions? [1]
   A Decarboxylation and oxidation
   B Reduction and oxidation
   C Decarboxylation and reduction
   D Redox

8 One molecule of glucose yields two molecules of pyruvate. Deduce how many turns of the Krebs cycle are required. [1]
   A One
   B Two
   C Three
   D Six

9 State the number of carbon atoms that are fed into the Krebs cycle as the result of the oxidation of one molecule of pyruvate. [1]
   A 1
   B 2
   C 3
   D 4

10 Which of the following parts of the mitochondrion are folded to form cristae? [1]
   A Inner membrane
   B Outer membrane
   C Intermembrane
   D Cytoplasm

11 Which of the following is the best definition of chemiosmosis? [1]
   A The production of ATP as protons move down the concentration gradient
   B The production of ATP as protons move up the concentration gradient
   C The production of ADP as protons move down the concentration gradient
   D The production of ATP as protons move across the concentration gradient

12 Identify the sentence that describes what happens in Photosystem II of photosynthesis. [1]
   A Light energy excites electrons in the mitochondrial membrane
   B Protons are passed along the membrane to generate energy
   C Electrons lost are replaced by electrons derived from water
   D Electrons are gained by the splitting of carbon dioxide

13 Chemiosmosis was first outlined by Peter Mitchell in 1961.
   a Distinguish between chemiosmosis in mitochondria and in chloroplasts. [4]
   b Distinguish between the light-dependent reactions and the light-independent reactions of photosynthesis. [2]
   c Outline the process of photoactivation. [3]
   d **i** Sketch a diagram of a chloroplast that shows its basic structure. [4]
       ii Annotate your sketch to show how a chloroplast is adapted to its function. [3]

14 **Figure 8.11 shows the effect on the rate of reaction of an enzyme in the presence of two inhibitors.**

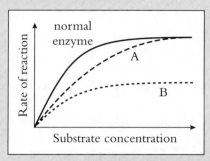

Figure 8.11 The effect of inhibitors on the rate of reaction of an enzyme.

a   Compare and contrast the effect of the two types of inhibitor shown in Figure 8.11. [3]
b   Distinguish between the method of each of the inhibitors when binding to the enzyme. [1]
c   Define *allosteric site*. [2]

9 [HL] Plant biology

KEY TERMS AND DEFINITIONS

Auxins – hormone responsible for the regulation of plant growth.

Fertilisation – the fusion of male and female gametes to produce a zygote.

Phloem – tube that conducts food and other substances throughout the plant from source to sink.

Xylem – hollow tube that allows the conduction of water through it from roots to leaves.

Exercise 9.1 – Transport in the xylem of plants

1 Read the article below and answer the questions that follow.

The desert, with its arid conditions, is an extremely hostile habitat for plants. Many desert plants are xerophytes and display adaptations such as extensive root systems to get as much water as possible from the scarce amounts available in such conditions. Water loss by transpiration is a factor that plants must battle every day, usually by adapting their leaves to minimise the rate of transpiration. Recently, studies of a species of desert moss have shown it to survive in even the hottest, driest surroundings; such as the Gurbantünggüt Desert in China. *Syntrichia caninervis* uses its leaves to collect water from the surrounding raindrops, fog, dew and mist. Each leaf has tiny hairs that extend from the leaf (much like the root hair in root hair cells). The hairs contain tiny micro-grooves and folds that allow water molecules to condense. This allows the plant to get that little bit of extra water compared to other plants in the same area. Scientists plan to use the natural structure of the leaf as a template for possible man-made versions that could be used to extract maximum moisture from a humid environment. Remarkably, the technology could be used to reduce splashing in public urinals; an expensive and unhygienic problem that could be solved by studying the leaves of moss in the desert. What an amazing subject biology is!

a Define *transpiration*.

b Outline why transpiration is inevitable as a consequence of gas exchange in the leaf.

c Define *xerophyte*.

d Outline how *Syntrichia caninervis* is able to adapt to its surroundings in the desert for water conservation.

e Compare how *Syntrichia caninervis* is able to adapt to its surroundings in the desert in terms of conserving water with other plants.

f Design an investigation to measure the rate of transpiration in a typical plant when placed in different temperatures. You should consider the following in your plan.
- The independent variable.
- The dependent variable.
- Control variables.
- How a potometer can be used to measure the rate of transpiration.

g Imogen carries out a similar investigation to measure the effect of humidity on the rate of transpiration. She transfers her results and plots the graph shown in Figure 9.1.

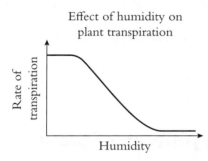

Figure 9.1 The effect of humidity on plant transpiration.

   i Describe the effect of humidity on the rate of transpiration of this plant.

   ii Explain why humidity has this effect on the rate of transpiration for the plant.

h Suggest other environmental factors that can have an effect on the rate of transpiration in plants.

i Halophytes are generally found on salt marshes and mud flats.

   i Define *halophyte*.

   ii Describe how halophytes are adapted to their surroundings.

   iii Predict what might happen to a plant if excess salt was **not** removed.

2 Plants transport water from the roots to the leaves to replace losses from transpiration. The cohesive and adhesive properties of water encourage upwards movement of the water through the xylem.

a State the type of pressure that results because of the loss of water vapour from the stomata.

b The walls of the xylem contain a substance that gives the xylem strength and prevents the collapse of the stem. State the name of this substance.

c Explain how cohesion and adhesion allow water to be drawn up through the xylem.

d Outline what happens in the roots as a result of transpiration.

e Construct a flow chart to show the movement of water from the soil to the leaves.

f Water moves into the roots by osmosis. Define *osmosis*.

g Identify the minerals required by plants that are described in the table.

Mineral ion	Usefulness to plant
	Part of cell walls
	Used to make chlorophyll
	Important co-factor for many enzymes

Table 9.1

h For each of the following methods, explain how it helps mineral ions move into plants.
  i Mass flow of water.
  ii Facilitated diffusion.
  iii Active transport.

3 Models of water transport in xylem can be created using simple apparatus including blotting paper, porous pots and capillary tubing.
  a Sketch a diagram of how you might use blotting or filter paper to model water transport in the xylem.
  b Predict what would happen to your model if left for a few hours.
  c Explain how the model demonstrates the passive nature of transpiration.

Exercise 9.2 – Transport in the phloem of plants

1 Read the article below about the use of radioactively-labelled carbon dioxide. This sort of investigation only became possible when radioisotopes became available.

How Science Can Track Plant Responses

Scientists might have discovered another use of radioactive carbon dioxide that could be used to make our lives better. Since the discovery of isotopes in 1921 (by Frederick Soddy) and the more regular use of them in the 1950s, scientists have been able to look closely at how certain reactions in organisms occur. A common example of this is the quantification of proteins.

Scientists tagged a particular plant hormone to show how quickly it moves throughout the plant transport system. The hormone is produced during times of stress and leads to the plant taking action to combat stress, or prepare for the consequences of the stress. The hormone has also been shown to move more sugar throughout the plant, creating a 'sugar rush' that is arguably the energy behind the defensive response of the plant.

The research team used radioactive carbon-11-labelled carbon dioxide and allowed maximum photosynthesis to happen. The team then tracked the movement of carbon-11 sucrose as it moved through the plant. It was possible to watch the sugars move through the phloem to the various sinks of the plant. There was also some observation of the movement of the hormone in water and dissolved minerals through the xylem from source to sink. Positron autoradiography was used to create imaging of the movement and produce a visualisation of what was happening.

The advantages of using carbon-11 are that it is non-invasive to the plant and the half-life is so short that the plant becomes radioactivity-free very quickly. Prior to this technique, the plant had to be cut into small pieces and dried out.

The scientists hope that their new understanding will lead to developments such as cleaning up pollutants and enhancing biofuel yields from crops.

a Define *translocation*.
b Outline the role of the following in translocation.
   i Source.
   ii Sink.
c Outline how hormones, such as the one mentioned in the article, are moved throughout the plant.
d Describe the role of active transport in the loading of organic compounds into phloem sieve tubes at the source.
e Once the materials enter the phloem, explain how the hydrostatic pressure of water allows transport by mass flow.
f The hormone in the article is able to move sugars around the plant.
   i State the name of the sugar that is moved throughout the plant.
   ii Suggest why the product of photosynthesis is **not** moved throughout the plant instead.
   iii It is suggested that the 'sugar rush' helps to provide energy for the plant's defensive response. Deduce why the movement of sugar helps to provide energy for the plant.
g Suggest the names of the sinks that the sugars were moved to after photosynthesis.
h State the name of the new technology/development that is named in the article for observing the movement of the hormones and the radioactive sugars.
i Previous techniques involved cutting up plants to observe the radioactive movements. Discuss why the new techniques and developments are more beneficial to the scientists carrying out the investigations.
j *This research sounds lovely and fun but will serve no real purpose in real life.* Evaluate this statement.

2 Copy and complete the table to distinguish between the xylem and the phloem.

	Xylem	Phloem
Materials moved	Water and	
Cause of movement	Transpiration	
Structure		
Source to sink example	Water from roots to leaves	
Direction of flow	Typically, one way	

Table 9.2

a Figure 9.2 shows a microscope image of a plant transport vessel.

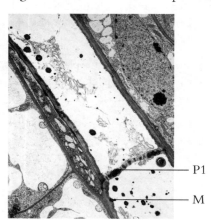

Figure 9.2 A plant transport vessel.

    i Identify the vessel shown in Figure 9.2.
    ii Outline the reasons for your answer to part i.

b Figure 9.2 is annotated with initials for the different parts shown.
    i Identify the name of the structure labelled as P1.
    ii Describe the structure of P1.

c **i** Suggest the identity of the structure labelled as M.
    ii Describe the role of M in plant transport.
    iii Explain why the role of M is important in plant transport.

3 The rate of movement through the phloem can be measured using radioactive sucrose and aphid stylets. In a simple investigation, the time taken for the radioactive sucrose to move between two points is observed and recorded in the table below. Answer the questions below. You need to copy and complete the table for part c.

Plant	Distance travelled by sucrose (mm)	Time taken for sucrose to travel (minutes)	Rate of transport (mm/min)
1	410	90	
2	430	98	
3	441	103	

Table 9.3

a Suggest how the radioactive sucrose was made for use by the plants.
b Outline how aphid stylets are used to help measure the rate of phloem transport.
c Calculate the rate of transport for each of the plants. Write your answer in your table.
d Calculate the mean rate of transport for the plants.
e Suggest a possible sink for the sucrose in this investigation.
f The mean rate of transport was different for each of the plants.
    i Evaluate the investigation to suggest reasons why this happened.
    ii Design an investigation that will minimise these errors.

Exercise 9.3 – Growth in plants

1 The need for food has motivated developments in plant growth since the beginning of humankind. Developments in scientific research have followed on from improvements in analysis and deduction as analytical techniques enable scientists to detect even the smallest of substances. This has had a major impact on our understanding of plant hormones and how they affect gene expression. Read through the text in the boxes below about hormones and gene expression in plants, and then answer the questions that follow.

Whoever thought of mapping the genome of a Christmas tree? Well, given that trees are shipped to many different cultures and countries, including Bangkok and Dubai, it is no surprise that there is big business to be uncovered if you can create the perfect tree. That is what one research group have done by creating a 'smart' tree that is real but has features that everyone wants (such as fragrance, needle retention, needle size, etc.). The genetic markers were identified through a transcriptomics analysis, a technique that allowed the team to compare the many different genes responsible for these traits under the many different environmental conditions that the trees experience. Once the most desirable traits are identified, the trees are then cloned so that thousands of 'perfect' trees are created and sold for maximum profit (or will be once the trees have actually grown in a few years!). The analysis even accounted for the way that photosynthesis and hormones affected growth to make sure that the biggest and best trees are produced.

Tomatoes are a wonderful food. Eaten in so many forms and in almost every type of culinary culture of the world, there is also considerable money to be made if you can produce outstanding tomatoes. However, the increasing temperatures of our planet are making this more difficult in some cases so an American laboratory has used genetic methods to improve current yields. The team have made changes to the genes of a popular tomato so that they flower faster and produce ripe fruit more quickly than any other commercial tomato. The consequences are that these tomato growers can plant more tomato plants in one season and produce a far greater yield than previously possible. The development of fruit from a tomato plant varies very little as this is tightly regulated by the plant's own hormone system. However, the laboratory has been able to identify a gene that might induce early flowering by using plants that grow in areas of the world with less sunlight. This gene was then introduced into varieties of cherry and Roma tomatoes, causing them to flower and ripen much earlier than they had ever done before. The team hope to develop the gene analysis and expression in other crops, such as maize and soybean.

Auxins are also big business if you can make them work for you!
Auxins have a major role to play in the growth of flowers, fruits, roots and stems. Some plants are more in demand than others, such as medicinal plants which are undergoing a resurgence in demand and usage. There are many companies now producing auxins in high quantities to promote plant growth. Auxins are cultivated within plants themselves but then distributed to various wholesalers and pharmaceutical companies. By introducing auxins to the plants that these companies need, they can produce a greater yield of bigger, better, useful plants for them to cultivate and use/sell.

a Describe the role of auxins in plant growth.

b List the parts of the plant where you would expect to find auxins controlling this growth.

c Suggest why mitosis and cell division in the shoot apex is important.

d Explain how auxins are able to influence cell growth rates by changing the pattern of gene expression.

e Suggest why the development of tomato-growing techniques will help to combat the increasing temperatures of some parts of the world.

f The tomato laboratory hope to develop their gene technology for use in crops such as maize and soybean. Comment on the usefulness of this idea in meeting the food demands of the world population.

g Meristems are the growing parts of flowering plants where cells divide by mitosis.

   i Distinguish between the apical meristem and lateral meristem in dicotyledonous plants.

   ii Outline how plant stems and roots are able to grow thicker.

h Discuss why the scientists working on the 'smart' Christmas trees are keen to develop their new 'breed' of trees.

i Evaluate the cultivation, and sale, of auxins to large pharmaceutical companies.

j Outline how hormones, such as auxins, are able to move around a plant.

k Hormones, such as auxins, have been difficult to identify and locate for scientists. Suggest **one** reason why this has been so difficult until recent developments in research and analysis.

l Design a method to show how the research teams could use micropropagation techniques to grow the new versions of the tomatoes and the Christmas trees described in the text.

m Comment on the advantages of using micropropagation techniques.

2 Plants are responsive to hormones, light, water and gravity. The movement towards, or away from, these stimuli is called tropism.

a Define *positive phototropism*.

b Outline what you would expect in the case of negative phototropism.

c Deduce the type of tropism shown by plant shoots towards light and gravity.

d Sketch a diagram to show the effect of positive phototropism on a plant shoot.

e Explain how unilateral light causes a plant to bend towards the light source.

f Roots grow differently to plant shoots.

   i Describe the type of tropism that plant roots will show.

   ii Explain why these types of tropism are important for plant growth.

Exercise 9.4 – Reproduction in plants

1 More than 85% of the world's 250 000 species of flowering plants depend on pollinators for reproduction. The honey bee is able to produce and store honey. In doing so, it is one of the most important pollinators, capable of pollinating plants such as okra, kiwifruit, celery, beet, mustard, broccoli and cauliflower. Plant reproduction depends on successful pollination – for the Brazil nut, it is essential – and fertilisation.

a 85% of the world's 250 000 species are pollinated by pollinators such as the honey bee. Suggest how the other 15% might be pollinated.

b There has been a paradigm shift as entire ecosystems are now protected, rather than individual species.

   i Outline what is meant by *paradigm shift* in this example.

   ii Explain why this *paradigm shift* is important for plant survival.

c Construct a table to show the characteristics that plants use to attract pollinators and an explanation of how each characteristic is able to do this.

d Outline the process of fertilisation in plants.

2 It is not just land animals that can help with pollination. Recent studies have shown that some underwater crustaceans are also capable of pollination. It is common for the pollen of seagrass to move around in the various currents and tides beneath the water. However, some of the pollen grains attach themselves to tiny underwater invertebrates that can then be transferred to other plants for fertilisation.

Seagrasses are an important part of the underwater ecosystem as they are food for some organisms, and they are also the habitat for many other organisms – such as the longhorn cowfish, the emerald leatherjacket and horned sea stars. Amazingly, seagrass is able to stabilise coastlines by anchoring sediment with their roots. Scientists have shown that pollinators can help seagrass by carrying out investigations to compare water tanks with and without these pollinators.

a State the names of the **three** organisms that rely on seagrass for their habitat.

b Describe the mutualistic relationships that the seagrass plant is involved in.

c The investigation to show the importance of the pollinators used two separate water tanks, with and without the pollinators. Deduce the important variable that had to be controlled to show that the pollinators were indeed the cause of pollination in the seagrass.

d There is currently a world decline in seagrass due to coastal development projects, runoff from agriculture, and other types of pollution.

   i Discuss the impact that this will have on the underwater ecosystems.

   ii Construct a plan to protect an area that relies on seagrass, such as the mangroves of the UAE.

3 Plants undergo a change in gene expression in the shoot apex in order to begin flowering.

a The apical meristem must be converted into a floral meristem for the parts of the flower to begin to grow.

   i Distinguish between the apical meristem and the floral meristem.

   ii State the different internal and external factors that affect the change of the apical meristem.

b Define *photoperiodism*.

c Distinguish between long-day plants and short-day plants.

d Describe how plants use photoreceptors to determine the relative length of day and night.

e The tomato farms mentioned in Exercise 9.3 use genes from short-day plants to induce flowering in typically long-day plants, especially during out-of-season times. Determine the benefits of encouraging tomato plants to flower in fewer sunlight hours than usual.

4 This section requires that you apply your biological understanding to certain required skills.

    a Figure 9.3 shows the half-view of an animal–pollinated flower.

        i Copy Figure 9.3 and label it to show the different structures.

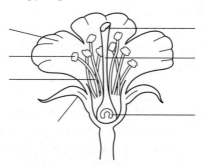

Figure 9.3 A half-view of a flower.

        ii Construct a table to briefly outline the function of each part of the flower that you have labelled.

    b i Draw and label the internal structure of a dicotyledonous seed.

      ii Outline the role of the cotyledons.

     iii Explain why the testa is important to the survival of the seed.

      iv State the role of the micropyle.

      v Define *germination*.

    c Design an experiment to test hypotheses about the following factors of germination.

        i Temperature.

      ii Water.

     iii Oxygen.

    d Explain why each of the following is important for germination to take place in seeds.

        i Temperature.

      ii Water.

     iii Oxygen.

? Exam-style questions

1 **Which of the statements below, A–D, correctly describes what variables must be at the optimum level for successful germination to take place? [1]**

    I Temperature

    II Oxygen

    III Carbon dioxide

    IV Water pressure

    A I only

    B I and II

    C I and III

    D I, II and II

2 Identify the bonding that is responsible for cohesion among water molecules. [1]

 A Ionic

 B Hydrogen

 C Disulfide

 D Covalent

3 Identify the part of a plant that most water is lost from during transpiration. [1]

 A The roots

 B The leaves

 C The fruits

 D The flowers

4 Identify the abiotic conditions that will result in the maximum rate of transpiration. [1]

	Light intensity	Temperature	Humidity	Wind speed
A	High	Low	Low	Low
B	High	High	High	Low
C	High	High	Low	High
D	Low	High	Low	High

5 Which of the following are plants that thrive in areas of high salt concentration? [1]

 A Halophytes

 B Xerophytes

 C Angiosperms

 D Cotyledons

6 Identify the mineral ion that has the correct function written next to it. [1]

 A Calcium – needed to make cell walls

 B Magnesium – needed to make cell membranes

 C Iron – stops enzymes from working

 D Potassium – provides a nice colour for the leaves

7 A plant has been placed in soil that has a very low concentration of potassium ions. Identify the mode of transport that uses ATP to help move ions such as potassium against the concentration gradient. [1]

 A Active transport

 B Passive transport

 C Osmosis

 D Facilitated diffusion

8 Which of the following is the movement of organic molecules through the phloem tissue? [1]

 A Transcription

 B Transpiration

 C Translation

 D Translocation

9 **Identify the type of vessel being described in the following sentences.** *The vessel is made up of dead cells and its continuous nature allows water to move through it. The vessel is made of lignin to help support it against negative pressure.* [1]

   A Phloem

   B Vascular bundle

   C Vascular cambium

   D Xylem

10 **Which of the following is commonly used to radioactively label substances in a plant?** [1]

   A ^{14}C

   B ^{14}P

   C ^{24}C

   D ^{12}C

11 **Which of the following best describes the growth of a plant shoot?** [1]

   A Positive phototropism and negative geotropism

   B Negative phototropism and negative geotropism

   C Positive phototropism and positive geotropism

   D Neutral phototropism and negative geotropism

12 **Identify the mechanism that controls the direction of movement of plant growth.** [1]

   A Auxins

   B Auxin efflux pumps

   C Auxin proteins

   D Auxin growth regulators

13 **Which of the following is not a common method of pollination in flowering plants?** [1]

   A Wind pollination

   B Insect pollination

   C Self-pollination

   D Temperature pollination

14 **Which of the following best describes the process of pollination?** [1]

   A Transfer of pollen from anther to the stigma

   B Transfer of female gametes from anther to the stigma

   C Transfer of pollen from stigma to the anther

   D Transfer of gametes from anther to the style

15 **Which of the following is the term used to describe how a plant responds to the relative periods of darkness and light?** [1]

   A Phototropism

   B Photoperiodism

   C Photosynthesis

   D Photo time period

16 **Xerophytes are plants that are able to live in arid conditions.**

  a List **three** ways in which xerophytes are adapted to survive in these conditions. [3]

  b Figure 9.4 shows a potometer set up to estimate the rate of transpiration.

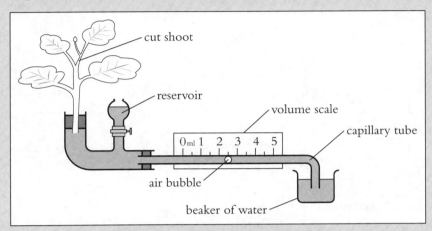

Figure 9.4 Measuring the rate of transpiration using a potometer.

    i Estimate the amount of water taken into the plant as shown in Figure 9.4. [1]

    ii Anna observes the movement of the air bubble every two minutes and records her results as shown.

Time (mins)	0	2	4	6	8	10
Volume of water (ml)	0.0	0.3	0.6	0.9	1.2	1.5

Calculate the transpiration rate for Anna's experiment. [2]

    iii Anna performs the same experiment but this time she does so under conditions of less light intensity than the first experiment. Estimate the results that you might expect Anna to get in the table below. [2]

Time (mins)	0	2	4	6	8	10
Volume of water (ml)	0.0					

    iv Analyse the effect of decreasing light intensity on the rate of transpiration. [4]

    v List other factors that affect the rate of transpiration in plants. [4]

    vi Design an investigation to estimate the rate of transpiration when changing **one** of the factors in your answer to part v. [5]

17 **Figure 9.5 shows two halves of a bean seed.**

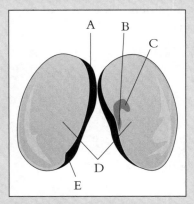

Figure 9.5 Two halves of a bean seed.

  a Identify the parts of the bean labelled A to E. [5]
  b Describe each part you have identified to outline their role in germination. [5]
  c Outline how the absorption of water through the micropyle leads to germination and growth. [3]
  d Figure 9.5 is a large diagram of a real seed that has been observed.
    i Measure the length of the bean seed in Figure 9.5. [1]
    ii The magnification of the bean seed in Figure 9.5 is ×1.8. The bean has been magnified to a size of 31 mm tall and 17 mm wide.. Calculate the size of the real bean seed that was drawn in Figure 9.5. [2]

18 **Explain how flowering is controlled in long-day plants and short-day plants. [6]**

19 **Compare and contrast the roles of auxin in geotropic and phototropic responses in plants. [3]**

HL Genetics and evolution 10

Chapter outline

In this chapter you will:
- explain how meiosis leads to independent assortment of chromosomes and unique composition of alleles in daughter cells
- explain how genes may be linked or unlinked and are inherited accordingly
- describe how gene pools change over time.

KEY TERMS AND DEFINITIONS

Evolution – the cumulative change in the heritable characteristics of a population.

Gene pool – all of the different genes in an interbreeding population at a given time.

Inheritance – the passing of heritable characteristics from parents to offspring.

Meiosis – cell division that results in each daughter cell receiving half of the number of chromosomes.

Speciation – the formation of new species from an existing population.

Exercise 10.1 – Meiosis

1 Meiosis is essential after fertilisation.
   a Define the following terms.
      i Fertilisation.
      ii Mitosis.
      iii Diploid.
      iv Haploid.
      v Chromosome.
      vi Allele.
   b State when chromosomes replicate before meiosis can begin.
   c Outline the two main functions of meiosis.
   d The word *chiasma* is derived from an Ancient Greek and modern Latin word that means 'cross-shaped mark'.
      i Sketch and label a diagram to show the location of a chiasma on a pair of homologous chromosomes.
      ii Describe how crossing over occurs between non-sister homologous chromatids.
      iii Explain how this crossing over results in new combinations of alleles on the chromosomes of haploid cells.
      iv State the plural term for chiasma.

e Random orientation of chromosomes produces a massive number of possible genetic combinations.

    i In humans, if the number of combinations is 2^n, where n is the haploid number, calculate the approximate number of possible combinations for just one gamete.

    ii *Giraffa camelopardalis* has a diploid number of 62. Calculate the approximate number of possible genetic combinations for one gamete of the giraffe.

f *When gametes are formed, the separation of one pair of alleles into the new cells is independent of the separation of any other pair of alleles.*

    i Identify the law that has been stated above.

    ii Construct a sentence that outlines this law in simpler terms.

g Outline the main reasons for the independent assortment of genes.

2 Figure 10.1 shows a microscopic image of the lily anther that has been stained. The lily anther is the male reproductive organ that contains four pollen sacs where haploid pollen grains are produced by meiosis. A thin cross-section of the lily anther was taken and stained, before being examined with a light microscope. Figure 10.1 shows a close-up image of the inside of one pollen sac. The different phases of meiosis are clearly visible.

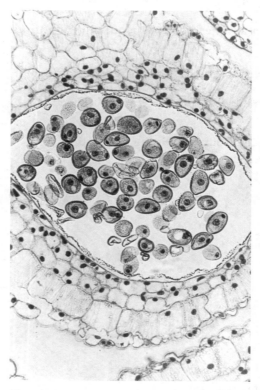

Figure 10.1 Microscopic image of the pollen sacs of a lily anther (magnification × 130).

a Draw and label a large diagram of any of the cells from Figure 10.1.

b Calculate the magnification of your drawing compared to the cell in the picture.

c Determine the phase that most of these cells are undergoing at the moment the image was captured.

3 It is important you are able to compare and contrast the processes of mitosis and meiosis. An excellent method of answering a 'compare and contrast' question is to construct a table. This ensures that you refer to both of the processes in your answer and avoids the loss of 'easy' marks.

  a Copy and complete Table 10.1 below to compare and contrast the processes of mitosis and meiosis.

Feature		Meiosis
Interphase	Occurs	Occurs
Order of division	Prophase, metaphase, anaphase, telophase	
Cell splits by		Cytokinesis
Number of divisions		Two
Independent assortment	Does not occur	
Crossing over		Occurs
Ploidy	Daughter cells are diploid	
Daughter cells	Identical	

Table 10.1

  b The formation of chiasmata during crossing over is outlined below. Copy and complete the information by inserting the correct terms into the spaces provided.

The chiasmata are formed during _____ I of meiosis. _____ chromosomes are paired and the chromatids break at the same location. Non-sister chromatids exchange _____. The chiasma is formed at the point where the over takes place and becomes visible when _____ separate.

  c Crossing over results in many new combinations of alleles being produced in haploid cells. Suggest why this is a potential advantage for a population.

  d As you know, the forefather of genetics is often known as Gregor Mendel.

    i State the three laws that were demonstrated by the work of Mendel in the 19th century.

    ii Identify the process that separates homologous chromosomes for the law of segregation.

    iii State the phase where the independent assortment aligns homologous pairs randomly.

  e Mendel used the garden pea to study the patterns of inheritance.

    i A pea plant with green peas and yellow flowers is crossed with a plant that has yellow peas and white flowers. All of the offspring from the first filial generation produced yellow peas and white flowers. Determine the genotype of the pea plant with green peas and yellow flowers.

    ii Pea plants with green peas and yellow flowers are crossed with pea plants that have yellow peas and white flowers. 264 peas in this cross produce the following offspring: 130 plants with yellow flowers and 134 plants with white flowers. From these flowers, 443 green peas were produced, and 448 yellow peas. Determine the genotype of the parent plant that had yellow peas and white flowers.

    iii Polygenic traits control more than one type of phenotype, such as hair colour, eye colour and skin colour. Identify the type of variation that is usually controlled by polygenic traits.

Exercise 10.2 – Inheritance

1 Read the article below and answer the questions that follow.

> ## Thomas Hunt Morgan links linked genes
>
> Thomas Hunt Morgan (1866–1945) is one of the most important geneticists and his legacy has spawned multiple Nobel Prize winners. Following the acceptance of Mendel's work on inheritance, Morgan became interested in the genetics of the fruit fly (*Drosophilia melanogaster*) and studied millions of fruit flies in his now-famous Fly Room at Columbia University.
>
> Morgan mated a white-eyed fly with the more common red-eyed fly. Only three of the first 1237 offspring had white eyes but this soon changed in the second generation. A large number of flies had white eyes and, quite remarkably, all of the white-eyed flies were male.
>
> This led Morgan to change the way he was thinking about inheritance and he began to accept parts of Mendel's work that he had previously distrusted. Morgan continued to investigate these traits and he eventually confirmed that it was the chromosomes that carry genetic information. Morgan developed the notion of linked genes to account for the previous anomalies of Mendel's work for the law of independent assortment. It was Morgan's careful observation and record-keeping that turned up anomalous data that could not be accounted for by Mendel's law of independent assortment.

a Outline why linked genes are often inherited together.

b Determine the linked genes that are described in the article.

c Deduce the sex chromosomes that you would expect a white-eyed fly to have.

d Some critics of Mendel's work have suggested that his data was too close to the expected 3:1 ratio and therefore was too good to be true. Some have suggested that he selected the data that best fitted his hypothesis. Comment on how the careful observation and record keeping of Morgan allowed him to develop the theories and ideas of gene linkage.

e State the number of chromosomes that a human has in each cell.

f Suggest why Morgan chose to work with the fruit fly for his experiments.

2 **a** Copy Table 10.2 below. Determine the possible gametes for the genotypes in the table.

Genotype	Gametes
BBRR	
bbRR	
BbRR	
Bbrr	

Table 10.2

b Remind yourself of how to construct a genetic diagram in the following examples and questions.

  i Purple flowers are dominant to pink flowers. State the phenotype if the genotype was Pp.

  ii Round seeds are dominant to wrinkled seeds in pea plants. Determine the phenotype if the genotype is rr.

   iii The dominant allele for grey fur is F and the recessive allele for black fur is f. Construct a Punnett Square to show the different genotypes of the offspring if a heterozygous dog and a homozygous recessive dog mate.

   iv Fruit flies can either have white eyes (e) or red eyes (E). A male fly has white eyes and is mated with a female fly that has homozygous dominant alleles for eye colour. Construct a Punnett Square and state the expected ratio of white eyes to red eyes that the F1 generation offspring will have.

   v Two fruit flies of the F1 generation in part iv are mated. Determine the likelihood of the F2 generation offspring having white eyes.

3 Mendel's famous pea plant experiment crossed plants that had unlinked genes on different chromosomes. A homozygous tall (T) plant with yellow seeds (g) was crossed with a short plant (t) that was homozygous for green seeds (G).

  a Identify the genotype that would be required for offspring to be tall plants.

  b Identify the genotype that would be required for offspring to have yellow seeds.

  c Determine the genotype of the tall plant with yellow seeds.

  d Determine the genotype of the short plant with green seeds.

  e Two plants with the same genotype (TtGg) are crossed.

   i Construct a genetic diagram that includes parental phenotypes, parental genotypes, possible gametes and a Punnett square for the F1 generation.

   ii Determine the ratio of the phenotypes shown in the F1 generation offspring.

  f A heterozygous plant is crossed with a short plant that is heterozygous for green seeds.

   i Construct a genetic diagram that includes parental phenotypes, parental genotypes, possible gametes and a Punnett square for the F1 generation.

   ii Determine the ratio of the phenotypes shown in the F1 generation offspring.

  g *Linked genes produce Mendelian ratios.* Analyse this statement.

  h Define the term *linkage group*.

4 In chilli plants, the gene for tall plants (T) is dominant to the gene for short plants (t). The gene for red chillies (R) is dominant to the gene for yellow chillies (y). A tall plant with yellow chillies (Ttrr) is crossed with a short plant with red peppers (ttRr).

  a Define the term *recombinant organism*.

  b Determine the genotypes of the offspring that will be recombinants.

5 Morgan's experiments on the fruit fly have already been discussed, but how did the obviously linked genes affect the ratios expressed in the offspring?

  a In a dihybrid cross, if **A** is linked to **B** and **a** is linked to **b**, show the notation that is used to signify that the two genes occur on the same chromosome.

  b A fruit fly that is homozygous for red eyes (R) and long wings (N) was crossed with a fruit fly that has the same genotype. The genes for these phenotypes are linked on the same chromosome.

   i Determine the parental genotypes of these fruit flies.

   ii State the possible gametes of the parents.

   iii Construct a Punnett square for the offspring of these two fruit flies.

   iv Determine the ratio of flies with red eyes and long wings to those with white eyes and short wings.

6 Variation is the differences that exist between individuals.
  a Identify the types of variation described below:
    i Has clear categories involving features that cannot be measured.
    ii Is not categorical and a range of measurements can be produced from one extreme to another.
  b Suggest examples of the two types of variation named in part a.
  c Compare and contrast between the causes of the two types of variation.
  d Meena measures and records the height of all her classmates. Sketch a graph to show the distribution of the variation that she would expect to see.
  e Meena then records the blood groups of her classmates as follows.

Blood groups	A+	A−	B+	B−	AB+	AB−	O+	O−
Frequency	16	3	5	1	2	1	13	3

Table 10.3

    i Determine the type of data that she has collected.
    ii Identify the type of graph that Meena should draw to show her results.
    iii Construct a graph to show her results.
    iv The expected ratios for blood type are shown below.

Blood groups	A+	A−	B+	B−	AB+	AB−	O+	O−
Frequency (%)	33	7	9	2	3	1	37	8

Table 10.4

       Analyse Meena's results in comparison to the expected ratios shown in the table.
    v Suggest how she might verify the significance of her own results.

7 Polygenic characteristics are controlled by many different genes at different loci on different chromosomes. It is more common for phenotypes to be controlled by polygenes as opposed to being controlled by just one gene.
  a Identify the type of variation that is usually exhibited by polygenes.
  b Suggest examples of phenotypes that are usually coded for by one gene.
  c Suggest examples of phenotypes that are polygenic and result in continuous variation.
  d Sadiki determines that three genes interact to control the colour of a particular seed. He crosses two plants with the following triploid heterozygous genes (AaBbCc).
    i Determine the possible gametes of the parent plants.
    ii Construct a Punnett square to show the range of colours of seed that will be present in the many offspring of the F1 generation.
    iii Circle all of the offspring that will have the dominant colour (ABC).
    iv Annotate the square to show which offspring will have the least dominant colour (abc).

8 The chi-squared test is a statistical test used in genetic investigations that compare the observed results with your expected results.
  a State the type of variation that chi-squared tests are used for.
  b State the formula for calculating the chi-squared value.
  c The null hypothesis states that there is no significant difference between the observed results and the expected results. Deduce what this would tell you about your results.
  d Mendel's famous experiments on pea plants produced the following results in the F2 generation: 5474 smooth seeds and 1850 wrinkled seeds.

   i Calculate the expected numbers that Mendel would have expected, assuming that this monohybrid cross was expected to produce a ratio of 3:1 of smooth seeds to wrinkled seeds.

   ii Calculate the chi-squared value for this investigation.

   iii Calculate the degrees of freedom for this investigation.

   iv The critical chi-squared value at the 5% significance level is 3.841. Comment on whether Mendel should accept or reject the null hypothesis that there is no expected difference between the observed and expected results.

e A geneticist was attempting to cross two different species. She predicted the following phenotypic results: 4:3:9 for the fur colours black, white, and grey, respectively. After performing the cross, the geneticist observed that 91 organisms had black fur, 40 had white fur, and 112 had grey fur. The critical values of chi-squared distribution are shown in Table 10.5. Use this to answer further questions.

Degrees of freedom	p-value at 0.05
1	3.841
2	5.991
3	7.815
4	9.488
5	11.070

Table 10.5

   i Calculate the chi-squared value for this cross.

   ii Calculate the degrees of freedom for this investigation.

   iii Comment on whether the geneticist should accept the null hypothesis or not. Give your reasons why.

f The results of the following investigation were due to independent assortment and were expected to follow the 9:3:3:1 rule on a 16-square Punnett square. In the tomato plant, tall plants are dominant to short plants and hairy plants are dominant to smooth plants. Crossing of two plants produce the following results:

  – Tall, hairy plants: 278

  – Short, smooth plants: 30

  – Short, hairy plants: 92

  – Tall, smooth plants: 97

   i Deduce what the independent assorting of the genes tells you about the linkage between the genes.

   ii Calculate the chi-squared value for this cross.

   iii Calculate the degrees of freedom for this investigation.

   iv Comment on whether the null hypothesis should be accepted or not. Give your reasons why.

9 Melissa and Rohan are cat breeders. They decide to breed two of their most prized cats to sell in the local area. Melissa wants to know what the expected phenotypes of the cats might be so that she can advertise the likely sales well in advance of the kittens being born. A cat with ginger fur is crossed with a cat that has grey fur. The allele for ginger fur (G) is dominant to that of grey fur (g).

a Identify the genotype that would be required for offspring to have ginger fur.

b Identify the genotype that would be required for offspring to have grey fur.

   c Determine the genotype of the cat with ginger fur.

   d Determine the genotype of the cat with grey fur.

   e It is determined that the offspring will be 50% likely to have ginger fur.

     i Determine the genotypes of the parents in this cross.

     ii Construct a genetic diagram that includes parental phenotypes, parental genotypes, possible gametes and a Punnett square for the F1 generation.

     iii Determine the ratio of the phenotypes shown in the F1 generation offspring.

10 Rudy is working on practice problems for his upcoming genetics test. He has to determine the likely offspring ratios for a SsYy x SsYy genetic cross.

   a Construct a genetic diagram that includes parental genotypes, possible gametes and a Punnett square for the F1 generation.

   b Determine the ratio of offspring that will be heterozygous for both traits.

   c Determine the ratio of offspring that will be homozygous recessive.

11 Smooth peas (S) are dominant to wrinkled peas (s) and yellow pea colour (Y) is dominant to green pea colour (y). A dihybrid cross is carried out between two heterozygous pea plants. The phenotypic frequencies are observed:

- Smooth, yellow peas: 561
- Smooth, green peas: 163
- Wrinkled, yellow peas: 194
- Wrinkled, green peas: 54

   a Determine the genotype of the two parent plants.

   b Construct a dihybrid cross to determine the expected frequencies of the offspring.

   c Calculate the chi-squared value for this cross.

   d Calculate the degrees of freedom for this investigation.

   e

Degrees of freedom	p-value at 0.05
1	3.841
2	5.991
3	7.815
4	9.488
5	11.070

Table 10.6

Comment on whether the null hypothesis should be accepted or not. Give your reasons why.

Exercise 10.3 – Gene pools and speciation

1 State the key term being described by the definitions below.

   a The cumulative change in the heritable characteristics of a population.

   b All of the different genes in an interbreeding population at a given time.

   c The frequency of a particular allele as a proportion of all of the alleles of that gene in a population.

   d When the same alleles are selected to maintain a stable population.

   e When environmental conditions change and organisms with favourable alleles survive and reproduce.

f Natural selection results in two new forms from a single existing population.

g A change in allele frequency in a gene pool due to chance events.

h The formation of new species from an existing population.

i Speciation that occurs in different geographical areas.

j Speciation that occurs in the same geographical area.

k The slow process of steady changes in an organism that accumulate over many generations and lead to speciation.

l Evolution that occurs in rapid bursts but interspersed with long periods of stability.

2 The evolution of the pepper moth in 19th century England showed that light-coloured moths allowed them to hide from predators by camouflaging themselves against light-coloured trees in their environment. The Industrial Revolution caused the light-coloured trees to darken, and suddenly the light-coloured peppered moths were easy targets for their predators. Over a period of time, the frequency of the dark peppered moth increased as they had a higher survival rate than the light peppered moth.

A population of insects in a woodland use the natural colours and environment to blend in and avoid being eaten by predators. The insects that have the closest colour to the general features of the wood are most likely to survive. Any insects that carry alleles making them darker or lighter will most likely be spotted and eaten. The variance within this population generally decreases.

Coho salmon are divided into two types of males – the hooknoses and the jacks. The hooknoses are large and will compete directly for the right to mate with the female salmon. The smaller jacks rely upon stealth to mate with the female without the larger hooknoses noticing. Salmon that are not big enough to compete, or small enough to be stealthy, have lower survival rates and reproduce less often.

a Determine which organism from the text above is an example of disruptive selection.

b Determine which organism is an example of stabilising selection.

c Determine which organism is an example of directional selection.

3 Around 5 to 6 million years ago, the Grand Canyon of Arizona was formed as the Colorado River carved through it. Many animals, including squirrels, found themselves divided from their original population by the canyon. The Grand Canyon proved to be a physical barrier and the squirrels were not able to communicate or reproduce with each other across this barrier. The original population of squirrels eventually evolved into two new species: the kaibab squirrel and the abert squirrel.

a Describe how geographical speciation led to the formation of two new squirrel populations.

b Outline how sympatric speciation can occur through temporal and behavioural isolation.

c Explain how temporal isolation is able to form new species.

d Distinguish between allopatric speciation and sympatric speciation.

e Polyploidy is one of the most common causes of sympatric speciation. Speciation in the genus *Allium* is caused by polyploidy. *Allium oleraceum* (field garlic) is commonly found in Europe.

   i Define *polyploidy*.

   ii If a cell has three sets of chromosomes, state the term used to describe this.

   iii If a cell has four sets of chromosomes, state the term used to describe this.

iv *Allium* often has four or five sets of chromosomes. Outline how this polyploidy leads to speciation in *Allium*.

v Suggest how polyploidy in *Allium* has allowed it cover a larger area of Europe than the original diploid versions.

f The gap in the fossil record that confused many scientists was explained by Gould and Eldredge. They supposed that punctuated equilibrium was behind the lack of fossil record for the intermediate stages between one species and another.

i Explain how punctuated equilibrium occurs.

ii *The evolution of the peppered moth in England in the 19th century is an example of punctuated equilibrium.* Discuss whether you think this statement is a good example of punctuated equilibrium or not.

4 As stated in the previous question, polyploidy is common in plants and can lead to speciation. The gilia plant in the Mojave Desert in California is an example of speciation by polyploidy. Artificial speciation is common in plants and species such as tulips and primroses have been created in this manner. Species of coffee plant with 22, 44, 66, and 88 chromosomes are known. Other common plants, such as the domestic oat, the peanut, tobacco and cotton are examples of polyploidy speciation. The Russian geneticist Karpechenko famously produced a new species after crossing a cabbage with a radish. The original hybrids were infertile but some fertile plants were formed by polyploidy gametes.

a List the organisms in the text above that are evidence of speciation by polyploidy.

b Predict the number of chromosomes in the original coffee plant.

c The plants produced by Karpechenko could breed with each other but not with the original cabbage or radish species. Explain how this shows evidence of speciation.

5 Population bottlenecks occur when an event causes a dramatic reduction in the size of a population. A classic example of a population bottleneck is the northern elephant seal. Human activity caused this bottleneck in the 1890s as the seals were hunted vigorously. The population of the seals fell to as low as 20 elephant seals but has since recovered to over 30 000. The southern elephant seal was not hunted as much and so has retained a relatively stable population.

a Suggest examples of an environmental event that may cause a population bottleneck.

b Suggest examples of a human-caused activity that may cause a population bottleneck.

c Suggest how the genetic diversity of the northern elephant seals compares to that of the southern elephant seal.

d Explain why the genetic diversity of the northern elephant seal will be affected in this way.

e Identify the key term that is described when a small group breaks away from a larger population to colonise a new area or territory.

f Distinguish between a population bottleneck and the founder effect.

g State the range by which allele frequencies will be expressed as a numerical value.

h The allele frequencies for wet or dry earwax is a much-researched area of population genetics (surprisingly!). Some Asian populations are amazed by the wet ear wax produced by some Western populations. There is also a link, perhaps even more incredibly, between the type of earwax and the emittance of body odour. There is a correlation between East Asian populations who sweat less and have dry earwax. There is a single mutation (guanine for adenine) that means people with aa genotype will have dry earwax, and those with aG or GG will have wet earwax.

i   Identify the dominant allele for type of ear wax.

ii Wet earwax is found in almost all populations, other than in northern Han Chinese and Koreans. Suggest how this dry form of earwax might have come about.

iii *Dry earwax offers an evolutionary advantage to those that produce it.* Comment on this statement.

? Exam-style questions

1   **Which of the statements below, A–D, correctly describes the functions of meiosis? [1]**

I   Halving the chromosome number

II   Doubling the chromosome number

III Producing genetic variety

IV   Stabilising the gene pool

A   I only

B   I and II

C   I and III

D   I, II and II

2   **Identify the phase of meiosis that you can see in Figure 10.2. [1]**

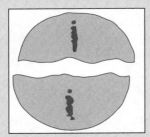

Figure 10.2 A cell undergoing meiosis.

A   Metaphase I

B   Metaphase II

C   Prophase I

D   Prophase II

3   **Identify the gametes that would be produced by the genotype AABB. [1]**

A   All AB

B   All aB

C   AB and ab

D   AB and aB

4   A female dog with black fur is crossed with a male dog with black fur. Predict the most likely phenotype ratio of the offspring. Grey fur is dominant to black fur. [1]
    A   100% black fur
    B   75% black fur
    C   50% black fur
    D   100% grey fur

5   A dog suffers from deafness caused by the recessive gene (d). Louis has a hearing dog and intends to breed it with the deaf dog. Identify the two possible genotypes of the hearing dog. [1]
    A   DD and dd
    B   DD and dD
    C   Dd and dd
    D   dd and dd

6   Identify the number of chromosomes in a human haploid cell. [1]
    A   23
    B   46
    C   23 pairs
    D   44

7   Which of the following do not follow Mendel's laws of independent assortment? [1]
    A   Linked genes
    B   Linked loci
    C   Matching alleles
    D   Homologous chromosomes

8   Identify the name of the organism that was famously used by Thomas Morgan to study linked genes. [1]
    A   *Simuliidae*
    B   *Glossina*
    C   *Drosophilia*
    D   *Tipulidae*

9   Which of the following is an example of discrete variation? [1]
    A   Blood group
    B   Height
    C   Mass
    D   Milk yield from cattle

10 Which of the following is an example of continuous variation? [1]
    A   Presence of freckles
    B   Eye colour
    C   Left and right handedness
    D   Hand span

11 There are three different genes involved in the colour of seeds in the wheat
    plant. Which of the following is the key term that describes this number of genes
    controlling a particular phenotype? [1]
    A Multiple gene inheritance
    B Monogenic inheritance
    C Polygenic inheritance
    D Polyploidy

12 Which of the following is the most suitable definition of a gene pool? [1]
    A The cumulative change in the heritable characteristics of a population
    B The frequency of a particular allele as a proportion of all of the alleles
    C All of the different genes in an interbreeding population at a given time
    D The selection of genes within a stable population

13 A new road is built that passes through a wooded area. A population of moths are
    split into two. Over time, one of the populations evolves to become darker and
    blends into the new environment. Eventually, the two populations are no longer
    able to interbreed and produce fertile offspring. Deduce the type of speciation that
    has taken place. [1]
    A Behavioural speciation
    B Temporal speciation
    C Sympatric speciation
    D Allopatric speciation

14 A homozygous brown cat with long fur is crossed with a homozygous black cat
    with short fur. The allele for black fur (B) is dominant to brown fur (b). The allele
    for short fur (s) is recessive to the allele for long fur (S).
    a State the possible genotypes of the parents. [1]
    b Determine the possible gametes of the parents. [2]
    c Determine the F1 genotype of the offspring. [1]
    d Two of the F1 offspring are mated. Construct a Punnett Square to show the potential
       genotypes of the offspring. [4]
    e Determine the phenotypic ratio of the F2 offspring. [4]

11 HL Animal physiology

Exercise 11.1 – Antibody production and vaccination

1 One of the most important developments in medical history took place in 1796. Read the following article which reports the events as if they happened in 2016 – with some creative licence to make the story more modern. Answer the questions that follow.

Outrage as Jenner tests cure for disease on small boy

The war on smallpox took a remarkable turn yesterday, as Edward Jenner successfully completed medical trials that will prevent the spread of smallpox. Smallpox is a contagious disease that has killed millions over the past few hundred years, devastating entire communities in some areas without sufficient medical care.

This sounds remarkable but ethics committees and science communities around the world are outraged. Reaction on social media has gathered pace and a video mocking Jenner has gone viral, with over 2 million views in less than 24 hours.

Jenner carried out his trials on James Phipps, an eight-year-old son of Jenner's gardener, from Jenner's hometown of Berkeley in Gloucestershire, UK. Jenner had noticed that milkmaids on a local farm, who had previously contracted cowpox, did not catch smallpox. Cowpox leads to fewer symptoms than the more virulent smallpox. On 14 May, Jenner took fluid from a cowpox blister and scraped it onto the skin of James Phipps. Over the next few days, the boy developed a small blister but recovered quickly.

What happened next might conceivably be one of the greatest discoveries of recent times in the long battle against smallpox, or it might be the most shocking outrage upon a young boy ever to be seen. On 1 July, Jenner introduced a sample of smallpox to young James. This would usually result in horrible symptoms, and like millions of others, lead to a fatal conclusion.

However, James did not develop smallpox, meaning that the presence of cowpox must have somehow protected him from developing smallpox. Doctors around the world are already vowing to use this innovative technique on their own communities, despite the public furore at testing on a child. It is hoped that this new technique might help to fight against other diseases, such as polio, measles, typhus and hepatitis B.

Jenner initially reported his findings in an article for the Royal Society, who refused to publish his work. Jenner remained resolute and, through his peers and social media, he was able to have his work recognised and accepted; but not without controversy regarding his ethics and working methodologies.

The World Health Organization is already setting up trials to find how out exactly how cowpox (a disease that really only affects cows) can prevent smallpox, one of the greatest killers of modern history. It has been reported that initial tests in the laboratory have shown the presence of white blood cells that are able to neutralise the disease. These white blood cells appear to present themselves around 10 days after the introduction of the cowpox virus.

It may be that Jenner has saved millions of lives and, already, people are suggesting that he is a hot favourite for a Nobel Prize, or possibly a knighthood. However, if Jenner had been wrong, he may have faced prison for the murder of an eight-year-old boy.

August 2nd, 2016

a Define *pathogen*.

b Resistance may be developed to an infection. State the key term that describes this resistance.

c State the name of the procedure that Jenner carried out on James Phipps.

d The article mentions that white blood cells appear after 10 days in laboratory tests.

   i Deduce the type of white blood cells that present themselves in order to fight disease.

   ii Identify the proteins that your answer to part i are able to recognise.

   iii Outline where you would expect to find the proteins that are your answer to part ii.

e The production of antibodies to fight disease involves B-cells and T-cells. List the following stages in order to explain how antibodies respond to pathogens.

   A B-cells divide into clones: plasma cells and memory cells.

   B Plasma cells secrete large numbers of antibodies into the bloodstream to destroy pathogens.

   C Memory cells remain to allow a large, rapid response to the same pathogen.

   D Activated helper T-cells divide into clones of active T-cells and clones of memory cells.

   E B-cells process antigen proteins from the pathogen and place them on their outer surface.

   F Active helper T-cells activate the B-cells by binding to them.

   G Helper T-cells are activated by binding to the macrophages.

   H Antigen presentation on the outside of macrophages.

f In 1967, the World Health Organization began a programme of vaccination to eradicate smallpox. Remarkably, they succeeded with this in 1975 as the last recorded case was in Bangladesh. This means that smallpox was the first infectious disease to have been completely eradicated by vaccination. Explain how vaccines prevent infection of known diseases, such as smallpox.

g Jenner risked the life of James Phipps, as well as the lives of other members of his own family that he tested his vaccination on. Analyse whether the risks that Jenner took were worth it, or not.

h The scientific community of 1796 (when Jenner originally carried out his vaccination trials) criticised and ridiculed Jenner for his ideas. Comment on whether the scientific community were right to criticise Jenner for his work at that time.

i Define *active immunity*.

j Using examples, outline how passive immunity protects the body from disease.

k Distinguish between an antibody and an antigen.

2 Epidemiology is the study of how diseases are distributed and caused within populations. This usually involves the study of how diseases spread, the patterns that develop, and how the disease was originally caused.

Tuberculosis (TB) is an infectious disease that is caused by the bacterium *Mycobacterium tuberculosis*. There is evidence that suggests that TB has been present in humans for thousands of years, and today it poses a serious threat to public health. Approximately 14 million people worldwide have TB, many of them in developing countries where the populations are more susceptible to such diseases. The BCG (Bacillus Calmette-Guérin) vaccine helps to protect against TB, especially among young children who may be vulnerable to the disease. Figure 11.1 shows how the number of TB deaths has changed in a period of 100 years (1913–2012). This is an example of epidemiology as the disease is mapped and observed to collect data. It is possible to draw some conclusions from the correlations shown in the graph. The Medical Research Council, formed in Britain in 1913, made the study of TB its initial focus for research.

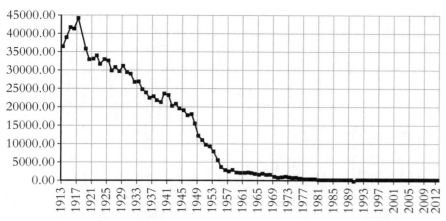

Figure 11.1 TB deaths in the UK, 1913–2012.

a   Describe how the number of TB deaths in the UK changed between 1913 and 2012.

b   Suggest why the general decrease in deaths from TB began from 1913 onwards.

c   There is a steep decline in deaths from TB from the early 1940s. Determine why such a decline occurred at this time.

d   The Bacillus Calmette-Guérin vaccine was introduced on a wider scale from the early 1950s.

   i   Describe the effect that the BCG vaccine had on the number of deaths by TB in the UK.

   ii Outline how this vaccine helps to fight against the disease.

e   Analyse the epidemiological data in Figure 11.1 to support the idea that the BCG vaccine was successful in preventing large numbers of cases of TB in the UK.

f   TB is an airborne disease that is spread quickly when people with TB cough, spit, speak or sneeze. People with AIDS or those who smoke are more likely to have an active infection of TB. Design a plan that could have been used in the early 1920s to help prevent the spread of TB in the UK.

3   Monoclonal antibodies to HCG (human chorionic gonadotrophin) are used in pregnancy test kits. HCG is secreted by the early embryo to maintain the corpus luteum and progesterone production. This means that a pregnant woman will have HCG present in her bloodstream and urine.

a   Outline how HCG is detected by pregnancy testing kits.

b   If the person is **not** pregnant, suggest why the pregnancy testing kit does not show a coloured line in the window.

Exercise 11.2 – Movement

1   The musculoskeletal system is responsible for movement, support and protection.

a   Identify the structures being described in the sentences below.

   i   A place where two or more bones meet.

   ii   The framework that supports the body and protects vital organs, such as the heart.

   iii Tough, fibrous structures that attach bones to one another at a joint.

   iv   Tough bands of connective tissue that attach muscles to bones.

   v   Work in antagonistic pairs to provide the force needed for movement.

   vi   Coordinate and monitor movements and stimulate the contraction of muscles.

b Outline how antagonistic pairs of muscles help to cause movement.

c Synovial joints allow certain movements but not others. The elbow joint is an example of a synovial joint and is formed by the radius, the ulna and the humerus. The muscles involved in elbow movement are the biceps and the triceps. Use this information to annotate the diagram in Figure 11.2 to show how the elbow is an example of a synovial joint that uses antagonistic pairs of muscles for movement.

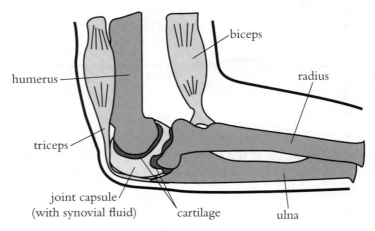

Figure 11.2 The hinge joint of an elbow.

d The table below distinguishes between the shoulder joint and the elbow joint. This is the sort of table that you should draw when comparing or distinguishing between two different structures. It is very clear and helps you to refer to both structures throughout the answer. In this case, your task is simply to deduce the features being compared in the table.

Feature	Shoulder joint	Elbow joint
	Synovial, ball-and-socket	Synovial, hinge
	Shoulder blade and humerus	Ulna, radius, humerus
	Rotational	Flexion and extension

Table 11.1

e Outline the role of ATP in muscle contraction.

2 In the late 1960s, Ashley and Ridgeway studied the role of calcium ions (Ca^{2+}) in the coupling of nerve impulses and muscle contraction. Thanks to improvements in apparatus, scientists like Ashley and Ridgeway made rapid developments in scientific research that might not have been previously possible. It was their use of aequorin that made their work possible. Aequorin emits light when it binds to Ca^{2+}. The light emission reaches a peak between the arrival of an electrical impulse at a muscle fibre and the contraction of that muscle fibre. Use of modern apparatus, such as microscopes and cameras, enabled detection of the light emissions; but some scientists use radioactive dyes to be able to see the rapid movements in muscle cells.

a Outline how calcium ions contribute to the control of muscle contractions.

b Explain how actin and myosin filaments produce the striped appearance of skeletal muscle.

3 The grasshopper is an insect with three pairs of legs. It makes use of this as its hind legs are specialised for jumping and some grasshoppers can jump as high as 20 times their own body length. If a human could do this, an average-sized man could jump over

30 metres in the air, or leap the length of a football field! Figure 11.3 shows the anatomy of grasshopper legs in comparison to human arms.

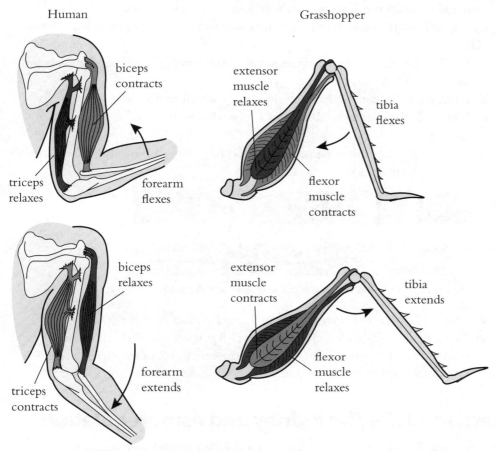

Figure 11.3 Human and grasshopper reflexes.

a Describe how the muscles of the grasshopper leg allow it to jump so high in the air.
b Describe how antagonistic pairs of muscles in the human arm allow the forearm to flex.
c Deduce why a grasshopper can jump much higher than a human can.

4 You are expected to be able to label a diagram of the structure of a sarcomere (Figure 11.4).

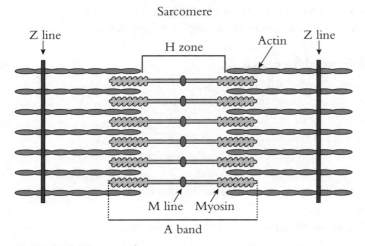

Figure 11.4 Diagram of a sarcomere.

a A sarcomere is the part of a myofibril between which **two** points?

b Identify the band that surrounds the Z-line.

c State the name of the filament that is connected to the Z-lines.

d Contraction of the skeletal muscle is achieved by the sliding of actin and myosin filaments.

   i Outline what happens when the myosin filaments pull the actin filaments towards the centre of the sarcomere.

   ii Energy for this contraction is derived from which molecule?

   iii Distinguish between the Z-lines of a relaxed sarcomere and a contracted sarcomere.

   iv Deduce whether the sarcomere at the top of Figure 11.5 is relaxed or contracted. Explain the reasons for your answer.

Figure 11.5 A relaxed sarcomere and a contracted sarcomere.

   v Outline how cross-bridge formation occurs during muscle contraction.

   vi The length of the sarcomere in Figure 11.5 was measured on an electron micrograph and found to be 9.7 mm. If the actual size of the sarcomere is 1 micrometre, calculate the magnification of the electron micrograph.

Exercise 11.3 – The kidney and osmoregulation

1 Part of being a scientist is being curious and wanting to find how things work, especially if that knowledge can be used in real life. Curiosity about particular phenomena led scientists to investigate how desert animals prevent water loss in their wastes. Without sufficient water, survival can be difficult for many desert organisms. Animals, in particular, are vulnerable to water loss as the range at which animal bodily tissue functions is within a very small range. If temperatures go above, or below, this temperature range then the organism may die. Animals have a variety of physiological, structural and behavioural strategies to cope with this and conserve water.

a Identify whether the following behaviours are examples of physiological, structural or behavioural adaptations.

   i Burrowing into moist soil during daylight.

   ii Producing highly concentrated urine.

   iii Obtaining enough moisture from the food that is eaten.

   iv Excreting metabolic wastes in the form of uric acid.

   v Living in underground habitats that are sealed off.

   vi Hairs in the nostril causing water from respiration to condense and then reabsorbed.

   vii Specialised kidneys with extra microscopic tubules to extract water from urine and return it to the bloodstream.

   viii Waxy, waterproof covering to prevent water loss by sweating and evaporation.

   ix Drinking water when it becomes available.

b The giant-striped mongoose (Grandidier's mongoose) stays in caves and burrows during the day. At night, they leave their caves and hunt for prey. Deduce how the giant-striped mongoose is able to conserve water in the arid conditions of its home in Madagascar.

c Some organisms will purposely find a cooler microclimate within their habitat. Examples of this are a falcon nesting on the ledge of a cliff that is less exposed to direct sunlight. An animal such as the white-throated wood rat will build a den from the random bits of woodland litter available to it. Compare and contrast how the falcon and the wood rat protect themselves against water loss.

d Animals such as the camel can produce very concentrated urine in their longer loop of Henle.

   i Outline the role of the loop of Henle in urine content regulation.

   ii Comment on the relationship between the length of the loop of Henle and the need for water conservation in animals.

e The type of nitrogenous waste in animals is correlated with evolutionary history and habitat. For each of the organisms below, state the type of nitrogenous waste that the organism would produce in their habitat.

   i Organisms that live in an aquatic habitat, such as fish.

   ii Birds and insects that reside in a terrestrial habitat.

   iii Some fish and amphibians that have terrestrial and some aquatic habitats.

   iv Explain why aquatic organisms are able to excrete ammonia as their waste product.

f The American kangaroo rat is one of the best-known organisms for reducing their water loss. Explain how the American kangaroo rat is adapted to minimise water loss and conserve water.

2 All animals are either osmoregulators or osmoconformers.

   a Define *osmoregulation*.

   b Outline how animals that are osmoregulators achieve osmoregulation.

   c Osmoconformers, such as marine vertebrates, **cannot** osmoregulate in the same way as osmoregulators. Explain how the osmotic pressure of these organisms is related to their surroundings.

3 a Urea is produced by mammals as a waste product from the metabolism of amino acids. The kidneys filter out waste molecules from the blood that passes through them.

   i State the name of the process described in this question.

   ii Outline the main roles of the kidney.

   iii Draw and label a diagram of the human kidney.

  b Kidney failure is an occurrence for many people, whether due to diseases like diabetes, or through conditions such as high blood pressure. For the following paragraph, deduce the type of treatment being described and answer the associated questions. An artificial kidney is required due to real kidneys not being able to filter the waste products. A steady flow of blood is passed over an artificial partially permeable membrane of the dialysis machine. The blood that has been purified is returned to the patient via a vein.

   i Deduce the treatment described.

   ii Describe what happens to the blood as it passes over the artificial partially permeable membrane of the dialysis machine.

c Sometimes, a patient will receive a working kidney from another person in order to replace their kidney that is not working.

 i State the name of this procedure.

 ii Suggest why a living donor is possible for this treatment.

 iii Evaluate this type of treatment; is it better or worse than the option in part b?

d Distinguish between the composition of the blood in the renal artery and the blood in the renal vein.

e Identify other substances that are **not** excretory products but are removed from the blood by the kidney.

4 a Copy the table and identify the structure that is part of the nephron by the description of the function in the corresponding row. The functions are the information that you should use to label a diagram of the nephron.

Structure	Function
	Porous wall that collects the filtrate
	The knot-like capillary where ultrafiltration takes place
	Tube shaped like a hairpin (or loop); has a descending limb and an ascending limb; water and salt reabsorbed here
	Carries filtrate to the renal pelvis
	Twisted section of the nephron with many mitochondria
	Twisted section of the nephron, but with fewer microvilli and mitochondria
	Brings blood from the renal artery
	Restricts blood flow to generate high pressure in the glomerulus
	Low pressure capillary bed absorbing fluid from the convoluted tubules
	Unbranched capillaries with a descending limb that carries blood into the medulla and an ascending limb that brings it back to the cortex

Table 11.2

b Use the information from the table to copy, label and annotate Figure 11.6.

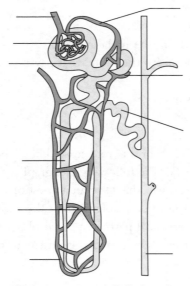

Figure 11.6 An unlabelled nephron.

c Describe the function of ADH.

d The solute concentration of the blood is too low. Not very much water is reabsorbed from the filtrate. A large volume of water, with a low solute concentration, is produced.

   i Predict the effect that this series of events will have on the solute concentration of the blood.

   ii When the solute concentration of the blood is too high, outline how ADH helps to maintain a more appropriate level of solute concentration.

   iii State the name of the process described in part ii.

5 Jordan is exercising hard on a hot day as part of his preparation for a summer athletics tournament. When he takes a break and visits the toilet, he notices that his urine is a much darker colour than normal. He is also feeling quite tired and feels that his heart rate is much higher than it usually is after exercise. Jordan checks his smart-watch which confirms that his heart *is* beating faster than his usual exercising heart rate.

a Based on the text above, determine the condition that Jordan might be suffering from.

b Jordan's friend, Matt, joins him for a run the following day. Matt is aware that Jordan was suffering yesterday and, although he is a much fitter athlete, Matt makes sure that he drinks plenty of water.

   i Outline the consequences that Matt will suffer if he overhydrates.

   ii Explain how overhydration can be avoided.

6 Kidney stones are formed when your urine contains too much uric acid and calcium, which your urine fails to dilute. These crystal-like substances can stick together, causing immense pain. However, kidney stones can be removed by ultrasound. NASA have recently developed specialised equipment that can locate and break down these kidney stones with a hand-held ultrasound device – even in space! The traditional method of locating, and breaking down kidney stones is not possible in space as the equipment is too big and bulky. In this instance, the astronaut would have to return to Earth to have the procedure.

a Identify the substances that urine fails to dilute, causing kidney stones.

b Outline how ultrasound breaks down kidney stones.

c Discuss the usefulness of NASA developing the ability to take a handheld ultrasound machine to space stations.

7 The recent ban of some Russian athletes from Olympic competition highlighted the importance of regular urinary testing of athletes.

a Urine analysis can be used to detect drug abuse. Identify the other uses of urine tests.

b A patient carries out a test and a high level of glucose is detected. Suggest what this patient might be suffering from.

c The following symptoms are identified when carrying out urinary tests. Suggest the conditions that might be causing these symptoms.

   i Presence of white blood cells with a visible nucleus.

   ii Presence of red blood cells in urine.

Exercise 11.4 – Sexual reproduction

1 Figure 11.7 shows a conversation between two friends.

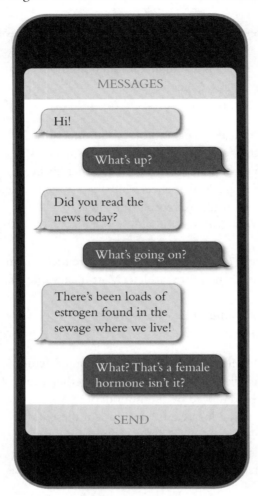

Figure 11.7 A conversation about estrogen in water.

a Suggest how concentrations of estrogen found their way into sewage and waste water in built up communities.

b A study in the 1990s showed that human sperm counts had declined by around 50% in recent years. A study by the UK government's Environment Agency in 2004 showed that the majority of fish tested were showing signs of feminisation. Analyse the relationship between these two seemingly related patterns.

c Design a plan that could help to prevent the concentrations of female hormones being found in waste water and sewage.

2 **a** Define *mitosis*.

b Define *meiosis*.

c State the names of the processes that involve both meiosis and mitosis, as well as cell growth and differentiation.

d Outline what happens in spermatogenesis.

e State the location of oogenesis.

f Explain how different numbers of gametes with different amounts of cytoplasm occur in spermatogenesis and oogenesis.

3 You are expected to be able to annotate diagrams of a seminiferous tubule and ovary to show the stages of gametogenesis.

   a Copy and annotate the stages on the diagram of spermatogenesis in Figure 11.8.

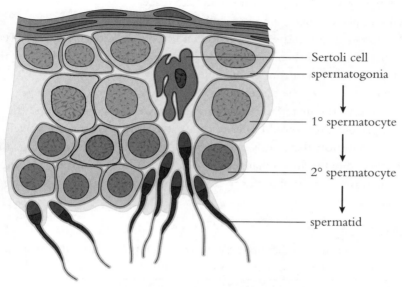

Sertoli cell
spermatogonia

1° spermatocyte

2° spermatocyte

spermatid

Figure 11.8 Spermatogenesis.

   b Copy and annotate the diagram of oogenesis shown in Figure 11.9.

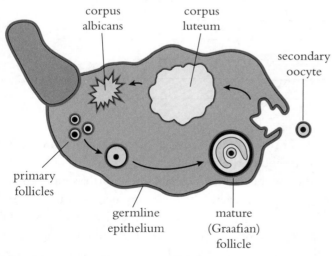

corpus albicans   corpus luteum   secondary oocyte

primary follicles

germline epithelium   mature (Graafian) follicle

Figure 11.9 Oogenesis.

   c Sketch, label and annotate a diagram of mature sperm and egg to indicate their functions. You are only expected to annotate the diagrams in the examination but this question is a challenge for you as we come to the later stages of the course.

4 a Define *fertilisation*.

b Suggest an example of an organism capable of external fertilisation.

c Suggest an example of an organism capable of internal fertilisation.

d Outline how mechanisms in fertilisation prevent polyspermy.

e Seven days after fertilisation, the embryo reaches the uterus. It is now made up of around 125 cells, thanks to mitosis. State the name of the embryo at this stage.

f The next stage is implantation.

   i State the structure where implantation will take place.

   ii Suggest why implantation of the blastocyst is so important.

g Usually, the endometrium is disposed of at the end of the menstrual cycle. However, if the egg has been fertilised then the lining must be maintained. Describe how the endometrium is maintained during pregnancy.

h Outline the primary roles of the placenta.

i Compare and contrast the materials that are passed between the mother and the fetus across the placenta. You should refer to the materials that are passed, as well as the method of transport that is used to do so. For example, the gas exchange of oxygen and carbon dioxide are exchanged by diffusion. When answering a 'compare and contrast' question, you should refer to both items in each part of your answer to achieve full marks.

5 a Define *gestation period*.

b Using the information in the table below, construct a graph to show the relationship between gestation period and average mass of the animals.

Organism	Gestation period (days)	Average mass (kg)
Elephant	640	5000
Bear	210	295
Goat	150	15
Sheep	148	35
Leopard	94	100
Rabbit	33	1
Cow	285	730

Table 11.3

c Deduce the trend that the data in your graph shows about the correlation between animal size and the gestation period of the mother.

d State the missing words in the text below that describes how birth is induced.
Signals from the _____ prevent further production of progesterone, triggering the secretion of _____, which is produced by the posterior lobe of the _____ gland. Estrogen levels rise and induce the development of oxytocin receptors on muscles of the _____ wall. Uterine contractions are initiated by the secretion of _____ from the endometrium. Oxytocin stimulates the myometrium to contract. The _____ become progressively stronger as more oxytocin is released until the baby is ousted from the uterus, during _____.

1 Which of the statements below, A–D, correctly describes entities that may carry antigens that trigger an immune response? [1]

   I   Protein

   II Virus

   III Parasite

   IV Antibiotic

   A I only

   B I and II

   C I and III

   D II and III

2 Identify the process that is shown in the photo of red blood cells in Figure 11.10. [1]

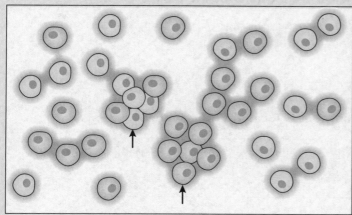

Figure 11.10 Red blood cells.

   A Agglutination

   B Red blood cells

   C Mitosis

   D Immunity

3 Identify the key term that describes the coating of a pathogen with antibodies to promote and enhance phagocytosis. [1]

   A Opsonisation

   B Agglutination

   C Memory cells

   D Inflammation

4 Which of the following is injected into a body in order to vaccinate that person against a disease? [1]

   A Antigens from a bacterium

   B A weakened version of the pathogen or toxin that causes the disease

   C Extra white blood cells that are specific to that disease

   D Cowpox

5 Who was the scientist who successfully vaccinated a young boy against smallpox in 1796? [1]

    A Edward Jenner

    B Louis Pasteur

    C James Watson

    D Alexander Fleming

6 Identify the term that is the study of the distribution, patterns and causes of diseases in a population. [1]

    A Oncology

    B Pathology

    C Epidemiology

    D Biomonitoring

7 Identify the correct antagonistic pair that is responsible for the flexing of the human forearm. [1]

    A Biceps contract and triceps relax

    B Triceps contract and biceps relax

    C Biceps and triceps relax

    D Biceps and triceps contract

8 Identify the function of the synovial fluid that is located in the synovial cavity of the elbow joint. [1]

    A Connects to the triceps

    B Keeps the radius in place

    C Reduces friction at the joint

    D Lubricates the tendon

9 The sarcomere is the unit of the myofibrils that start and end at which point? [1]

    A The H zone

    B The dark band

    C The Z-lines

    D The thin filaments

10 When a muscle contracts, identify what happens to the sarcomere. [1]

    A Relaxes

    B Contracts

    C Nothing

    D Doubles in size to create more force

11 Which of the following is not a possible consequence of overhydration? [1]

    A Swollen body cells

    B Nausea

    C Confusion and disorientation

    D High sodium levels

12   Riyadh analysed the body fluid of a marine organism. The body fluid was found to have identical concentration of solutes as the sea water. Deduce the type of organism that Riyadh is analysing. [1]
   A   Osmoregulator
   B   Predator
   C   Osmoconformer
   D   Fish

13   Identify the part of the nephron that is being described: this is a twisted section of the nephron where water, nutrients and salts are reabsorbed back into the blood. This part of the nephron also contains many microvilli and mitochondria. [1]
   A   Bowman's capsule
   B   Loop of Henle
   C   Distal convoluted tubule
   D   Proximal convoluted tubule

14   Which of the following terms means the production of female gametes? [1]
   A   Oogenesis
   B   Spermatogenesis
   C   Gametogenesis
   D   Implantation

15   Which of the following terms refers to fertilisation of an ovum by more than one sperm? [1]
   A   Implantation
   B   Polyspermy
   C   Polyploid
   D   Polygamete

16   Gametes are produced by spermatogenesis and oogenesis.
   a   Compare and contrast spermatogenesis and oogenesis. [7]
   b   Draw a labelled diagram of a mature sperm. [5]
   c   Outline the role of HCG in the early stages of pregnancy. [2]
   d   Explain how the structure and function of the placenta are linked during pregnancy. [8]

17   a   Draw and label a diagram that shows the structure of a sarcomere. [4]
   b   Describe the stages of how skeletal muscle contracts. [6]

18   a   Define *immunity*. [2]
   b   Explain how vaccination is successfully carried out. [8]
   c   Evaluate whether vaccinations are considered to be safe or dangerous. [4]
   d   Outline the main stages involved in the production of monoclonal antibodies. [3]

12 Neurobiology and behaviour (Option A)

KEY TERMS AND DEFINITIONS

HL **Ethology** – the study of animal behaviour under natural conditions.

HL **Natural selection** – when behaviours that favour survival and reproduction are passed on.

HL **Neuropharmacology** – a branch of pharmacology that investigates and researches how drugs act upon the nervous system.

Neurulation – the folding of the neural plate into the neural tube.

Stimulus – a change in the external environment of an organism.

Exercise A.1 – Antibody production and vaccination

1 It is difficult to see what happens inside the brain because if you were to open up the brain of a living person, it is likely that the person would die! Read the following text about how neuroscientists are able to use models as representatives of the real world.

> Developmental science uses a variety of animal models to model what is happening inside the human brain. This allows us to develop a better understanding of how the brain is formed in its early years, from embryo to fully grown adult. Human brains cannot be observed in the same way because this is unethical and would take far too long to observe. The human brain is also incredibly complex and much more difficult to understand than the brains of other, smaller organisms. The human embryo develops in the uterus, making it extremely difficult to closely observe what is happening in the developmental stages.
>
> One of the most popular organisms observed by neuroscientists is *Xenopus laevis* (the African clawed frog). Xenopus carries relatively large eggs, with a transparent yolk, that are easy to

observe and manipulate. The embryo will typically develop in less than 48 hours and it is generally considered to be much more ethical to use these embryos rather than human embryos. Other organisms that have been used in scientific research are listed below.

- Mole rats were used to observe how their mothers cared for them.
- The house mouse is often studied; it shares many diseases with humans due to living in such close proximity to humans.
- The fruit fly is able to reproduce very quickly and only has a small number of chromosomes.
- *Danio rerio* (zebrafish) are used because they have transparent tissue.

a Neurulation has been well studied in *Xenopus laevis*. Define *neurulation*.

b List the animals in the above text that are used for observation in scientific research.

c The text states that the human brain takes too long to fully form to be observed. Deduce what make *Xenopus laevis* more suitable than humans for observing neural development.

d Outline the other reasons why *Xenopus laevis* is ideal for research into neural development.

e Many studies in the past 100 years have used animals such as cats and dogs for experimentation. Discuss whether domesticated animals, such as cats and dogs, should be experimented on to observe neurulation.

f Suggest another reason why experimenting on animals to observe neurulation in humans might **not** be entirely reliable.

g As the neural tube elongates, cells at the anterior end become part of which structure?

h Identify the layer of cells described by the structures that they will eventually form.
   i Forms the skin and neural tissues.
   ii Becomes the muscle and bone.
   iii Forms the inner cells of the digestive and respiratory systems.

i Construct a flow chart to correctly rearrange the following stages of how the neural plate develops.
- Fusion.
- Folding.
- Thickening and elongation.
- Elongation.
- Convergence.

j Annotate your flow chart to outline what happens at each stage of the development of the neural plate.

k Define *neurogenesis*.

l Incomplete closure of the embryonic neural tube can cause *spina bifida*, a disorder that affects 5% of the population at birth.
   i Outline what happens as part of this incomplete closure that causes *spina bifida*.
   ii Suggest what a surgeon can do to treat a baby born with *spina bifida*.
   iii Once a baby with *spina bifida* has been treated by the surgeon in this way, they will be able to function as normal. Comment on this statement.
   iv Suggest what pregnant mothers should take as a dietary supplement in order to greatly reduce the risk of *spina bifida* and other neural tube defects.

m Describe how the neural tube is formed.

2 Read the article below and answer the questions that follow.

Cultural experiences, including the acquisition of a language, result in neural pruning. Newborn babies are believed to have many more neurons than their own adult brains will in later life. The brain decides which neurons it needs to keep, based on which connections are being used. This is known as neural pruning. As a person grows older, it may be that they try new things or undergo new experiences. An example of this would be liking a new type of food, or even developing a liking for a new style of music. People who are good at learning languages use different areas of the brain in order to learn new words and switch easily between the languages that they know. However, if the human brain makes errors during the pruning process, it can lead to important connections being lost. It is believed, but not proven, that it can lead to psychiatric disorders, such as schizophrenia. Teenagers are sometimes known to be emotionally volatile as they grow and learn how to deal with new experiences. It may be that some teenagers have difficulty empathising with other people and their brains must develop the ability to think about other people, rather than themselves.

a Define *neural pruning*.
b Suggest why neural pruning is beneficial to humans.
c Define *plasticity*.
d Identify the areas of the brain that are responsible for the following:
  i Comprehension of words.
  ii Articulation of words.
e Outline how bilingual people are able to learn a second language.
f Suggest how teenagers' brains might develop as they develop higher-level skills such as empathy.

Exercise A.2 – The human brain

1 Different parts of the brain have specific roles.
  a Identify the parts of the brain being described in the table below. Copy and complete the table.

Part of the brain	Specific role
	Controls the gut muscles, breathing and heart rate.
	Coordinates muscular activity responsible for posture, movement and balance.
	Hormones made here and body temperature, thirst and hunger are controlled.
	Hormones made in the hypothalamus secreted here to regulate bodily functions.
	The main centre for high-complexity functions such as language, learning, memory and emotions.

Table 12.1

b Parts of the brain, and the activity that it undertakes, have been identified through use of animal experiments, autopsies, lesions and fMRI.

i In the 19th century, after the death of a patient who could only say one word, a French neurologist identified a large tumour which had damaged the side of the patient's brain. Deduce what the neurologist could work out from this information.

ii Parkinson's and multiple sclerosis have been observed and studied in animals by the severing of connections in the brains of the animals. The effects are then observed and scientists are able to learn a great deal about these serious diseases. Evaluate whether testing on animals in this case is acceptable or not.

iii MRI is commonly used to observe, not just the brain, but many types of injury and conditions. The presence of tumours and other abnormalities can be detected. Scientists also use fMRI to link the activity of the brain in specific parts with the thought processes and actions being undertaken. State the full name of MRI and fMRI.

iv Outline how fMRI scans are able to link brain activity to the thought process of the person involved.

v The brains of people were scanned while they listened to different sounds of atmospheric music. The fMRI scans are shown in Figure 12.1. Analyse the scans to suggest what they might be showing.

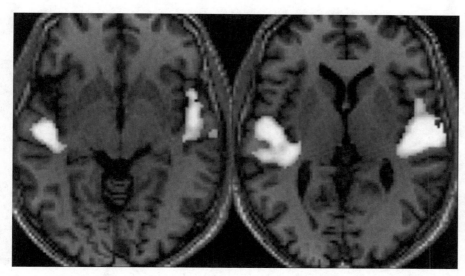

Figure 12.1 An fMRI scan of people who were scanned while they listened to different sounds of atmospheric music.

vi Discuss whether fMRI and MRI scanning is proof of causation when observing how parts of the brain are more or less active during different situations.

c Perhaps the most famous brain study is that of Phineas Gage. Read the series of 'live' tweets below that could have been sent if Gage had been around in the 21st century. Answer the question that follows.

Figure 12.2 Social media posts about Phineas Gage.

The case of Phineas Gage was one of the first to suggest a link between brain trauma and personality change. Gage's skull is one of the most famous items at the Harvard Medical School campus. Imagine you were one of the first neuroscientists at the time to make this link and construct a 'tweet' of your own. Remember, tweets are a maximum of 140 characters.

2 The correlation between body size and brain size in different animals can be analysed by comparing the weight of the brain (E) with the weight of the body (S). This produces the ES ratio and the table below shows the ES ratio for many different animals.

Animal	ES ratio
Human	1:50
Cat	1:110
Mouse	1:40
Elephant	1:560
Ant	1:7

Animal	ES ratio
Horse	1:600
Small bird	1:14
Hippopotamus	1:2789
Squirrel	1:150

Table 12.2

a Analyse the data in the table to draw conclusions about the relationship between body size and brain size.

b Compare the relative brain sizes of the mouse and the hippopotamus.

c Predict the ES ratio for a dog.

d Suggest a possible reason for this correlation between brain size and body size.

3 Figure 12.3 shows a doctor checking the pupil reflex of a patient.

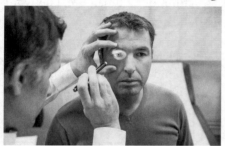

Figure 12.3 Checking the pupil reflex.

a Identify the part of the nervous system that the pupil reflex is a part of.

b Explain why the pupil reflex is a useful tool for making a quick assessment of brain function in patients.

c A doctor shines his light into the eyes of a patient with suspected brain damage. The pupils fail to constrict immediately. Deduce the part of the brain that has been damaged.

d Suggest other tests that a doctor may carry out to assess the brain functionality of a patient.

Exercise A.3 – Perception of stimuli

1 Figure 12.4 shows a chef picking up a hot pan. The chef is **not** wearing any protective layers on his hands.

Figure 12.4 A chef picking up a hot pan.

a Predict what happens next in the scenario with the chef.

b Define *receptor*.

c Identify the type of receptor involved when the chef realises that the pan is too hot for his bare hands.

d Identify the type of receptor described in the following examples.

   i   Responds to light energy.

   ii Responds to chemical substances.

   iii Responds to forces and movement.

   iv Type of chemoreceptor in the nose that detects different smells and scents.

e Humans cannot detect as many different smells underwater as a marine organism such as a shark.

   i   Suggest why humans do **not** have as a good sense of smell as a shark.

   ii Explain why it is more important for a shark to have such a good sense of smell.

2 You are expected to be able to label a diagram of the structure of the human eye.

   a Copy and label Figure 12.5 to show the main structures of a human eye. The word box below will help you to complete this.

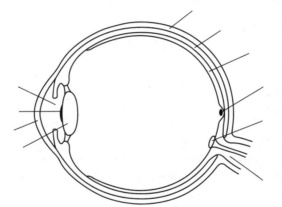

sclera	iris
blind spot	retina
pupil	lens
choroid	fovea
optic nerve	cornea

Figure 12.5 The human eye.

   b Copy the table. Complete it by identifying the part of the eye being described by its function.

Part of the eye	Function
	Gelatinous fluid that holds the back of the eye in shape
	A fluid that holds the front of the eye in shape
	Refracts light as it enters the eye
	Gap in the iris that light passes through
	Controls the size of the pupil
	Controls the diameter of the lens
	Holds the lens in position
	Contains melanin and absorbs light
	Carries action potentials back to the brain
	Contains only cone cells
	Tough outer layer
	Sensory area where rods and cones are found

Table 12.3

c Describe how rods and cones are arranged on the retina of the eye.

d Deduce the type of cell that is being described in each column in the table below.

Highly sensitive to light	Less sensitive to light
Works best in dim light	Works well in bright light
One type responds to all wavelengths of light	Each cell is connected to its own bipolar cell
Not present in fovea	**Not** present at the edges of the retina

Table 12.4

3 a A hearing person will detect sound waves using the following steps. The steps have been mixed up; your task is to list the stages in the correct order to show how a hearing person detects sound waves.
- Cochlea releases a neurotransmitter.
- Electrical impulse sent to the brain.
- Neurotransmitter crosses a synapse and stimulates a sensory neuron.
- The brain detects the wavelength of the sound wave by the relative movement of the basilar membrane.
- Movement caused by pressure waves stimulates hair cells in the cochlea.

b State the name of the nerve through which electrical impulses are transmitted to the brain.

c Deaf patients may be fitted with cochlear implants. The understanding of the underlying science is the basis for technological developments; the discovery that electrical stimulation in the auditory system can create a perception of sound resulted in the development of electrical hearing aids and ultimately cochlear implants. Experiments have been carried out on humans since the 1950s to help understand which frequencies are important for speech recognition.

    i Outline how cochlear implants are able to assist deaf people.

    ii Investigations were carried out on humans to find out how their ears worked, and what frequencies and sounds could be heard. Discuss whether you think it was ethical to investigate humans like this.

    iii The cochlear implants are able to bypass the part of the hearing system that is at fault. Determine which part of the ear might **not** be functioning properly in a patient that is wearing cochlear implants.

d Many people who are deaf, or 'hard of hearing', cannot hear everyday sounds and this can be frustrating. However, when those sounds are fire alarms, the hearing loss can be potentially deadly. At a recent electronics device show in Las Vegas, hearing aids have been showcased that can link directly to smart devices. The new technology will allow deaf people to hear the doorbell and the fire alarm, as well as isolate desired sounds, such as the television. The hearing aids contain a sound processor that alters parts of the sound signal that the person usually does not hear so well and boosts speech and voice signals. Future applications of the technology expect to include connection to a range of smart devices, such as televisions, radios, lighting, safety equipment, mobile telephones and most household appliances.

   i   Compare the technology described with that of a regular cochlear implant.

   ii Discuss the implications for the safety of deaf patients if the new technology becomes available.

   iii Comment on a possible barrier to the technology being available to all patients.

HL Exercise A.4 – Innate and learnt behaviour

1 Pavlov's experiments into reflex conditioning in dogs is one of the most famous biology experiments. Read the article below where Pavlov is interviewed by a national newspaper about his work.

Newspaper interviewer: Hello Ivan, how are you?
Pavlov: Good, thank you. I have been very busy.

We hear that you have been experimenting on the salivation of dogs?
Pavlov: Yes, I was actually researching the gastric systems of different animals, and while measuring the salivation rates of dogs I noticed something that piqued my interest.

So, you would bring the dogs food in order to make them produce saliva. As our readers know, we produce saliva to help us to digest our food. What happened next?
Pavlov: I noticed that the dogs were producing saliva *before* I fed them. They had started to anticipate that food was coming so I started to set up different situations to measure this effect.

You played different sounds to them, is that correct?
Pavlov: It is, yes.

Why did you play those sounds to the dogs *before* feeding?
Pavlov: The dogs would hear the sounds, then receive food. After a period of time, they started to produce saliva when they heard the sounds. This carried on even when I did not bring them any food.

That's amazing. So, the dogs produced saliva even when no food actually arrived?
Pavlov: Yes, this shows me that the dogs can be conditioned to respond to different stimuli.

What other stimuli did you use to test this theory?
Pavlov: Quite a few: a buzzer, a metronome and electric shocks.

Do you think humans can be conditioned in this way?
Pavlov: Of course, by repeating a stimulus, the human will behave in a way that shows they are anticipating the stimulus. A great example of this is if someone holds a pin next to a balloon. What does the other person do? Of course, they automatically flinch because they are expecting the balloon to be popped and a loud noise to be produced.

Hmmmm, yes, very clever. Anyway, do the dogs keep the conditioned response forever?
Pavlov: That is what we are trying to find out. I hope to let you know how this goes in my new paper at the end of the year.

---

a Identify the neutral stimulus before conditioning in Pavlov's experiment.

b Identify the unconditioned response to the food in Pavlov's experiment.

c Outline how Pavlov conditioned the dog to salivate during conditioning.

d Determine the conditioned stimulus of Pavlov's experiment.

e Explain why it was important that the sound was played *before* the food was produced, rather than afterwards.

f Predict what happened when Pavlov continued to play the sounds, but without bringing the dogs any food.

2 Copy the table and complete it by identifying the different types of neuron described.

a

Type of neuron	Cell body	Function
	Located at the centre of the neuron.	Carries impulse from receptors to the central nervous system.
	Makes up the majority of the neuron.	Allows communication between the central nervous system and the other neurons.
	Located at the end of the neuron.	Carries electrical impulse from the central nervous system to an effector.

Table 12.5

b State an example of an effector in a reflex arc.

c The pain withdrawal reflex is an example of innate behaviour.

  i Define *innate behaviour*.

  ii Sketch and label a reflex arc for a pain withdrawal reflex of your choice.

  iii The table below contains the steps of the pain withdrawal reflex. Use this to construct a step-by-step summary of how the pain withdrawal reflex triggers a protective response.

Muscle fibres contract, causing the part of the body to withdraw from the pain stimulus.	Relay neurons continue the impulse.
Receptors in the skin detect pain stimulus.	The motor neuron receives the impulse and sends it to a muscle near the pain stimulus.
Sensory neuron sends the impulse to the CNS.	Receptors convert signal into an electrical impulse that is sent along the sensory neuron.

Table 12.6

3 Birdsong provides evidence of inheritance and learning as it is developed in young birds. Read the text below and answer the questions that follow.

> Birdsong is partly innate and partly learnt behaviour. Some notes within birdsong are recognised by birds from other species, even when reared in isolation. Mating and territorial calls are usually learnt from parents. Birds have also been known to display evidence of regional dialects. Songbirds learn their songs during the nesting period as they replicate the behaviour and songs of the adults around them. Quite amazingly, some songbirds are able to mimic other species, such as frogs, and sounds from inanimate objects, such as car alarms.

a Deduce what is evident when birds are able to produce songs from other species, even when kept in isolation.

b Give another example of innate behaviour that is **not** mentioned in the text above.

c Explain why the quality of the mating call is important for the survival of a bird.

d Determine what can be deduced from the evidence that some birds have regional dialects.

e Identify **one** other piece of evidence from the article that supports the notion that songbirds are able to learn to produce different sounds.

f Outline the main reasons that birds are born with the innate ability to sing songs and make certain calls.

4 Konrad Lorenz demonstrated the bonds that are formed between parent and offspring occurs during the early hours of their life. Lorenz separated a group of new-born geese into two groups; one group was hatched with the mother, the others was hatched in an incubator. The young goslings from the first group followed their mother but the goslings that were hatched in the incubator followed Lorenz around as if he was their mother.

a Predict what happened when Lorenz mixed up the goslings from the two groups.

b State the critical time period for imprinting in most birds.

c Deduce the biological advantage that is provided by imprinting.

5 Jabari is playing his favourite computer game. He keeps 'dying' as he gets to a certain level and this frustrates him. However, over a number of attempts, Jabari realises that there are a number of ways to avoid the dreaded monster that keeps ending the life of his character. He eventually moves to the next level of the game, and is absolutely delighted. In fact, next time he plays the game, he passes straight through the difficult level easily each time.

a Determine the type of conditioning demonstrated by gamers like Jabari.

b Outline the experiences that this type of conditioning relies on.

c This type of conditioning is used when training dogs to behave a certain way. For each of the descriptions below, state the type of reinforcement that is being described.

   i The behaviour of the dog causes a good thing to happen. The behaviour of the dog continues to improve.

   ii The behaviour of the dog causes a bad thing to cease. The behaviour of the dog improves.

   iii The behaviour of the dog causes a bad thing to happen, and the behaviour of the dog gets worse.

   iv The behaviour of the dog causes a good thing to stop, and the behaviour decreases.

HL Exercise A.5 – Neuropharmacology

1 Read this paragraph and answer the questions that follow.

> The American House of Congress have recently passed a bill that aims to speed up approval of new medicines and medical devices. There has been plenty of criticism that the bill has been rushed through, without the relevant parties giving it the thorough scrutiny that such a bill deserves. The bill aims to provide billions of dollars for research into drug abuse and the safety of medical drugs. Part of this bill is specifically designed to combat abuse of opioids, such as morphine, methadone, oxycodone and heroin. Some people who are drug addicts seem to get addicted more easily than others. Some people begin using drugs due to peer pressure, or because their socioeconomic circumstances make them more likely to try drugs in the first place. Once users start abusing drugs, the user feels high and euphoric, causing them to continue to continue to seek the high that was achieved.

  a Explain why patient advocates often press for the speeding up of drug approval processes.

  b Suggest why the speeding up of the drug approval process encourages more tolerance of risk.

  c Outline what the drug approval process aims to achieve.

  d Sometimes, a medical trial may be abandoned early and treatment administered to those who need it. Comment on the disadvantages of such a decision.

  e Opioid abuse is a result of drug addiction. Outline what a drug addict is, and why addicts are not able to overcome their addiction.

  f Identify the **three** factors outlined in the above text that contribute to addiction.

  g In the Pacific region, *kava* is used for medicinal and cultural purposes in order to relax after a hard day. Comment on why this use of a drug is acceptable in the Pacific region.

2 Read this paragraph about some different examples of psychoactive drugs and answer the questions that follow.

> Nicotine is obtained from *Nicotiana tabacum* and is consumed via the smoking of cigarettes. The effect felt is similar to that of taking cocaine and amphetamines, although not as intense. However, there are drugs, such as benzodiazepines, alcohol and tetrahydrocannabinol that affect the body in a completely different way.

  a List the **three** examples of excitatory drugs in the text above.

  b List the **three** examples of inhibitory drugs in the text above.

  c Outline the effect of cocaine on the nervous system.

  d Identify the inhibitory drug described as follows: this drug is present in cannabis and binds to receptors in the presynaptic membranes of the hippocampus, inhibiting the release of excitatory neurotransmitters. The overall effect is an impairment of short-term memory and a stimulation of appetite.

  e Outline the effect of dopamine.

f A lot of the information for this question comes from a branch of pharmacology that investigates and researches how drugs act upon the nervous system. Determine which branch of pharmacology this is.

g Compare and contrast the effect of stimulants and sedatives on the nervous system.

HL Exercise A.6 – Ethology

1 The UK population of the black peppered moth was relatively small prior to the Industrial Revolution. The Industrial Revolution caused more soot and pollution to be produced and trees with pale bark in the area became darker. Within months, the population of the black peppered moth increased dramatically, while the population of the white peppered moth greatly decreased.

   a Suggest why the population of black peppered moths was so low prior to the Industrial Revolution.

   b Explain why the population of the white, and black, peppered moths appeared to switch.

   c Explain how the offspring of the black peppered moth benefit from the survival of their parents.

   d The theory of the black peppered moth was eventually proven through ethology. Define *ethology*.

2 Read the text in the boxes below about different ethological studies; then answer the questions that follow.

> The migratory behaviour of blackcaps has long been argued about among ethologists, until an experiment was devised to test the range of hypotheses. Blackcaps were hatched from birds that spent their winter in Spain and in Britain. The offspring were reared away from their parents and their migratory patterns were monitored by tagging. The blackcaps migrated to the same place as their parents.

> Vampire bats feed on the blood of mammals. However, if a bat cannot locate enough food then a fellow bat might regurgitate some of their own food. The bats will then be likely to return the favour at another time when the roles are reversed.

> Shore crabs use their strong claws to crack open mussels, their favourite prey. However, shore crabs only attack mussels of a certain size that will yield a suitable amount of energy. It would not be worthwhile for the shore crabs to eat very large or very small mussels.

There are two types of coho male salmon: jacks and hooknoses. The jacks are small and hide before sneaking out to mate with the female salmon. Hooknoses are larger and tend to fight other salmon to mate with available females.

The innate release of pheromones causes female lions to achieve synchronised estrus, increasing their chances of survival and reproduction.

Blue tits like to feed on cream from milk bottles. They used to do this by piercing the aluminium foil caps on milk bottles. This behaviour was then observed in areas of the UK and Europe that were beyond the flying range of the blue tits.

a Deduce whether the migratory patterns of the blackcaps are innate or a learnt behaviour.

b The behaviour of the bats is an example of a type of altruism.
   i Define *altruism*.
   ii State the type of altruism that is evident in the bats when they expect to receive the favour back at a later date.

c Determine the benefit to the shore crab of their foraging behaviour.

d Outline how each of the types of salmon are able to survive.

e Suggest why the synchronisation of estrus in female lions is beneficial to survival.

f This question is about the learnt behaviour of the blue tits.
   i Explain how the behaviour of the blue tit was able to be observed in areas far beyond their range of flight.
   ii In more recent years, the milk bottles with aluminium foil caps were replaced by bottles with hard, plastic caps. Predict what happened to the learnt behaviour.

? Exam-style questions

1 **Which of the statements below, A–D, correctly describes stages in the development of the neural plate? [1]**
   I Elongation
   II Fission
   III Convergence
   IV Cross-bridge formation
   A I only
   B I and II
   C I and III
   D I, II and II

2 **Neurulation is the folding process that develops the neural plate into which structure? [1]**
   A Neural tube
   B Notochord
   C Ectoderm
   D Embryo

3 Which of the following is the key term that refers to the natural death of a cell? [1]

    A Neural pruning

    B Neurogenesis

    C Apoptosis

    D Cell migration

4 Which part of the brain is most likely to be affected in a person who struggles to express their thoughts as words? [1]

    A Wernicke's area

    B Synapses

    C Broca's area

    D Medulla oblongata

5 Which of the following is an example of plasticity? [1]

    A Liking a new food

    B Elimination of synapses

    C Birdsong

    D Palmar grasp reflex

6 Identify the food supplement that pregnant women can take that reduces the chances of spinal defects, such as *spina bifida*. [1]

    A Omega-3 fatty acids

    B Folic acid

    C Turmeric

    D Potassium

7 Which of the following is not a reason why animals such as *Xenopus* are used in observation of neurulation? [1]

    A Embryo is more accessible

    B Eggs are easily manipulated

    C Embryo development is rapid

    D Animals do not feel pain

8 Identify the part of the brain that is responsible for the control of breathing and heart rate. [1]

    A Cerebellum

    B Hypothalamus

    C Medulla oblongata

    D Cerebral hemispheres

9 Identify the function that is carried out by parietal lobe. [1]

    A Regulation of higher intellectual functions and social behaviours

    B Movement, spatial awareness and sense of touch

    C Judges distance and perspective

    D Involved in speech and memory

10 Which of the following are characteristics of rod cells in the eye? [1]

I   Highly sensitive to light
II **Not** present in the fovea
III Less sensitive to light
IV Each cell is connected to its own bipolar cell

A I only
B I and II
C I and III
D I, II and II

11 Which system is responsible for the production of reflex reactions? [1]

A Autonomic nervous system
B Parasympathetic nervous system
C Central nervous system
D Respiratory system

12 Which of the following are not a part of a cochlear implant? [1]

A Processor
B Receiver
C Stimulator
D Auditory nerve

13 Choice chambers were set up to observe taxis and kinesis in woodlice. Which of the following chambers are woodlice most likely to move towards? [1]

A Dark and dry
B Light and dry
C Dark and damp
D Light and damp

14 Identify the example of an excitatory drug from the list below. [1]

A Nicotine
B Ethanol
C Cannabis
D Valium

15 Which of the following diseases can be treated using the stimulant pramipexole? [1]

A Parkinson's
B AIDS
C Diabetes
D Multiple sclerosis

16 **a** Define the term *neural pruning*. [1]
   b Outline the functions of the following parts of the brain.
      i Cerebellum. [1]
      ii Hypothalamus. [1]
   c Explain the effects of psychoactive drugs on synaptic transmission. [3]

17 a Explain the role of innate and learnt behaviour in the development of birdsong in young birds. [4]
    b Outline why it is useful for young birds to develop birdsong. [3]
    c Outline how Lorenz was able to show the effect of imprinting in geese. [5]

18 a Define the term *stimulus*. [1]
    b Draw a labelled diagram of a reflex arc for the pain withdrawal reflex. [7]
    c Describe the different types of receptors that humans use to detect changes in their external environment. [4]

Biotechnology and 13
bioinformatics (Option B)

Chapter outline

In this chapter you will:

- explain how microorganisms can be used and modified to perform industrial processes
- describe how crops can be modified to increase yields and to obtain novel products
- outline how biotechnology can be used in the prevention and mitigation of contamination from industrial, agricultural and municipal wastes
- **HL** outline how biotechnology can be used in the diagnosis and treatment of disease
- **HL** outline how bioinformatics is the use of computers to analyse sequence data in biological research.

KEY TERMS AND DEFINITIONS

Bioinformatics – the use of computers to analyse sequence data in biological research.

Bioremediation – the treatment and removal of pollutants using microorganisms.

HL **Biotechnology** – the use of biological processes for industrial purposes.

HL **Quorum sensing** – the regulation of gene expression in response to an increase in bacterial cell populations.

Exercise B.1 – Microbiology: organisms in industry

1 Citric acid is commonly used as a preservative and for flavouring of food. Citric acid is produced by continuous fermentation by the mould *Aspergillis niger*. Citric acid is produced in a metabolic pathway by growing it using simple sugars.
   a State the metabolic pathway by which citric acid is generated.
   b Outline the ideal conditions that are required for citric acid production.
   c The food industry had to develop large-scale deep tank fermenters to provide the high levels of oxygen required to promote the rapid respiration and growth of *Aspergillis niger*. The fermenters contained large paddles to agitate the mixture. State the main benefit of using the giant paddles.
   d Penicillin is used to treat many types of infections, such as skin infections and ear infections, that are caused by bacteria.

    i   Sketch and label a diagram of a typical bacterial cell. Your diagram should include: flagellum, nucleoid region, 70s ribosomes, cytoplasm, plasma membrane, cell wall and pili.

    ii   State what has developed as a result of the overuse of antibiotics, such as penicillin.

    iii   Antibiotics, such as penicillin, are grown in large fermenters under controlled conditions. Identify the major benefit of using large fermenters in this way.

    iv   Outline the conditions that must be monitored by probes during a fermentation run.

    v   Distinguish between batch fermentation and continuous fermentation. To help you with this, the differences are shown in the table below. Your task is to identify the correct method of production.

A.	B.
Compounds are extracted at the end of the run	Products (and waste) removed during the fermentation process
Process is completed with a fresh addition of microorganisms and nutrients	Nutrients are added into the fermented mixture at a regular, measured rate

Table 13.1

    vi   State a method that can be used to monitor the number of microorganisms being produced in a fermenter.

e The metabolic diversity of microorganisms allows them to survive the diverse range of conditions and factors that they might encounter. Identify the related key words by the descriptions below.

    i   The sum total of all of the chemical reactions that occur within a living organism (anabolic and catabolic).

    ii   Linked reactions where the products of one reaction become the reactants for the following reaction; requires a number of enzymes to catalyse the stages.

    iii   Organisms that receive their energy through chemicals by modifying inorganic molecules.

    iv   Microorganisms that carry out photosynthesis, using light energy from the Sun to create organic compounds.

    v   The chemical process that converts an atmospheric gas molecule to a stable form for use in the metabolic pathways.

f Classification of bacteria is carried out by Gram staining and observing the reaction to see if the bacteria can be classified as Gram-negative or Gram-positive. The cell wall of a Gram-positive bacterium is thicker than that of Gram-negative one, and the difference is easily observed by use of crystal violet.

    i   Distinguish between the cell walls of Gram-positive and Gram-negative bacteria.

ii The procedure for Gram-staining is shown below. List the procedure in the correct order. The bacteria being tested in the hypothetical method below are *Staphylococcus aureus, Mycobacterium tuberculosis* and *Escherichia coli*.
- Final wash with water to remove any unwanted counterstain.
- Wash the slide with 95% alcohol.
- Stain bacteria with crystal violet for 30 seconds.
- Rinse with water, then cover with Gram's iodine to react with the crystal violet.
- Prepare bacterial smear over the heat of a Bunsen burner.
- Counterstain with safranin.

iii State the colour that Gram-negative bacteria will be after the final rinse.

iv State the colour that Gram-positive bacteria will be throughout this process.

v Outline why the colour is **not** removed from the Gram-positive bacteria.

vi *Staphylococcus aureus* and *Mycobacterium tuberculosis* remain a dark blue/purple colour after Gram staining. *Escherichia coli* turns pink after Gram staining. Deduce the classification of *Staphylococcus aureus, Mycobacterium tuberculosis*, and *Escherichia coli*.

2 The idea of serendipity often appears in this book, as well as in the IB syllabus. It seems that many a scientist has experienced good fortune in their quest for knowledge and evidence. The discovery of penicillin is one of the most important medical discoveries and it all started with a messy laboratory! Dr Alexander Fleming noticed that a mould (*Penicillium notatum*) had contaminated his Petri dishes of *Staphylococcus aureus*. The *Penicillium notatum* had somehow prevented the regular growth of the *Staphylococcus aureus*. It took nearly 15 years for the first civilian to be treated with penicillin; without this 'fortunate' contamination, the discovery of antibiotics and the resulting protection against disease might not have happened for many years.

a Define *antibiotic*.

b Outline how antibiotics target bacteria in order to protect the body against disease.

c *Was Dr Fleming's discovery a lucky observation, or do we only perceive what we are 'open to'?* Discuss this statement and compare your view with that of a classmate.

d The mass production of penicillin uses *Penicillium chrysogenum* instead of the *Penicillium notatum* that Fleming first used. Suggest the benefit of using *Penicillium chrysogenum* instead of *Penicillium notatum* for mass production of penicillin.

e In order to ascertain which antibiotic is best for which bacterial infection, it is possible to measure the zone of inhibition. These zones of inhibition were observed by Fleming when he made his initial discovery. You can carry out this lab experiment using antibiotic discs but it is possible to make your own by using disc shapes from a hole puncher. Soaking the discs in different disinfectants or substances (garlic kills some bacteria) should allow you to compare your own zones of inhibition for your own bacterial culture.

i Figure 13.1 shows the zones of inhibition for a range of different antibiotics.

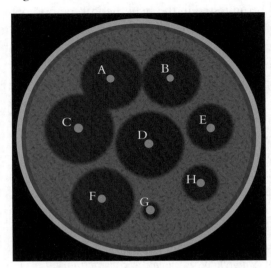

Figure 13.1 Results of an experiment to show the zone of inhibition of bacterial growth for different antibiotics.

Measure the zone of inhibition for the antibiotics labelled A–H. Copy the table below and record your results.

Antibiotic	Diameter of the zone of inhibition (mm)
A	
B	
C	
D	
E	
F	
G	
H	

Table 13.2

ii Identify the antibiotic that is the most effective against this particular bacterium.

iii Identify the antibiotic that is the least effective against this particular bacterium.

Exercise B.2 – Biotechnology in agriculture

1 Almost 85% of the corn grown in the United States is genetically modified. The corn is modified so that it is resistant to a particular herbicide (glyphosate) that usually attacks weeds. Controversially, food producers are not bound to label food as being genetically

modified or not; even though these foods are banned in some countries. Other common examples of genetic modification include:

- Soy: one of the most heavily genetically modified foods and can also reduce the amount of 'bad' cholesterol in the body.
- Zucchini: protects the plant against viruses.
- Tomatoes: genetically modified tomatoes can grow throughout the year to be bigger and juicier.
- Milk: milk in the United States is often modified with a growth hormone, even though this is banned in Europe, Japan and Australia.
- Apples: genetically modified apples have been shown to avoid browning for up to two weeks. Typically, apples will become brown within minutes.

a i Outline how glyphosate affects the growth of crops, such as corn.

ii Figure 13.2 shows how the use of glyphosate affects the resistance of weeds in the same area.

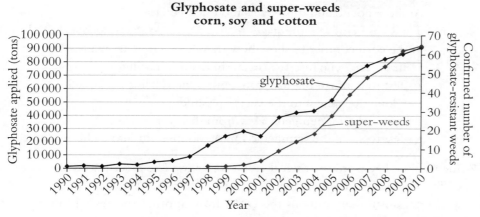

Figure 13.2 The use of glyphosate on corn, soy, and cotton and how glyphosate-resistant weeds respond.

Describe how the resistance of glyphosate changes in Figure 13.2.

iii Usage of other herbicides has reduced, thanks to the use of glyphosate-tolerant plants. Using the evidence from part ii, and the previous statement, comment on whether farmers should continue to use glyphosate on their crops.

b It is very difficult, sometimes impossible, to differentiate between genetically modified food and organic food. Comment on whether this is a good thing or a bad thing for consumers.

c Explain how the delayed browning of apples is beneficial for humans.

d Identify the food in the text above that is genetically modified to overcome environmental resistance and increase crop yields.

e Genetically modified foods are rare in Europe due to political and environmental pressures. The potato is a source of starch for millions of people around the world, with the starch also being used for a range of commercial and industrial purposes. Most potatoes are made up of a combination of amylose and amylopectin. The thickening of amylose is not helpful to many industrial processes because the thickening hinders many of the processes. Amylopectin is difficult to obtain but it does not thicken and is highly desirable for industry. Hence, the Amflora potato was developed as a potato plant that was genetically modified so that the starch in the potato only contained the desired amylopectin. Even though the Amflora potato was not designed for human consumption, it took 13 years to gain approval from the European Commission.

   i   The Amflora potato used an antibiotic-resistance gene to inhibit the production of amylose. Determine the main reasons that the European Commission did not wish to grant approval to the Amflora potato.

  ii   The transfer of antibiotic resistance from the potato back to the bacteria is almost certainly **not** going to happen. Suggest why this encouraged the European Commission to eventually grant approval.

 iii   The European concern about the resistance gene was eventually resolved by the use of biotechnology. Another strain of the potato has been created that does **not** have the resistance gene in any part of the DNA. Distinguish between the Amflora potato and this newly-modified potato.

  iv   The steps below are the stages required in making transgenic crops. List the stages in the correct order to show how transgenic crops are made.

- Insert the gene into the organism that is receiving it.
- Test to confirm that the transgenic gene is being expressed.
- Clone the gene into the vector plasmid.
- Isolate the foreign gene away from the host species.
- Test to see if the transgenic DNA was inserted into a chromosome.

2 Identify the key words by their description below. The descriptions have been kept deliberately vague in some cases to make you think deeply about them.

  a An organism that contains the DNA from another species within its chromosomes.

  b The entire set of proteins in the lifetime of an organism.

  c Herbicide that prevents the synthesis of amino acids in treated plants.

  d Circular DNA molecule that combines foreign DNA into a plasmid and transfers it into the DNA of an organism.

  e Genetically engineered DNA that combines DNA from two different species.

  f Sequence of nucleotides that codes for a protein sequence that will be produced in a transgenic organism.

  g The section of a gene that codes for the protein sequence of the target gene.

  h The chemical structure that is responsible for the colour of a compound.

3 Tobacco is a drug that contribute to the ill health and death of millions of people. However, the tobacco plant has been used to help produce a vaccine for hepatitis B. Hepatitis B is a viral infection that attacks the liver and is responsible for the deaths of millions of people through cirrhosis and liver cancer.

  a State why tobacco plants are ideal for producing vaccines and antibodies.

  b A genetically modified mosaic virus has been used to mass produce a hepatitis B vaccine. Outline how the tobacco mosaic virus was used to make the vaccine for hepatitis B.

Exercise B.3 – Environmental protection

1 Identify the key words that are described by the sentences below.
   a The treatment and removal of pollutants using microorganisms.
   b The regulation of gene expression in response to an increase in bacterial cell populations.
   c New features that emerge when microorganisms associate together.
   d A virus that is capable of infecting bacteria.
   e The use of bacteriophages to target specific bacteria.

2 The Gulf War oil spill of 1991 was one of the largest oil spills in history. The spill was a deliberate war tactic designed to slow the advancement of the enemy. It was estimated that up to $500\,000$ m^3 of oil was spilt and conditions at the time meant that the 60-mile long slick of oil remained in one place. It is estimated that the ongoing clean-up operation has cost well over 200 million US dollars.
   a Suggest the physical remediation methods that might have been employed to prevent further spillage of the oil spill.
   b Outline how an absorbent, such as peat moss, is used to deal with oil slicks.
   c If the chemicals of a spill do **not** dissolve in water, then chemical remediation may be required. Outline the main types of chemical remediation that can be used to treat chemical spills.
   d Bioremediation is an effective method of treating chemical and oil spills. Some microorganisms are capable of metabolising oil and, if the population is large enough, the microorganisms can make considerable progress into the clean-up. Outline how a clean-up company can facilitate the increase of an oil-eating microorganism population.
   e Oil spills contain hydrocarbon molecules that can be broken down by a wide range of enzymes. One bacteria, in particular, is capable pf producing these enzymes to break down the petroleum products.
      i State the name of the bacterium that is an excellent microbe for bioremediation.
      ii Explain the main advantage of using these bacteria for bioremediation.
      iii Describe the method required to increase the population of the bacteria, in the event of an oil spill.
      iv Suggest how the bacteria obtain the energy required for reproduction and metabolism of the oil spill.
      v The bacteria are versatile enough to clean up other pollutants, too. Mercury compounds are incredibly toxic; due to the complex chemical imitation that it exhibits, the mercury compounds can be very dangerous to plants, pond life, and humans as it is passed along the food chain. Outline how the bacteria named in part i are able to carry out bioremediation to break down the mercury compounds.

3 Quorum sensing allows cell-to-cell communication between bacteria when there are enough of them to actually constitute a quorum.
   a State the mechanism that allows bacteria to detect the chemical signals of other bacteria that are close by.
   b Quorum sensing aids the control of symbiosis, spore production, ability to infect other organisms, cell aggregation, and the formation of biofilms. Define *biofilms*.

c Quorum sensing allows dangerous pathogens to communicate and can lead to a coordinated attack on the human body. Dental plaque is just one example of how biofilms cane be problematic. Dental plaque consists of a complex array of microorganisms, including a multitude of bacterial and fungal species. Suggest some other problems that may be caused by biofilms.

d The emergent properties of communicating bacteria are different to those of the individual bacteria that work together. Identify the advantages to the bacteria of the biofilm formation and the associated emergent properties.

e The matrix that forms as part of a biofilm can be inhibitory to the drugs that are prescribed to combat certain infections. Describe the main emergent properties of biofilms that make them so difficult to target and treat.

f A biofilm that is on the inside of a water pipe should **not** be removed by use of antibiotics. Deduce why using antibiotics should not be used on biofilms in this sort of example.

g Suggest what damage might be caused by the presence of biofilms on water pipes and other similar surfaces.

h Viruses are able to infect bacteria to resolve the problem of biofilms. The success rate of combining bacteriophages with chlorine is very high. The T4 bacteriophage is one such example of a virus that is able to destroy bacteria by attacking it from inside the biofilm. State the name of the bacteria that is targeted by the T4 bacteriophage.

HL Exercise B.4 – Medicine

1 Identify the key words described by the sentences below.
   a Small molecules that are formed during metabolism.
   b Metabolites that are essential for growth and reproduction.
   c Molecules that are used for specialised functions.
   d Segment of DNA that is in close proximity to a specific genetic disease allele.
   e The sequence differences in the DNA code that makes each genome unique.
   f Substances that stimulate the production of antibodies and bind with the antibodies.
   g When a pathogen infects many people in a local area.
   h When a pathogen infects people worldwide
   i All of the messenger RNA molecules expressed by an organism.
   j The use of DNA to treat diseases that are caused by a missing or dysfunctional protein.

2 Developments in scientific research follow improvements in technology, and innovation in technology has allowed scientists to diagnose and treat diseases. Many years ago, doctors simply had their experience, a few reference books, and the symptoms presented to them to determine how best to treat their patients. The spread of infectious diseases was difficult to control because diagnosis was slow, and communication between communities even slower. The traditional methods of analysis have previously been:
   • Microscopic analysis to observe parasitic infections.
   • Urine samples, and swabs from infected areas, were used to identify bacterial infections and observe their growth. This would take time to gain results, by which point the disease might have spread far and wide.
   • Clinical observation has allowed for diagnosis of genetic diseases, sometimes coupled with detection of metabolites in blood samples.

The recent advances in medical biotechnology allow the problems outlined above to be diagnosed more accurately and with a much greater reliability.

a Infections by a pathogen can now be detected by the presence of its genetic material or by its antigens. An ELISA test is able to detect the presence of antibodies to pathogens. State the full name of the ELISA test.

b Identify one of the issues with the use of the ELISA test.

c An ELISA test is carried out on a patient suspected of carrying the HIV virus. The array shows that the colour for a positive test remains. Analyse the results to determine whether the person has contracted the HIV virus.

d Advances in technology make the world a safer place. Comment on this statement, basing your judgement on the content of this chapter so far.

e Genetic markers can be used to identify the predisposition to a genetic disease of an individual. Comparison of the genetic markers in many people allows for diseases to be linked to specific markers. List the useful functions that genetic markers have.

f PCR can be used to detect genetic markers. State the full name of PCR.

g List the components required for PCR to take place.

h The influenza virus (flu virus) is tracked by PCR. The virus rapidly evolves and must be carefully monitored to prevent sudden epidemics from becoming pandemics. State the molecule that the influenza virus lacks, meaning that it can only be tracked by its RNA sequences.

3 Diseases can be indicated by metabolites found in samples of urine and blood.

a Copy and complete the table below to show the names of common diseases that can be detected in blood and urine. The possible diseases are listed below for you to choose from (you may have to research them if you have not covered them in class).
  • Phenylketonuria (PKU).
  • Hepatitis B.
  • Zellweger syndrome.
  • HIV.
  • Alkaptonuria.
  • Lesch–Nyhan syndrome.

Disease	Metabolite detected	Metabolite pathway
	Elevated levels of phenylpyruvate	Absence of phenylalanine hydroxylase enzyme
	Uric acid crystals detected in the urine	Purine production
	Long fatty acid chains detected in the blood	Peroxisome assembly
	High levels of homogentisic acid detected in urine and blood	Breakdown of tyrosine

Table 13.3

b Suggest how a baby diagnosed with phenylketonuria can be treated in order to avoid the severe intellectual disabilities that may occur.

c Deduce whether phenylalanine is a primary metabolite, or a secondary metabolite.

d Newborn babies are tested by using a blood test to detect the levels of phenylketonuria. Explain why it is important that this test is carried out on newborn babies, rather than waiting until the child is older.

4 Biopharming uses genetically modified animals and plants to produce proteins for therapeutic use. Production of insulin and human growth hormone have been achieved through the use of genetically modified bacteria. However, the production of more complex proteins is more difficult. The post-translational modifications required to make certain proteins work properly are not achievable by using bacteria. However, the proteins can be produced in transgenic animals and plants to ensure that the post–translational modifications take place. Antithrombin cannot be produced in bacteria as complex sugar chains are required to be made.

    a Outline the function of antithrombin.

    b State the risk that an antithrombin deficiency carries.

    c Describe how biopharming of antithrombin takes place in order to produce large quantities of the protein.

🄷🄻 Exercise B.5 – Bioinformatics

1 Identify the key words described by the sentences below.

    a The use of computers to analyse sequence data in biological research.

    b Collections of biological sequencing information, organised for rapid access and analysis.

    c Short, partial version of a cDNA sequence.

    d Species that is widely studied and is believed to have genetic similarities with other organisms.

    e The study of evolutionary relationships between genetic information and groups of organisms.

    f A phylogenetic tree diagram with branches of equal length.

2 Databases store information in an orderly fashion and make a search for patterns and trends easier. This allows for genes to be mapped and relationships between organisms to be determined. Databases can help with the tracking of epidemics in order to prevent pandemics.

    a Outline how the body of data in databases is increasing.

    b Explain why the body of data in databases is increasing at such a rate.

    c Collaboration between scientists is essential to the development of databases and the spirit of scientific discovery. *The commercialisation of bioinformatics databases is going to enhance worldwide discovery and collaboration.* Comment on this statement.

    d State the name of the search tool that allows for the identification of similar sequences in different organisms.

    e State the name of any of the major nucleotide or protein databases.

    f Compare and contrast a BLASTn search and a BLASTp search.

    g A researcher has determined a sequence of unknown function.

        i Outline the next stage that the researcher can carry out to find out more about the unknown sequence.

        ii The researcher has a protein sequence. Suggest which type of search he should carry out.

        iii Predict what the researcher might be able to determine by searching other databases to search for a match for his unknown sequence.

    h Expressed tag sequences (ESTs) are used to identify the exon regions of DNA as part of gene discovery techniques.

        i Outline the advantages of using ESTs.

        ii State the name of the enzyme that is used to produce cDNA.

3   Model organisms are used to help scientists observe how some human functions
     occur. Some examples are listed below.
     •   Yeast (*Saccharomyces cerevisiae*)
     •   Western clawed frog (*Xenopus tropicalis*)
     •   Zebrafish (*Danio rerio*)
     •   Fruit fly (*Drosophila melanogaster*)
     •   Soil roundworm (*Caenorhabditis elegans*)
     •   House mouse (*Mus musculus*)
     •   *Escherichia coli*
     •   Thale cress (*Arabidopsis thaliana*)
     a   Describe some of the features that make model organisms, such as the ones
         listed above, ideal for being model organisms.
     b   Some studies on model organisms take place *in vivo*. Explain why model
         organisms are used instead of humans for such experiments.
     c   Using your knowledge from other chapters, identify the studies that have
         been carried out on the following model organisms.
         i   Western clawed frog (*Xenopus tropicalis*)
         ii   Fruit fly (*Drosophila melanogaster*)
         iii   Yeast (*Saccharomyces cerevisiae*)

? Exam-style questions

1   **Metabolism is the sum total of which type of reactions that occur in a living
    organism? [1]**
    A   Chemical
    B   Physical
    C   Mitochondrial
    D   Metabolic

2   **Organisms that gain energy through chemicals by modifying inorganic molecules
    are known as which group? [1]**
    A   Chemoautotrophs
    B   Photoautotrophs
    C   Heterotrophs
    D   Bacteria

3   **Which of the following does not need to be monitored during fermentation? [1]**
    A   pH
    B   Substrate levels
    C   Oxygen levels
    D   Nitrogen levels

4 Identify the type of fermentation that removes products during the fermentation process, as and when they are ready. [1]

    A Fermentation

    B Batch fermentation

    C Continuous fermentation

    D Inoculation

5 Determine which of the following microorganisms grows best at room temperature. [1]

    A Pyschrophiles

    B Mesophiles

    C Thermophiles

    D Hyperthermophiles

6 Identify the condition that is essential for the production of biogas. [1]

    A Large surface area

    B High levels of oxygen

    C Oxygen not present

    D High levels of carbon dioxide

7 Identify the substance that is widely used today as a preservative. It is fermented by the mould *Aspergillis niger*. [1]

    A Soap

    B Citric acid

    C Toothpaste

    D Ethanoic acid

8 Identify the key word that refers to the entire set of proteins of an organism. [1]

    A Genome

    B Proteome

    C Progenome

    D Recombinant DNA

9 Glyphosate-tolerant crops have a range of positive and negative impacts. From the list below, identify the positive impact of glyphosate-tolerant crops. [1]

    A Leads to reduced use of herbicides by farmers on their soils

    B Nitrogen-fixing is inhibited by the harming of nitrogen-fixing bacteria

    C Glyphosate-tolerant crops may become weeds themselves

    D Glyphosate-tolerant crops are too expensive to be grown by some farmers

10 The target gene is ligated into which plasmid during *Agrobacterium* transformation? [1]

    A Ti

    B Pi

    C Ai

    D T4

11 **Which of the following is** not **a physical method of remediation? [1]**
    A Skimming
    B Washing
    C Vapour extraction
    D Solvent extraction

12 **Which of the following is a highly versatile bacterium that is ideal for bioremediation? [1]**
    A *Lactobacillus casei*
    B *Enterococcus durans*
    C *Actinomyces israelii*
    D *Pseudomonas*

13 **Reverse transcriptase is commonly used in biotechnology.**
    a State the function of reverse transcriptase in biotechnology. [1]
    b Outline the main uses of reverse transcriptase in biotechnology. [3]
    c Outline the uses of a named bacteria in bioremediation. [5]

14 Ecology and conservation (Option C)

Chapter outline

In this chapter you will:

- explain why community structure is an emergent property of an ecosystem
- outline the human activities that impact on ecosystem function
- describe how entire communities need to be conserved in order to protect biodiversity
- **HL** outline the dynamic biological processes that impact on population density and population growth
- **HL** explain how soil cycles are subject to disruption.

KEY TERMS AND DEFINITIONS

Biodiversity – the range and variety of plant and animal life in a particular habitat.

Community – group of populations living and interacting with each other.

Ecosystem – a community and its abiotic environment.

HL **Population** – a group of organisms of the same species that live in the same area at the same time.

Species – group of individuals that can interbreed and produce fertile offspring.

Exercise C.1 – Species and communities

1 The relationship between *Zooxanthellae* and reef-building coral reef species is mutualistic, or symbiotic. *Zooxanthellae* is photosynthetic algae, and lives in the tissues of the corals.

  a Outline what it means if two organisms have a symbiotic relationship.
  b Describe how *Zooxanthellae* and the corals have a symbiotic relationship.
  c Explain why it is beneficial for the *Zooxanthellae* to have this relationship with the corals.
  d State the word and chemical equations for photosynthesis.
  e Determine the useful compounds that are provided by *Zooxanthellae* to the corals.

2 State the key terms described by the following descriptions (some of these are to remind you of what was studied in Chapters 4 and 5):

a A factor that is less available than the amount required by an organism.

b Group of populations living and interacting with each other.

c Group of organisms of the same species, living in an area at the same time.

d Group of individuals that can interbreed and produce fertile offspring.

e A community and its abiotic environment.

f How a species obtains its food.

g The sum total of a species' use of the abiotic and biotic resources in the environment.

h Where a species lives in its ecosystem.

i A species that has an overly strong effect on a community but without being very large in terms of population numbers.

j The interaction between organisms in which both are adversely affected.

k Interaction between primary consumer and producer.

l Interaction between living organisms where one of them is caught, killed and eaten by another.

m Interaction where both species benefit.

n Interaction between two organisms where one benefits but the other neither benefits nor is harmed.

3 a The table below lists some of the limiting factors that affect plants. Determine the limiting factors being described in each example.

Limiting factor	Example
i	Carrots grow best at around 20 °C.
ii	Some trees need hundreds of litres of water per day.
iii	The tea plant grows best in a soil of around pH 5.5.
iv	Some plants grow away from light in order to locate other materials.
v	Species that grow in mangroves are able to survive in water that is twice as saline as seawater.
vi	Plants require potassium, nitrogen and phosphorus for healthy growth.

Table 14.1

b The table below lists some of the limiting factors that affect animals. Deduce the limiting factors being described in each example.

Limiting factor	Example
i	Some animals can survive extreme highs or lows, as low as -50 °C, or as high as 50 °C.
ii	Large animals require large amounts of this in order to rehydrate.
iii	Some species only eat one, or two, different types of food. These species need to live in an area with a good supply of their prey.
iv	Pacific salmon return to their birthplace in order to reproduce.
v	Some animals occupy an area between a few km^2, right up to hundreds of thousands of km^2.
vi	Some species can survive in areas with extremely high levels of salts dissolved in water.

Table 14.2

c One organism has evolved over thousands of years to adapt to its environment. The organism has a very thick layer of fur and insulating fat to survive in temperatures as low as –40 °C. The metabolism of this Arctic creature allows it to break down stored fats to access water reserves, rather than trying to find water in their hostile surroundings. After breeding on sea ice, these large animals will dig dens where they can, depending on their habitat and conditions. The size of their territory can vary as ice caps may break off or melt. One of their favourite foods/prey are seals because they get a relatively large energy yield from such a large animal.

    i Deduce the species of animal that is described in the passage above.

    ii Identify the limiting factors that are outlined in the passage.

d Your teacher, Mr Lee, takes you to the Arctic for a biology field trip. While you are there, he wants you to correlate the distribution of the polar bears with an abiotic variable.

    i Suggest the possible transects that you could choose for your investigation.

    ii Design the method that you might follow to gather data about the distribution of polar bears with an abiotic factor of your choice.

    iii Suggest some biotic factors that might affect the distribution of polar bears in the area of the Arctic that you are sampling.

    iv On your trip, you learn about some examples of symbiotic relationships. State **three** examples of symbiotic relationships.

4 Keystone species are essential to their ecosystem and their numbers can dramatically affect the overall ecosystem. The mountain lion of Canada is capable of roaming hundreds of kilometres and regularly interacts with other animals, such as deer, rabbits and birds.

  a Define *keystone species*.

  b Suggest how the feeding behaviours of the deer and the rabbit might be controlled by the mountain lion.

  c Predict what might happen in the absence of the mountain lion.

d The theory of keystone species was first established by Robert Paine in 1969. Paine showed that the removal of one species had a major effect on the ecosystem. He did this by removing the sea star (*Pisaster ochraceus*) from a tidal plain on Tatoosh Island in Washington, US. The sea star is a predator of the mussel in this ecosystem.

   i Predict what happened to the population of mussels after the removal of the sea star.

   ii Explain why the population of the mussel changed in this way.

   iii Suggest what happened to all other species in the ecosystem after the removal of the sea star.

   iv Deduce the keystone species in this ecosystem.

Exercise C.2 – Communities and ecosystems

1 a Construct a food web based on the information below. (Warning: this could get quite complex, so it is best to lightly use a pencil so that you can make changes and corrections.)

> An ecosystem has three main producers: carrots, grasses and grains. The grasses are consumed by rabbits and grasshoppers but the rabbit also eats the carrots. The grasshoppers eat the grains and are consumed by owls and birds. Birds also eat the grains and are often consumed by foxes. Mice eat the grains and are eaten by owls. The fox is one of the top consumers and is also responsible for eating rabbits.

b Sketch **one** food chain from the food web in part a.

c Compare and contrast food chains and food webs. 'Compare and contrast' questions are ideal for a table to show the similarities and differences between them.

d Outline what the arrows in the food web and food chains shows.

e Determine the trophic level of the owl in this food web.

f Suggest reasons why different organisms might occupy different trophic levels.

g 80-90% of the energy is **not** passed on through each trophic level. Explain what happens to the energy that is not passed on from one trophic level to another.

h Identify which animal(s) in the food web are both a primary consumer and a secondary consumer.

i Identify the groups of organisms described by the following descriptions.

   i Produces complex organic compounds by using light energy.

   ii Obtains organic molecules from other organisms.

2 Pyramids of energy show the amount of energy that is passed through a food chain.

a State a typical unit for pyramids of energy.

b Draw and label a pyramid of energy for the following food chain:

     clover → snail → thrush → sparrow hawk
     The clover takes in 1 000 000 J of energy from sunlight.

3 Analysis of a Whittaker climograph that shows the relationship between temperature, rainfall and ecosystem type is required for the following exercise. The climograph was first devised by Robert Whittaker and shows the types of ecosystem that are most likely to emerge in the climactic conditions shown. You are expected to be able to analyse the relationship between the temperature, rainfall and ecosystem type. Use Figure 14.1 to answer the questions that follow.

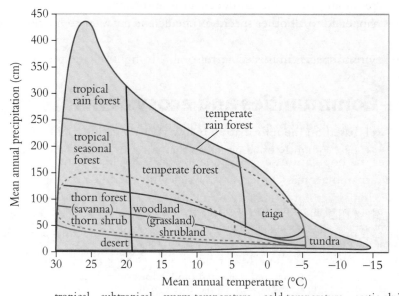

Figure 14.1 A climograph.

a Determine the types of ecosystem that can exist with a mean annual precipitation of 250 cm.
b Determine the range of conditions that a tundra is likely to form under.
c Determine the ecosystems that are likely to form above temperatures of 20 °C.
d State the factors that the climate of a region might be influenced by.

Exercise C.3 – Impacts of humans on ecosystems

1 Human activity sometimes involves the introduction of alien species into an area or ecosystem. One of the most famous examples of alien species is the introduction of the cane toad (*Rhinella marina*) to Australia. The toads originated from Central America and South America, before ending up in Puerto Rico and Hawaii. A total of 101 cane toads were brought to Australia to combat the damage caused by cane beetles to the sugar crops of Queensland. This protection of the cane crop explains how the cane toad got its name. However, the destruction of the cane beetle never really happened and, instead, the cane toad began to affect other species and organisms. Many species of crocodile and turtles were adversely affected and the cane toads have now killed entire populations of some species. Cane toads are notorious for being prolific breeders as their females lay up to 35 000 eggs at a time – that is an immense number. Such was the speed of their migration, that they spread rapidly; up to 70 000 eggs a year were laid and cane toads spread all the way down the coast of Australia. This happened at a rate of up to 10 km a year at first but soon increased rapidly to over 50 km per year.

a Define *alien species*.

b Suggest why the increase in population of an alien species might be an issue.

c Suggest why alien species are sometimes introduced to an ecosystem.

d Explain what is meant by an endemic species.

e Outline the evidence that biologists could use to determine the origin of the cane toad.

f The cane toads were introduced to Australia in the 1930s; suggest why they were preferred to other methods that might have been around at the time.

g Analyse why the cane toads were able to spread so rapidly and grow in such large numbers.

h Explain why the cane toad is so dangerous and also, able to fight off any predators that it might come across.

2 *Anoplolepis gracilipes* (crazy ant) is easily spotted by its chaotic movement patterns. The crazy ant has invaded many ecosystems from Hawaii to the Seychelles. On Christmas Island, they have even formed multi-queen super-colonies that are able to affect the populations of the red land crab, as well as many arthropods, birds and mammals that come into contact with them. Crazy ants cannot survive in extremely cold temperatures and are dangerous because of their ability to protect against the venom of their predators. Recent studies have shown that the crazy ant has a protective acid sheath. Quite remarkably, crazy ants are even able to short-circuit electrical systems as they take shelter in fuse boxes and electrical power devices.

a Determine how the ant is able to protect itself against possible predators.

b Identify the groups of organisms that are affected by the crazy ant.

c The protective mechanism of the crazy ant also doubles as a weapon. Predict how the crazy ant might do this.

d The crazy ant typically targets spiders and centipedes. Suggest how this might affect other parts of the food chains and food webs of this ecosystem.

e Outline how crazy ants are able to affect the activity of humans.

f The crazy ant is not capable of travelling very far; usually less than 100 metres or so in one year. Suggest how crazy ants are able to spread as far and as wide as they do.

3 Sometimes, the introduction of an alien species might not be purposely carried out by humans. The brown tree snake (*Boiga irregularis*) was accidentally introduced to Guam by the US military and almost caused the extinction of some of the island's endemic species. The brown tree snake removed many of the native pollinators of the island, a factor that had a serious effect on plant life on the island. The brown tree snake uses its mild venom to immobilise its prey, which can include everything on the island from birds, rats, mice and lizards. In the natural habitat of the brown tree snake, the population is kept under control by disease, competition for food, and predators.

a Suggest how the destruction of pollinators affected the plant life of the island.

b Identify the limiting factors of the brown tree snake in its natural habitat.

c Outline why these limiting factors do **not** keep the population of the brown tree snake under control in Guam.

4 Read this shocking article about the Laysan albatross and answer the questions that follow.

> ### Laysan Albatrosses Dying in the Pacific!
>
> Think about that bottle cap you just threw away, that toothbrush you no longer use, or maybe the hundreds of plastic carrier bags that you and your family use each year. Where does this plastic go? Much of this land litter actually ends up in the seas and oceans; and here it becomes one of the biggest, and most dangerous, killers of marine life. A recent study has found that 97.5% of Laysan chicks had plastic in their stomachs, including items such as cigarette lighters, pens and buttons. It is estimated that up to 1 000 000 seabirds die each year from eating plastic.

a Distinguish between macroplastic and microplastic debris.

b The North Pacific Gyre is largely responsible for the transportation of large volumes of plastic. Outline what a 'gyre' is.

c The degradation of plastic in the oceans can release chemicals into the water that may bioaccumulate and biomagnify. Outline the processes of bioaccumulation and biomagnification.

d DDT (Dichlorodiphenyltrichloroethane) is often accumulated in living organisms by bioaccumulation. DDT was originally introduced as an insecticide in World War II to control the spread of malaria. These programmes were successful as malaria was eradicated from Europe and the USA. However, studies in the 1960s showed that DDT was linked to cancers and declines in certain species of birds, leading to many bans on the use of DDT. In future years, evidence would be provided that DDT was **not** actually carcinogenic and might not have been responsible for the decline in bird populations. Use of DDT was discontinued in the Kwa Zulu region of South Africa from 1991 to 2000. Figure 14.2 shows the number of malaria cases in the Kwa Zulu region of South Africa between 1971 and 2003.

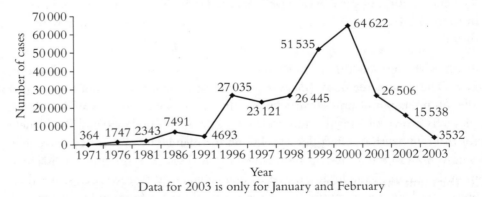

Figure 14.2 Malaria cases in the Kwa Zulu region of South Africa.

   i *It was the right decision to ban the use of DDT in the 1960s.* Evaluate this statement.

   ii Describe how the number of malaria cases changed between 1971 and 2003.

   iii Analyse the data shown in Figure 14.2.

e Design a plan that will help protect birds like the Laysan albatross from the dangers of macroplastics and microplastics.

Exercise C.4 – Conservation and biodiversity

1 Carrying out captive breeding is **not** an easy task to complete successfully, as low conception rates and problems with adapting behaviour lead to poor survival rates. However, many species have been bred very successfully and the success rates are very high in controlled conditions. Read the case studies that follow and answer the questions.

a

The Peregrine Falcon: Peregrine falcons often live a full life as they have few natural threats to their survival. The activity of humans was the greatest threat as humans hunted, destroyed eggs and ruined habitats. As the use of DDT increased, the numbers of falcons decreased; DDT is known to thin the eggs of birds. Eventually, DDT was banned from use in America, at a time when the Peregrine Recovery Plan was being implemented. Chicks were hatched in captivity and then released into the wild, gradually.

i Explain why the introduction of DDT led to a decrease in the number of peregrine falcons.

ii Identify the greatest threat to the number of peregrine falcons.

iii Describe how the numbers of peregrine falcons were increased.

iv The peregrine falcon was eventually removed from the endangered list. Suggest what humans can do in order to keep them off this list.

b

The Bald Eagle: The American Eagle Foundation (AEF) leads the way in the captive breeding of the golden eagle, having released nearly 150 eaglets in the past 20 years. The AEF does this by the translocation of wild eggs and the gradual release of offspring back into the wild. Only those eggs that are likely to produce fertile offspring are used, and the healthiest offspring are selected for release into the wild. The eggs that hatch are fed and monitored by humans wearing special camouflage clothing for the first few days before release into the wild.

i Outline the methods that the AEF uses to ensure that as many bald eagles as possible are produced.

ii Identify how the AEF enhances the survival rate of released eaglets.

iii Some people argue that endangered species are less likely to survive in the wild as they do not have the appropriate behaviours to survive. Based on the evidence and the work of the AEF, comment on this statement.

c

The Giant Panda: Possibly one of the most famous examples of captive breeding are the highly-publicised programmes across the world to maintain the giant panda population. Pandas in the wild have a very low birth rate and breeding began in China in the 1950s. It took eight years for the first ever giant panda, Ming Ming, to be born in captivity as part of a captive breeding programme. Development of programmes, coupled with extensive knowledge of mating cycles and panda behaviours has contributed to more regular success in modern times.

i Pandas have one estrus cycle per year and are usually fertile for between 24 to 36 hours. Discuss the implications of this to the panda breeding programmes.

ii Artificial insemination is often used to increase the chances of successful fertilisation. Discuss whether artificial insemination should be used like this.

iii In the 1960s, only 30% of panda cubs would survive but the figure is now closer to 90%. Suggest why there has been such a marked increase in the past 50 years.

iv Housing, and caring for, a giant panda costs around $2.6 million a year. The production of offspring raises this total to over $3 million a year. The online panda camera at Washington Zoo receives over 2 million hits a month, and visits increased by 50% during the first few months of giant pandas being at the zoo. Fewer than 2000 pandas are now found in China, with a couple of hundred distributed around the world. Evaluate whether zoos should continue with captive breeding programmes.

v One panda, Xiang Xiang, failed to survive upon release into the wild and it was believed that he died after struggling with other giant pandas. In 2014, Xue Xue was released but did not survive for more than a year. Both of Xue Xue's parents were bred in captivity. Suggest why these pandas, like many other endangered species, failed to survive after release into the wild.

d

> **Primates:** Nearly 75% of primate species, such as gorillas and gibbons, are in decline and as many as 60% are facing the possibility of extinction. Many primate species are quite specialised and are not flexible enough to adapt to their ever-changing environment. Many primates are hunted for their meat and, in some parts of the world, primate organs are transported as they are believed to have special healing powers. There is destruction of their natural habitat as cattle ranches, soybean fields, and palm oil plantations are built in their place. The consequences are much wider than just for the primates themselves. Some primates carry pollen between trees and any seeds in their droppings are distributed widely.

i Outline why it is **not** just the primates themselves that might suffer from dwindling numbers.

ii Construct a plan for local communities to help the primates.

iii Explain how scientists are able to identify new species of primate and how they can be linked to other species in other areas.

e Evaluate whether captive breeding programmes are worthwhile.

2 a State why biological diversity is important within an ecosystem.

b Define *indicator species*.

c Outline an example of an indicator species that you have studied.

d Define *biotic index*.

e Give an example of an abiotic factor.

f Compare and contrast in-situ conservation and ex-situ conservation.

HL Exercise C.5 – Population ecology

1 A group of scientists wish to determine the population size of a species in a particular area. The team decide that their two options are to count every single organism, or to count a sample and use this to estimate the total number.

  a Define *population*.

  b Sketch and label a graph to show how the population of humans has grown exponentially in recent years.

  c Identify the different types of sampling described in the table below.

Method of sampling	Description
	Grid mapped out, random grid points selected, and sampling carried out as close to the points chosen as possible.
	One transect line rolled out and regular interval samples taken.
	Two transect lines rolled out and species counted and recorded in each section.
	Study area mapped out, random squares used to count and record number of species.
	Within a certain area, a part of the population is captured, marked and released. This is repeated after a certain time interval and the population is estimated using the Lincoln Index.

Table 14.3

  d 200 birds are captured, marked and released. A few weeks later, 140 unmarked birds and 60 marked birds are captured.

    i Use the Lincoln Index to estimate the total population of birds in the area.

    ii The experiment was repeated, but this time 485 frogs were captured, marked and released. The second capture found 28 marked frogs and 43 unmarked frogs. Estimate the total population of frogs in the area.

    iii Outline the limitations of the capture, mark, release technique.

2 Not only are fish an important protein source for millions of people, but they are a significant part of the economy and linked to nearly 2 million jobs in the US economy alone. The National Oceanic and Atmospheric Administration (NOAA) analyses the trends in population sizes of different fish by using the following methods:

- Catch data – counting the number of fish caught by fishing.
- Abundance data – a measure of the mass of the fish.
- Biology data – information on the growth rates and mortality rates of the fish.

  a Outline how overfishing and underfishing threaten the long-term populations of the marine environment.

  b Explain how the NOAA could encourage sustainable fishing.

  c The NOAA carry out a survey and discover that the mean age of the fish in a particular area is very low. Predict what the impact will be on the sustainable fishing in this area.

  d The NOAA survey also determines that the reproductive status of the fish is low. Estimate how this will affect the population growth and the sustainable yield.

  e Determine the headings for the table below. The table shows information about the sampling methods used to monitor fish stocks.

Echo sounders	Sound pulses transmitted into water, producing a 3D image that measures the time interval between emission and the return of the pulse. The image is used to estimate the size of fish shoals.	Can only be used for shoals of fish, or areas where many fish are close to each other. Does not measure individual fish.
Fish catches	Using fish caught, the age profile of the fish can be estimated and used to estimate population size.	Bias in the estimate occurs as poor reporting of fish occurs, or if restricted fish are dumped.

Table 14.4

3 Figure 14.3 shows the growth curve for *Lemna*, a free-flowing aquatic plant. Answer the questions that follow.

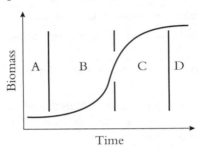

Figure 14.3 The growth curve for *Lemna*.

  a Identify the phase in part A of Figure 14.3.
  b Identify the phase in part B of Figure 14.3.
  c Identify the phase in part C of Figure 14.3.
  d Identify the phase in part D of Figure 14.3.
  e State the **four** factors that influence human population phases.
  f Determine which of the following scenarios will lead to the largest increase in human populations.
    A Natality and immigration < emigration and mortality.
    B Natality and mortality = emigration and immigration.
    C Natality and mortality > mortality and emigration.
    D Natality and immigration > mortality and emigration.
  g Explain why you chose your answer to part f for the largest increase in population.

🆅🅻 Exercise C.6 – Nitrogen and phosphorus cycles

1 Nitrogen is highly abundant in our atmosphere and is a vital building block for many proteins and cell structures.
  a Suggest why nitrogen must be converted to other compounds in order for it become accessible to plants and animals.
  b Identify the bacteria that helps to make nitrogen more accessible to plants.
  c State the word equation for the conversion of nitrogen in the air, with hydrogen, into ammonia.

d *Rhizobium* is **not** a free-living bacteria and associates with roots in a mutualistic relationship.

    i   Define *mutualistic relationship*.

    ii   Describe the mutualistic relationship between *Rhizobium* and the roots of the plants.

    iii State the term that describes the conversion of gaseous nitrogen into ammonia.

e State the other **two** nitrogen compounds that a plant is able to take in, other than ammonia.

2 a List the following stages of the nitrogen cycle in the correct order. As this is a cycle, you may start at any place as long as you get them all in the correct order.

- Plants take in ammonia and compounds by their roots.
- Ammonia and water form ammonium (NH_4^+).
- Plants convert the ammonia into nitrogen compounds.
- Nitrogen compounds are passed along the food chains to consumers.
- Saprotrophs return nitrogen to the soil as ammonia, via ammonification.
- Ammonia compounds broken down to nitrites, and then nitrates, by nitrifying bacteria, during nitrification.
- Nitrogen-fixing bacteria convert nitrogen in the atmosphere into ammonia and other ammonium compounds.
- Plants and animals die.
- Nitrates can then be taken up by plants.

b Saprotrophs break down dead plants and animals. State an example of a saprotroph.

c Define *ammonification*.

d Deduce the product formed in the following equation:

        ammonia + water $\rightarrow$ ....

e Define *nitrification*.

f Nitrates are sometimes broken down by denitrifying bacteria to form atmospheric nitrogen. State the name of this process.

g Draw and label a diagram of the nitrogen cycle, using the information from this exercise.

3 The phosphorus cycle can be influenced by the application of fertiliser, or by the harvesting of agricultural crops.

a Deduce what will happen to the levels of phosphorus as a result of:

    i   Harvesting of crops.

    ii   Addition of fertiliser.

b List the following stages of the phosphorus cycle in the correct order.

- Phosphorus found in marine sediments and mineral deposits (within phosphorite).
- Weathering of rocks releases phosphate ions into the soil and water.
- Phosphate ions and minerals taken up by plants.
- Plants consumed by animals and the phosphate is reused in molecules such as DNA.
- Plants and animals die.
- Decay of plants and animals releases phosphates back into the soil.
- Phosphates can now be taken up by plants.

c Identify the event described: *Phosphorus in the soil can be washed into waterways, rivers and oceans, causing it to be stored there for many years before returning to the cycle.*

? Exam-style questions

1 Which of the statements below, A–D, correctly describes interactions between organisms? [1]
   I   Predator-prey
   II   Herbivory
   III Mutualism
   IV   Parasitism
   A   I only
   B   I and II
   C   I, II and II
   D   I, II, III and IV

2 Identify the type of relationship that exists between a mosquito and a human being. [1]
   A   Predator-prey
   B   Herbivory
   C   Mutualism
   D   Parasitism

3 Identify the term that describes where a species lives in the ecosystem. [1]
   A   Spatial habitat
   B   Mutualism
   C   Ecosystem
   D   Ecological niche

4 Two species occupy fully overlapping niches. Which species will most likely become extinct from that environment? [1]
   A   The species that has the greater selective advantage
   B   The species that was there first
   C   The species that has the lesser selective advantage
   D   The bigger (or faster) species

5 Figure 14.4 shows a pyramid of numbers for a particular ecosystem. Deduce which level of the pyramid would represent a tree. [1]

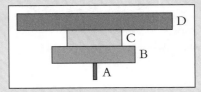

Figure 14.4 A pyramid of numbers.

   A   A
   B   B
   C   C
   D   D

6 **What does the arrow in a food chain show to the person looking at it? [1]**
   A   The direction of energy flow
   B   The direction of mass increase
   C   How the energy is lost at each level
   D   Who eats who

7 **Which of the following is the correct definition for biomass? [1]**
   A   The total energy of an organism
   B   The total mass consumed at each trophic level
   C   The number of organisms that have organic matter
   D   The total dry mass of organic matter

8 **Figure 14.5 shows a Whittaker climograph. Determine which ecosystem would be suited to a mean precipitation between 200 cm and 250 cm; and a mean temperature of above 20 °C. [1]**

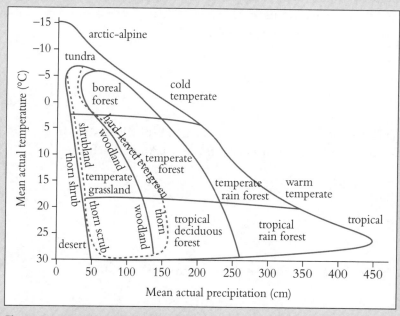

Figure 14.5 A Whittaker climograph.

   A   Temperate rainforest
   B   Tropical deciduous forest
   C   Tropical rainforest
   D   Tundra

9 **Identify the method that is not used to control alien species, such as the cane toad. [1]**
   A   Using predators or disease organisms to exert biological control.
   B   Removal of plants, or the trapping and destruction of animals as part of a physical removal programme.
   C   Addition of fertiliser to encourage plant growth.
   D   Chemical control, using herbicides and insecticides.

10 Grass that is growing in a field is eaten by a grasshopper. The grasshopper is consumed by a mouse, which is then eaten by a fox. The farmer who owns the field uses pesticides to control the number of pests that are damaging his crops. Deduce which animal will accumulate the greatest amount of pesticide over time. [1]

A   The grass

B   The fox

C   The grasshopper

D   Humans

11 Which of the following is not a chemical that can bioaccumulate in an organism? [1]

A   DDT

B   Methylmercury

C   Lead

D   Carbon dioxide

12 An endangered species is protected by being kept in captivity, and encouraged to breed, before being reintroduced back into its natural habitat. This process of captive breeding is an example of which type of conservation? [1]

A   In-site

B   Ex-situ

C   En-situ

D   Au-situ

13 Claudio uses Simpson's reciprocal index of diversity to measure the biodiversity of four different ecosystems. Using the results below, identify the ecosystem with the greatest biodiversity. [1]

A   1.18

B   2.34

C   4.18

D   6.01

14 Which of the following is not a method of sampling used to estimate population size? [1]

A   Line transect

B   Belt transect

C   Quadrat sampling

D   Random count technique

15 Which of the following is most likely to cause eutrophication? [1]

A   Fertilisers

B   Pesticides

C   Insecticides

D   Poisons

16 **a** Discuss the role of in-situ conservation of endangered species. [4]

    b Explain why it is important to preserve biodiversity. [5]

    c Design a plan that would promote the conservation of fish. [5]

17 **a** Define the following terms.

      i Ecological niche. [1]

      ii Fundamental niche. [1]

      iii Realised niche. [1]

    b Using a named example, explain why top consumers are more affected by biomagnification than organisms at lower trophic levels. [4]

    c Draw and label the nitrogen cycle. [7]

15 Human physiology (Option D)

Chapter outline

In this chapter you will:
- outline how a balanced diet is essential to human nutrition
- describe the nervous and hormonal mechanisms that control digestion
- explain how the chemical composition of the blood is controlled by the liver
- **HL** describe the external and internal factors that influence heart function
- **HL** outline how hormones are not secreted at a uniform rate and how they exert their effect at low concentrations
- **HL** explain how red blood cells are vital in the transport of respiratory gases.

KEY TERMS AND DEFINITIONS

Balanced diet – a diet that contains the appropriate proportions of carbohydrates, fats, proteins, vitamins, minerals and water in order to maintain a healthy body.

HL **Emphysema** – condition that causes the walls of the alveoli to break down.

High density lipoprotein – 'good' cholesterol that is responsible for transporting low density lipoprotein from tissues to the liver to be broken down.

HL **Hormone** – chemical messenger secreted by cells or glands that controls the activity of other cells or glands in the body.

Malnutrition – condition caused by a deficiency of nutrients in the diet of an individual.

Exercise D.1 – Human nutrition

1 Diabetes is an increasingly common condition and is affecting more and more people as our diets and lifestyles change. In 1980, there were an estimated 108 000 000 people with diabetes but the latest figures taken in 2014 suggest that there are now 422 000 000 people worldwide who suffer from the condition. Diabetes is more common in middle- or low-income families and can lead to blindness, heart attacks, strokes and loss of lower limbs. Type I diabetes accounts for around 5% of all diabetes patients but it is the more common type II that is controllable to some extent. Symptoms of type II diabetes include: being very thirsty, more regular urination, always feeling tired or hungry, sudden weight loss without trying.

   a Calculate the increase in number of people that suffer from diabetes between 1980 and 2014.

   b Explain what diabetes is and how it affects the blood sugar level of the blood.

c Distinguish between type I and type II diabetes. A table is a great way of presenting the differences between two different things. It is important you refer to both types in your answer and a table almost guarantees that you will do this. To help you, you can use the answers listed below to construct your own table to answer the question.
- Caused by insulin resistance.
- Onset in early years.
- Caused by lack of insulin.
- Treated by insulin injections.
- Onset in adulthood.
- Treated by lifestyle and diet change.

d Design a lifestyle plan for someone who might be at risk of type II diabetes.

e Your friend is worried that they might be suffering from diabetes and describes her symptoms to you. Outline the symptoms that you would expect her to describe if she was suffering from diabetes.

f *Schools are responsible for the onset of type II diabetes.* Discuss this statement.

g Diabetes sufferers have a great need for a healthy lifestyle and a good, balanced diet. Identify the key words related to healthy living and balanced diet, being described below.

   i A diet that contains the appropriate proportions of carbohydrates, fats, proteins, vitamins, minerals, and water in order to maintain a healthy body.

   ii Caused by a deficiency of nutrients in the diet of an individual.

   iii When a person does not have enough to eat and this leads to body tissue being broken down.

   iv Chemical substance taken in by an organism for growth and metabolism.

   v The substances that cannot be made by the body and must be taken in from food.

   vi Substance group that includes phosphorus, calcium, magnesium, sodium, iron.

   vii Substance group that includes A, C, D, K.

   viii Substance group that includes histidine, valine and tryptophan.

   ix Substance group that includes examples such as omega–3.

   x Not getting enough of the essential nutrients and can lead to malnutrition.

h Look at the foods listed below. For each list of foods, determine which food group they best belong to.

   i Salmon, soybean, kale, spinach, walnuts, corn, cottonseed.

   ii Liver, soya milk, pork, oatmeal, green beans, asparagus, broccoli, citrus fruits, spinach, egg yolks, mushrooms, eggs, fish, cereal, bananas.

   iii Look at the **three** daily food plans below. Determine which food plan would offer the most balanced diet to a typical adult male.

Food plan 1

Breakfast

Feta and spinach omelette, yoghurt, glass of milk

Lunch

Smoked chicken, lettuce and tomato sandwich, water

Dinner
Grilled salmon, lemon and almond, mashed potatoes, green bean salad, lemon juice and mint
Snacks
Cereal and honey, small chocolate bar

Food plan 2

Breakfast
Frosted cereal and milk

Lunch
Cheese and ham sandwich, can of lemonade

Dinner
Sausage, egg and chips, water

Snacks
Two packets of crisps, chocolate biscuits, apple

Food plan 3

Breakfast
None

Lunch
Hot dog, French fries, can of sweetened carbonated drink

Dinner
Burger, French fries, small salad, can of sweetened carbonated drink

Snacks
Sweets, raisins, candy, chocolate

   iv   Identify the food plan which puts people most at risk from diseases such as diabetes and heart disease?

2 Doctors sometimes use the body mass index (BMI) to determine whether a patient is within the healthy boundaries for their mass. Some people may be identified as being underweight, some as healthy, and some as being overweight, or even obese.

BMI is calculated by using the following formula:

$$\text{BMI} = \text{mass (kg)} / \text{height}^2 \text{ (m}^2\text{)}$$

The general rules for using the value are:

Below 18.5:   underweight

Between 18.5 and 24.9:   normal

Between 25.0 and 29.9:   overweight

Above 30.0:   obese

a Look at the details for the following people and calculate their BMI. For each person you should also deduce whether they are underweight, normal, overweight, or obese.
  i Victoria Beckham, 1.67 m, 49 kg.
  ii Serena Williams, 1.76 m, 74 kg.
  iii Michael Jordan, 1.98 m, 98 kg.
  iv Alicia Keys, 1.67 m, 56 kg.
  v Harry Potter, 1.65 m, 57 kg.
  vi Dwayne 'The Rock' Johnson, 1.96 m, 122 kg.
  vii Homer Simpson, 1.82 m, 142 kg.
b Some people have a BMI of over 30 but may **not** be considered to be obese or overweight. Explain, using a named example from the choices in part a, how this can be the case.

3 Anorexia nervosa is an eating disorder that is potentially life-threatening and can be identified by using BMI calculations, similar to those that you have carried out in the previous question. The disease, which carries an illogical outlook of weight gain and self-image, affects both men and women. The causes of anorexia are difficult to pinpoint but can often be related to:

- Media perception and promotion of healthy bodies
- Trying to meet the demands of a career, such as modelling
- Childhood trauma and psychological trauma
- Peer pressure to be thin
- Irregular hormones
- Inherited factors making one more susceptible to the condition
- Nutritional deficiencies.

There are many signs to look out for in someone that you suspect might be anorexic. These include: fanatical dieting despite being underweight, an obsession with food content, loss of menstrual cycle in females, depression, lethargy, thinning hair, hair loss, and avoidance of social functions.
a Identify the biological factors that can contribute to the development of anorexia in a person.
b Anorexia can have an effect on the human body, especially the skeletal system and the heart. Outline how anorexia affects the heart, and any other biological effect that you can think of.
c Explain why anorexia affects the heart muscle in the way that it does.
d Suggest which foods an anorexic person might benefit from in order to provide the nutrients required for a healthy heart.

4 For each of the descriptions that follow, you must identify the condition being described and suggest suitable foods that can help to alleviate the condition.
a Bleeding gums, loose teeth, lack of energy, mood swings, chronic joint pain, bruising occurs easily.
b Mental retardation, small head growth, lack of hair, regular seizures.
c Soft bones, malformed bones, development of body similar to Figure 15.1.

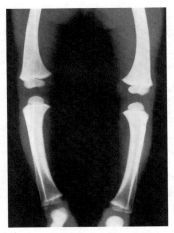

Figure 15.1 Malformed bones.

5 The energy content of food can be easily measured in the laboratory. By burning a known mass of food and measuring the temperature change of a known volume of water, you can use the following formula to measure the energy content of that food.

Energy (J) = temperature change x mass of water x specific heat capacity (4.18 J/g/°C for water)

a Meghan carries out an investigation to measure the energy content of three foods, A, B and C. She places 25 g of water at 26 °C into a boiling tube and burns the three foods to completion. Her results are outlined below.
   – Food A: final temperature 65 °C, mass of food 0.6 g.
   – Food B: final temperature 81 °C, mass of food 0.5 g.
   – Food C: final temperature 51 °C, mass of food 0.6 g.
      i   Calculate the energy content of 100 g of food A.
      ii   Calculate the energy content of 100 g of food B.
      iii Calculate the energy content of 100 g of food C.
b Suggest which food might have been used as food B.

Exercise D.2 – Digestion

1 Some of the developments in the understanding of digestion occurred, quite simply, through a hole in the stomach. Alexis St Martin was a fur trapper who suffered a gunshot wound to the stomach, enabling scientists to observe the mechanisms of digestion. William Beaufort was the physiologist responsible for caring for St Martin, and amazingly, he managed to help him to survive. St Martin had to give up his regular job and was hired by Beaufort, allowing him access to the wound and the idea that he could observe digestion through this. Daily samples were taken and analysed, allowing Beaufort to observe the role of hydrochloric acid in the stomach. Up until that point, it was believed that the stomach was responsible for grinding up food. Beaufort's methods were even copied by Ivan Pavlov, whose studies into digestion led to one of the most important discoveries of animal behaviour.

a Outline how acid in the stomach is produced.
b Gastric juice in the stomach contains an acid and an enzyme. State the name of the acid, and describe how the enzyme helps to break down food in the stomach.
c Some scientists imitated the work of Beaufort by making holes in the stomachs of other animals. This allowed them to observe digestion and make advances in medical

science and physiology. Comment on whether this sort of investigation is ethical, and if it would be allowed in today's society.

d Outline the role of hydrochloric acid in the stomach in protecting the body from dangerous pathogens.

e The stomach should digest itself if it contains hydrochloric acid that is pH2. State why this does not happen.

f Holly eats a lot of spicy food and as a result develops a gastric ulcer.

   i Outline how this gastric ulcer might have formed as a result of Holly's spicy food.

   ii Predict the symptoms that Holly might experience as a result of her gastric ulcer.

   iii State the name of the bacterium that can also cause stomach ulcers. This bacterium can be treated with a range of medications, including amoxicillin and clarithromycin.

2 Absorption mainly occurs in the small intestine, which is lined with villi that will help absorption to take place.

a Define *absorption*.

b Outline the main adaptations of the villi that maximise the rate of absorption of food molecules into the bloodstream.

c The small intestine consists of five main layers, as shown in Figure 15.2. Your task is to copy this diagram. Then label and annotate the five layers, using the information in the table below. Warning: some of the labels do **not** match the correct description, so you must decide how to use them in your diagram.

Layer	Description
Mucosa	Contains the epithelium (contains enterocytes, goblet cells, and endocrine cells).
Serosa	Contains blood vessels and connective tissue.
Circular muscle layer	Smooth muscle arranged in a circular way.
Submucosa	Smooth muscle arranged in a longitudinal way.
Longitudinal muscle layer	Single layer of epithelial cells with connective tissue.
Lumen	The hollow tube that the food and molecules flows through.

Table 15.1

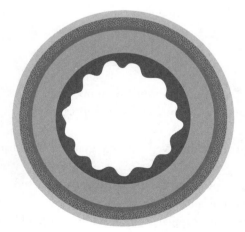

Figure 15.2 Transverse section of the small intestine.

   d Identify the food, or food group, being digested and absorbed by their descriptions below.

     i   Hydrolysed to glucose and absorbed by epithelial cells of the small intestine.

     ii Co-transported by facilitated diffusion with sodium.

     iii Digested by proteases into amino acids; amino acid carrier proteins carry them by facilitated diffusion into the blood in the capillaries.

     iv Emulsified in the intestines by bile, before lipases digest them into fatty acids and glycerol. Glycerol is absorbed and fatty acids will diffuse into the small intestine.

     v   Non-digestible carbohydrates do **not** get digested and will pass straight through to the rectum. Identify the food group described.

3 Cholera is caused by the ingestion of food or water that has been contaminated with *Vibrio cholera*. The toxin that is released can attach itself to enterocytes that are able to trigger water to leave the infected enterocytes. This excess of water can then lead to watery diarrhoea. The loss of water from the body leads to sever dehydration if large volumes of water are lost. Patients must be rehydrated and antibiotics may be provided to combat the bacteria.

   a State the name of the toxin that causes dehydration.

   b List the consequences and symptoms that someone who is suffering from dehydration may experience.

   c Identify the part of the digestive system that is usually responsible for absorbing water.

   d State the name of the bacteria that is responsible for causing a cholera infection.

Exercise D.3 – Functions of the liver

1 Some of the functions of the liver are outlined below.

- Produces bile, enzymes, hormones, cholesterol, triglycerides.
- Contains the gall bladder, which sends bile via the bile duct to the small intestine so that fats can be emulsified.
- Stores glycogen, vitamins and minerals.
- Synthesises amino acids and proteins.
- Is responsible for the removal of toxins and breaking down drugs and other harmful substances.
- Helps to maintain a constant blood pressure and temperature.
- Breaks down erythrocytes.
- Regulates blood clotting.
- Converts ammonia to urea.

   a Use the information above to construct a mini-essay about the importance of the liver. You should explain why each function of the liver is so important to maintaining a healthy body.

   b State the names of the blood vessels that supply the liver with oxygenated blood, and takes away deoxygenated blood.

   c State the name of the blood vessel that is responsible for bringing deoxygenated blood that contains glucose, minerals, vitamins and amino acids.

   d Compare and contrast the role of sinusoids and capillaries in providing a dual blood supply to the liver.

e Identify the structures described below.

 i Involved in many storage and metabolic processes, making up nearly 80% of liver cells.

 ii Proteins made in hepatocytes, in the endoplasmic reticulum and Golgi complexes.

 iii Macrophages that break down red blood cells so that the cells can be recycled.

 iv The tube that leads to the gall bladder where bile is stored.

 v Liver cells can be observed under a microscope by making a temporary specimen of the liver cells. List the following stages in the correct order to show a suitable method for preparing a temporary liver cell specimen.

   • Add 2 or 3 drops of suitable staining solution, such as iodine or methylene blue, to the cells.

   • Grind a piece of fresh liver with 10 ml salt solution.

   • Smear some of the liver salt solution across the microscope slide.

   • Cover with a cover slip.

   • Observe under a light microscope at a magnification of at least ×100.

 vi State why a staining solution was used.

 vii Lina observes some fresh liver cells under a microscope at ×100 magnification. She measures the observed cells to be 0.5 mm in diameter. Calculate the actual width of the liver cell that Lina observed.

f i The Kupffer cells of the liver are responsible for breaking down red blood cells so that they can be reused by the body. Explain why red blood cells do **not** reproduce like other cells.

 ii Hemoglobin is split into which functional parts?

 iii Globin is reused in the synthesis of which molecule?

 iv Which part of hemoglobin is transformed into iron and bilirubin?

 v Outline the roles of the iron and bilirubin that are broken down from the heme group.

g You will have heard of cholesterol as part of your diet, but it is not actually an essential nutrient because the body is capable of making its own cholesterol in the liver.

 i Outline the main uses of cholesterol in the body.

 ii Explain why cholesterol needs to be carried as plasma lipoproteins.

 iii Distinguish between high density lipoprotein and low density lipoproteins.

 iv Outline the main function of low density lipoproteins.

 v State the main function of high density lipoproteins.

 vi Coconut oil is rich in saturated fats that help to increase the amount of high density lipoproteins in the body. However, coconut oil also increases the amount of low density lipoproteins. High density lipoproteins are considered to be 'good' cholesterol because they transport bad cholesterol to the liver to be broken down and keep the arteries clear and unclogged. Evaluate whether a person at risk of clogged arteries should consume coconut oil to maximise their intake of 'good' high density lipoproteins.

h Jaundice is a condition that causes the skin and the whites of the eyes to turn yellow. The metabolism of hemoglobin accounts for nearly 80% of bilirubin production, which binds to albumin. If the liver cannot remove the bilirubin from the blood, the levels become too high and cause the skin and eyes to become jaundiced.

 i State the main cause of jaundice.

 ii Suggest what a person with jaundice might be suffering from.

     iii Newborn jaundice is more common. Outline the main causes of newborn jaundice.

     iv Outline how a baby with jaundice can be treated to reduce the levels of bilirubin and encourage optimal liver function.

2 An epidemiological study of liver disease (cirrhosis) in the 1980s highlighted the relationship between alcohol consumption and the chances of developing cirrhosis. Cirrhosis is a disease where damaged liver tissue is replaced by scar tissue.

  a Explain why the replacement of damaged liver tissue with scar tissue is so dangerous.

  b State some of the main symptoms of cirrhosis.

  c Outline how cirrhosis can be cured.

  d

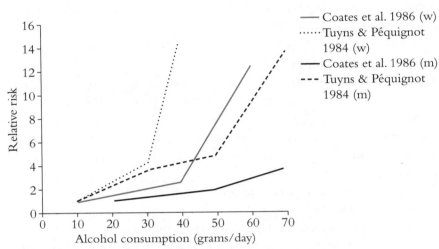

Figure 15.3 Graph to show the relationship between liver disease and alcohol consumption.

     i Analyse the graph in Figure 15.3 that shows how alcohol consumption is related to the risk of cirrhosis in adults.

     ii The graph shows how powerful an epidemiological study can be. Explain why combining the studies and patterns found is beneficial to changing public attitudes.

  e Alcoholics are at extreme risk of cirrhosis, and other liver diseases. The table below lists some of the reasons why alcoholics should, and should not, receive a liver transplant. Comment on whether you think alcoholics should be entitled to a liver transplant.

For	Against
Everybody deserves to live	It was their own fault for drinking
With a new liver, the patient might change their lifestyle	Other people might deserve the transplant more
Consideration of family and friends	They may damage the new liver
Family might rely on the patient financially	Costs too much money for someone who might not deserve it
Drinking is an addiction – a disease in itself	It was their fault for drinking in the first place

Table 15.2

Exercise D.4 – The heart

1 People with heart problems, such as bradycardia, arrhythmia or tachycardia, may have an artificial pacemaker implanted to maintain an acceptable heart rate.

  a Identify the type of heart problem that might be resolved by the action of the pacemaker that is described below.

    i The heartbeat is reduced via a reduction in signals being sent from the pacemaker.

    ii The heartbeat slows down too much and so the signals from the pacemaker begin, causing the heart to beat faster.

  b Outline how a pacemaker is fitted to a patient with heart problems.

  c Define *heart rate,* and suggest the range that a healthy resting heart rate should fall within.

  d The factors listed in the table below all contribute to an increase, or decrease, in heart rate. Consider each factor, and the description, and complete the table by deducing whether the factor increases or decreases the heart rate.

Factor	Description	Increase OR decrease of heart rate?
Age	Heart muscles struggle to pump as well in older people	
Body size	Larger area needs to be covered	
Temperature	Vasodilation occurs	
Potassium ions	Potassium ions can decrease action potentials	
Eating	Blood required to be pumped to the stomach	
Posture (upright)	Gravity has an effect on this	
Drugs	Caffeine and nicotine are stimulants	

Table 15.3

  e Action potentials are required for the heart to beat. Define *action potentials*.

2 If blood pressure falls outside a certain range, hypertension can develop. There are many causes of hypertension, many of which are related to lifestyle, genetic factors and diet. Read the descriptions of Michelle, Samaira and Prisha below and answer the questions that follow.

Michelle is an athlete who trains every day in the run-up to competitions. Her diet is very well balanced and she uses very little salt. Michelle has a BMI of 23.1, does not smoke or drink alcohol, but is often stressed before a big race.

Samaira is a student at university who consumes alcohol and occasionally smokes. She rarely gets stressed, even though she often has deadlines to meet. She has a BMI of 29.8 and enjoys exercise by walking 15 minutes to her university every day.

Prisha lives in the same student house as Samaira but has a terrible diet, often pouring lots of salt onto her food before eating it. Prisha usually stays out longer than Samaira on a night out, so she consumes more alcohol. Prisha also avoids stress by not going to all of her lectures.

  a From the descriptions, above, which person do you believe is most likely to be at risk of hypertension?

b Michelle is the least likely to develop hypertension but what could she do to reduce the risk even further? Suggest **one** change to Michelle's lifestyle that she could make in order to achieve this.

c Prisha eats more than Samair, and exercises less. They are the same height; estimate a BMI value that you might expect Prisha to have based on the evidence of the descriptions.

d Genetics is a considerable factor in the development of hypertension. Deduce which of the three girls is most likely to have genetic factors that increases the risk of hypertension.

e If one of the girls were to develop hypertension, suggest what the possible consequences might be.

f A sufferer from arteriosclerosis will have restricted oxygen flow to tissues due to the hardening of the arteries. The buildup of plaque causes platelets to release clotting factors that form a clot over the plaque. This is called a thrombus and blocks the flow of blood to tissues.

    i Determine the name of the condition that has just been described.

    ii Outline the consequences of the condition named in part i.

HL Exercise D.5 – Hormones and metabolism

1 Read the text below about footballer Lionel Messi and answer the questions below.

> A human growth hormone (somatotrophin) is taken by some athletes in order to gain muscle mass. One of the most famous examples of this is the footballer, Lionel Messi. Messi is one the most talented athletes in the world, but when growing up his size was considered to be a potential barrier to succeeding as a professional athlete. Messi suffered from a growth hormone disorder and his first contract with Barcelona stipulated that they would pay for the high expensive medical costs of his condition. These costs were as high as $900 a month; but the possibility of enhancing height, as well as pituitary function, alleviating skin and teeth issues, and boosting the immune system was too great for Messi to ignore. Messi is now an average-size man but at the time of beginning the treatment (aged 13) he was only 1.27 metres in height. The use of human growth hormone is also the source of some controversy, as the disgraced cyclist Lance Armstrong used it as part of his sophisticated doping system. Other athletes are rumoured to use it to gain an advantage in their sports; the line between medical requirements and enhancing performance appears to be a very fine line.

a Human growth hormone is proven to reduce body fat mass and increase sprint capacity when taken together with testosterone. Explain how this might help athletes to gain an advantage over their competitors.

b Some of the risks of using human growth hormone and testosterone (or other anabolic steroid treatments) include enlarged sexual glands and mental issues. Outline some of the other side effects associated with the use of anabolic steroids.

c *Leo Messi should **not** be allowed to use human growth hormone as this has allowed him to reach a level of competition that he could not reach without using them.* Comment on this statement.

d *All athletes should be allowed to use performance enhancing drugs if they have equal access to them with no limitations.* Comment on this statement and give your judgement.

e Human growth hormone has an obvious benefit to athletes like Messi. Define *hormone*.

f Hormones act to control bodily functions by using positive or negative feedback mechanisms. Define *negative feedback*, using a named example.

g Identify the hormone listed below by the main function described.
  i Fight-or-flight response.
  ii Promotes absorption and conversion of glucose.
  iii Coverts glycogen to glucose.
  iv Promotes growth.
  v Controls water reabsorption.
  vi Controls sexual development of males.

h Deduce which of the hormones in part g are examples of steroid hormones.

i Outline how steroid hormones are able to form a receptor-hormone complex.

j Outline how the hypothalamus controls hormone secretion.

k Identify the structure described as follows: *I am very small but extremely important. I have a role to play in endocrine function and can control many different systems of the body with my actions. One of my main roles is to control the release of several hormones by the pituitary gland. This allows me to regulate the temperature of the body and how much food the body needs. I can make you moody, or happy. I can influence your sexual behaviour and reproduction. Who am I?*

HL Exercise D.6 – Transport of respiratory gases

1 A person that smokes cigarettes is at risk from a wide range of diseases and conditions. Cigarettes contain many chemicals and carcinogens, including tar and nicotine. Efficient gas exchange requires oxygen and carbon dioxide to be exchanged at the surface of the lungs. A large surface area is important for this to take place. One of the most damaging conditions often suffered by long-term, heavy smokers is emphysema.

  a Define *emphysema*.

  b Smoking is one of the major causes of emphysema. State other factors that can also contribute to the onset of emphysema.

  c Outline the main consequences that an emphysema sufferer might experience.

  d Long-term exposure to smoking can lead to emphysema. List the following stages in order to show how emphysema is developed.
  - Inhibition of the proteases is reduced as the enzyme inhibitor (alpha–1–antitrypsin) is reduced.
  - Airways narrow and lung tissue may begin to break down.
  - Less oxygen can get into the bloodstream.
  - Increase in protease activity breaks down the alveolar wall.
  - Tissues of the lungs swell.
  - Surface area of the lung is reduced.
  - The alveoli become less elastic, affecting ventilation.

  e Outline some of the treatments that can be used to help people with emphysema.

  f A person with emphysema is on a waiting list for a lung transplant. The patient does **not** intend to quit smoking. Comment on whether this person should be allowed to have the lung transplant.

2 Myoglobin is a protein that binds oxygen in muscles.
  a Describe the structure of myoglobin.
  b Distinguish between myoglobin and hemoglobin.

c Some carbon dioxide is able to bind to hemoglobin to form $HbCO_2$. State the full name of $HbCO_2$.

d State the name of the enzyme that converts carbon dioxide to carbonic acid.

e State what is formed when carbonic acid is catabolised by the enzyme named in part d.

3 The Bohr effect explains how the increased release of oxygen by hemoglobin occurs in respiring tissues.

a Define the *Bohr effect*.

b Explain the Bohr effect.

c Deduce the effect of carbon dioxide concentration on the release of oxygen in tissues.

d During exercise, the amount of carbon dioxide in the blood affects the rate of ventilation. Outline how vigorous exercise affects the breathing rate.

e State how the ventilation rate of humans can be measured.

f The rate of ventilation is controlled by which part of the brain?

g Define the following key terms related to breathing rate.

   i   Total lung capacity.

   ii Residual volume.

   iii Tidal volume.

h State the range of pH that human blood is regulated to remain within.

i Athletes use altitude acclimatisation to enhance their performance as this makes the heart pump faster, increasing ventilation rates and increasing the number of erythrocytes in the blood. It is possible to gain a competitive advantage but there are possible complications that may be encountered. Construct a table to compare the advantages and disadvantages of high altitude training.

? Exam-style questions

1 **Which of the following is not an essential nutrient? [1]**
   A Carbohydrates
   B Vitamins
   C Water
   D Minerals

2 **A person is lacking an essential nutrient from their diet. Which of the following describes the condition that occurs as a result of this missing nutrient? [1]**
   A Starvation
   B Malnutrition
   C Balanced diet
   D Vitamin D

3 **Identify the condition caused by a vitamin C deficiency. [1]**
   A Rickets
   B Anemia
   C Scurvy
   D Emphysema

4   **Identify the symptom of a person that is suffering from a vitamin C deficiency. [1]**
A   Poor ventilation rate
B   Poor concentration
C   Too much energy
D   Bleeding gums

5   **Which of the following is not typically found in gastric juice? [1]**
A   Water
B   Mucus
C   Salivary amylase
D   Hydrochloric acid

6   **Which of the following is not an adaptation of the villi in the small intestine? [1]**
A   Large surface area
B   Thin epithelial lining
C   Lacteal carries away proteins
D   Network of capillaries

7   **Which of the following is not a symptom of stomach ulcers? [1]**
A   Stomach pain
B   Excess acid
C   Acid reflux
D   Joint pain

8   **Identify the blood vessel that is not connected to the liver. [1]**
A   Hepatic portal vein
B   Hepatic vein
C   Hepatic artery
D   Hepatic aorta

9   **A person has yellow skin and the whites of their eyes have turned yellow. Determine the condition that this person might be suffering from. [1]**
A   Jaundice
B   Cirrhosis
C   Heart disease
D   Rickets

10 **Identify the key terms that refer to the contraction and relaxation of the heart muscle. [1]**
A   Hypertension and relaxation
B   Contract and relax
C   Systole and diastole
D   Systole and hypertension

11 The pituitary gland is responsible for the release of many hormones that control the metabolism of the human body. Identify the hormone from the list below that is not **typically released by the pituitary gland. [1]**

    A Oxytocin

    B Luteinising hormone

    C Growth hormone

    D Dopamine

12 Which of the following decreases during high altitude training? [1]

    A Immunological response

    B Sprint speed

    C Ventilation rate

    D Blood viscosity

13 Hormones are produced by parts of the endocrine system but are not secreted at a uniform rate.

    a Define *hormone*. [3]

    b Outline how a hormone exerts an effect, using a named example. [2]

    c Compare and contrast gastric juice and pancreatic juice. [4]

    d Describe how the pancreas is able to affect blood glucose levels. [6]

14 Figure 15.4 shows a typical oxygen dissociation curve at various partial pressures of oxygen.

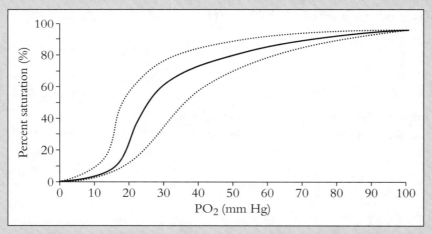

Figure 15.4 An oxygen dissociation curve.

    a Outline the possible causes of the curve shifting to the right. [2]

    b On the graph, label the curve that might represent myoglobin. [1]

    c Outline **four** roles of the liver. [4]

    d Describe how hemoglobin is broken down by the liver. [3]

Glossary

abiotic factors   non-biological factors, such as temperature or pH, that are part of the environment.

absorption   the taking up of a substance by a tissue; for example, the process by which nutrients pass from the lumen of the intestine into the lymph or blood, or by which the intensity of a beam of light energy is reduced as it passes through a leaf

activation energy   the energy a substrate molecule must achieve before it can change chemically

active site   the region on the surface of an enzyme to which the substrate molecule binds

active transport   transport of a substance across a membrane against the concentration gradient, involving a carrier protein and energy expenditure

aerobic respiration   respiration that requires oxygen, and produces carbon dioxide and water from the oxidation of glucose

alleles   different versions of a gene found at a locus of a chromosome.

amino acid   building block of proteins.

anaerobic respiration   respiration that occurs in the absence of oxygen in which glucose is broken down to lactic acid or to ethanol and carbon dioxide

antibody   protein produced by blood plasma cells, derived from B-cells, that binds to a specific antigen in order to destroy it.

antigen   a substance that stimulates the production of antibody

ATP (adenosine triphosphate)   a universal energy storage nucleotide formed in photosynthesis and respiration from ADP and Pi; when it is formed, energy is stored; when it is broken down, energy is released

ATP synthase/synthetase   an enzyme that catalyses the production of ATP

auxins   hormones responsible for the regulation of plant growth.

balanced diet   a diet that contains the appropriate proportions of carbohydrates, fats, proteins, vitamins, minerals and water in order to maintain a healthy body.

binomial system   system used to name organisms using the genus and species.

biodiversity   the range and variety of plant and animal life in a particular habitat.

bioinformatics   the use of computers to analyse sequence data in biological research.

bioremediation   the treatment and removal of pollutants using microorganisms.

biotechnology   the use of biological processes for industrial purposes.

carbon flux   movement of carbon between the carbon pools.

carcinogen   a substance that causes the transformation of cells to form malignant tumours (cancer)

cardiac muscle   specialised muscle found only in the heart

carrier   an individual who has one copy of a recessive allele that causes a genetic condition in individuals who are homozygous for the allele

cell cycle   the sequence of events that takes place from one cell division until the next; made up of interphase, mitosis and cytokinesis.

cell wall   firm structure that surrounds the plasma membrane of cells of plants, fungi and bacteria; it gives cells their shape and limits their expansion

cellulose   a polymer of glucose; it is the primary constituent of most plant cell walls

chlorophyll   the most important photosynthetic pigments of green plants, found in the grana of chloroplasts and responsible for trapping light energy (some bacteria have a chemically different form called bacteriochlorophyll)

chloroplast   organelle found in some plant cells that is the site of photosynthesis

chromosome   long structure of DNA that carries genetic information of the cell.

circulatory   system circulates blood around the body; blood is pumped by the heart through this double circulatory system.

cladistics   the system of classifying organisms according to their shared characteristics and based on ancestry.

community   group of populations living and interacting with each other.

condensation   reaction removal of water to form a larger molecule.

cytoplasm   contents of a cell enclosed by the plasma membrane, not including the nucleus

denaturation   a change in the structure of a protein that results in a loss (usually permanent) of its function

differentiation a process by which originally similar cells follow different developmental pathways because particular genes are activated and others are switched off

diffusion passive, random movement of molecules (or other particles) from an area of high concentration to an area of lower concentration

digestion system responsible for the breaking down of large, insoluble macromolecules into smaller, soluble monomers for absorption.

DNA profiling analysis of DNA from samples and compared to that of a known individual.

DNA replication double-stranded DNA is copied semi-conservatively to produce two identical DNA molecules.

ecology the study of the relationships between living organisms and their environment, including both the physical environment and the other organisms that live in it

ecosystem a community and its abiotic environment.

emphysema condition that causes the walls of the alveoli to break down.

endocrine gland a ductless hormone-producing gland that secretes its products into the bloodstream

endoplasmic reticulum a folded system of membranes within the cytoplasm of a eukaryotic cell; may be smooth (sER), or rough (rER) if ribosomes are attached

endosperm the food reserves found in a seed of a monocotyledonous flowering plant

endosymbiosis theory that proposes that mitochondria and chloroplasts evolved from bacteria.

enzyme biological catalyst, globular protein.

ethology the study of animal behaviour under natural conditions.

eukaryotic organism whose cell contains a membrane-bound nucleus.

evolution the cumulative change in the heritable characteristics of a population.

exocrine gland a gland whose secretion is released via a duct

fertilisation the fusion of male and female gametes to produce a zygote.

food chain a sequence of organisms in a habitat, beginning with a producer, in which each obtains nutrients by eating the organism preceding it

food web a series of interconnected food chains

fluid mosaic model the accepted model of the structure of a membrane that includes a phospholipid bilayer in which proteins are embedded or attached to the surface.

gene pool all of the different genes in an interbreeding population at a given time.

genome the complete genetic information of an organism or an individual cell

genotype the exact genetic constitution of an individual feature of an organism; the alleles of an organism

germination the growth of an embryo plant using stored food in a seed

greenhouses gases gases such as carbon dioxide, methane, and water vapour that trap heat energy in the atmosphere.

heritable characteristics traits passed on to offspring.

high density lipoprotein 'good' cholesterol that is responsible for transporting low density lipoprotein from tissues to the liver to be broken down.

homeostasis maintaining a constant internal environment.

homologous structures structures that are similar due to common ancestry.

hormone chemical messenger secreted by cells or glands that controls the activity of other cells or glands in the body.

hybrid the offpring of a cross between genetically dissimilar parents

hypotonic a less concentrated solution (one with a more negative water potential) than the cell solution

hypothesis a testable explanation of an observed event or phenomenon

immune system provides resistance and protection against infections, toxins and pathogens.

immunity resistance to the onset of a disease after infection by the pathogen that causes the disease.

inheritance the passing of heritable characteristics from parents to offspring.

karyogram a diagram or photographic image showing the number, shape and types of chromosomes in a cell

karyotype the number, shape and types of chromosomes in a cell

lipid a fat, oil, wax or steroid; organic compound that is insoluble in water but soluble in organic solvents such as ethanol

lysis breakdown of cells

malnutrition condition caused by a deficiency of nutrients in the diet of an individual.

mesocosm experimental tool that acts as a smaller version of an ecosystem in which conditions can be controlled and measured.

meiosis cell division that produces haploid number of chromosomes in daughter cell.

metabolic pathway chain or cycle of linked events catalysed by enzymes.

mitosis cell division that produces two daughter cells with the same chromosome compliment as the parent cell

monosaccharide simple carbohydrate.

muscle fibre a single muscle cell that is multinucleate in striated muscle

natural selection when organisms adapt to their environment in order to survive and reproduce.

neuropharmacology a branch of pharmacology that investigates and researches how drugs act upon the nervous system.

neurulation the folding of the neural plate into the neural tube.

nervous system the network of neurons, synapses and fibres that transmit nerve impulses around the body.

nucleus organelle found in eukaryotic cells that controls and directs cell activities; it is bounded by a double membrane (envelope) and contains chromosomes

organelle a cell structure that carries out a specific function – for example, ribosome, nucleus, chloroplast

osmoregulation control of the water balance of the blood, tissue or cytoplasm.

osmosis the diffusion of water molecules from an area where they are in high concentration (low solute concentration) to an area where they are in a lower concentration (high solute concentration) across a partially permeable membrane

phloem tube that conducts food and other substances throughout the plant from source to sink.

photosynthesis the process by which light energy is absorbed and stored as chemical energy in organic compounds.

polypeptide chain chain of amino acids.

polysaccharide natural polymers of sugars joined by condensation reactions.

population a group of organisms of the same species that live in the same area at the same time.

precautionary principle system in place to protect against potential damage in instances where scientific proof is not yet evident or absolute.

prokaryotic organism whose genetic materials is not contained in a nucleus.

proteome the complete set of proteins in an individual's genome.

quorum sensing the regulation of gene expression in response to an increase in bacterial cell populations.

respiration the controlled breakdown of food molecules to release energy.

respiratory system group of organs that work together to ensure that oxygen and carbon dioxide are exchanged and delivered to where they are needed.

ribosome a small organelle that is the site of protein synthesis

sarcomere contractile unit of skeletal muscle between two Z-lines

sexual reproduction the production and fusion of gametes.

skeletal (striated) muscle voluntary muscle tissue, which has multinucleated cells with arrangements of actin and myosin microfilaments

smooth muscle sheets of mononucleate cells that are stimulated by the autonomic nervous system

speciation the formation of new species from an existing population.

species group of individuals that can interbreed and produce fertile offspring.

stimulus a change in the external environment of an organism.

testa seed coat

transcription first part of gene expression where a section of DNA is copied into mRNA by RNA polymerase.

translation decoding of mRNA at a ribosome to produce an amino acid sequence.

vaccination injection of an antigen to induce antibody production before a potential infection

vacuole a liquid-filled cavity in a cell enclosed by a single membrane; usually small in animals

variation differences in the phenotype of organisms of the same species

vascular bundles a length of vascular tissue in plants consisting of xylem and phloem

vector a plasmid or virus that carries a piece of DNA into a bacterium during recombinant DNA technology; or an organism, such as an insect, that transmits a disease-causing organism to another species

vesicle a membrane-bound sac

xylem hollow tube that allows the conduction of water through it from roots to leaves.

zygote the cell produced by the fusion of two gametes

Acknowledgments

The authors and publishers acknowledge the following sources of copyright material and are grateful for the permissions granted. While every effort has been made, it has not always been possible to identify the sources of all the material used, or to trace all copyright holders. If any omissions are brought to our notice, we will be happy to include the appropriate acknowledgements on reprinting.

Cover Lotus_studio/Shutterstock; Figs. 1.1 and 1.2 based on data published by Cancer Research UK; Fig. 4.1 PeterEtchells/iStock/Getty Images; Fig. 5.2 Grafissimo/iStock/Getty Images; Fig. 5.3 Mihai Ivascu/Shutterstock; Fig. 5.5 rootstocks/iStock/Getty Images; Figs. 9.2, 10.1, 11.5b, 15.1 Biophoto Associates/Science Photo Library; Fig. 11.1 based on data published by the Office for National Statistics; Fig. 11.5a Don W.Fawcett/Science Photo Library; Fig. 12.1 PR Michel Zanca,ISM/Science Photo Library; Fig. 12.2 Science Source/Science Photo Library; Fig. 12.2(train) S. R. Gaiger/Topical Press Agency/Hulton Archive/Getty Images; Fig. 12.3 Image Point Fr/ Shutterstock; Fig. 13.2 ksass/E+/Getty Images; Fig. 14.2 based on data published by True Value Metrics